CW00921496

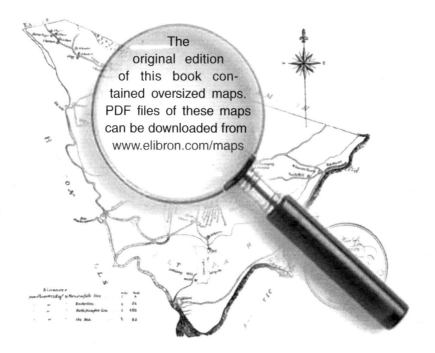

PEDRO SIMON

THE EXPEDITION

OF

PEDRO DE URSUA & LOPE DE AGUIRRE

IN SEARCH OF

EL DORADO AND OMAGUA

IN 1560-1

TRANSLATED BY

WILLIAM BOLLAERT

WITH AN INTRODUCTION BY

CLEMENTS R. MARKHAM

Elibron Classics
www.elibron.com

Elibron Classics series.

© 2005 Adamant Media Corporation.

ISBN 1-4021-9557-5 (paperback)
ISBN 1-4021-3727-3 (hardcover)

This Elibron Classics Replica Edition is an unabridged facsimile
of the edition published in 1861 by the Hakluyt Society,
London.

REPORT FOR 1861.

THE Council have great satisfaction in reporting that the Hakluyt Society, which has now completed the fourteenth year of its existence, continues in a prosperous condition, both as regards the number of its members, and the state of its funds; and that, for this year, as for every previous year excepting 1853, two volumes will be issued to the Members of the Society.

Since the last General Meeting, the following volumes have been delivered to Members:

"The Narrative of the Embassy of Ruy Gonzales de Clavijo to the Court of Timour at Samarcand, A.D. 1403-6." Translated for the first time, with Notes, a Preface, and an Introductory Life of Timour, by Clements R. Markham, Esq.

"A Collection of Documents, forming a Monograph of the Voyages of Henry Hudson." Edited, with an Introduction, by George Asher, Esq., LL.D.

Two volumes are in course of preparation, which will be delivered to Members, for the year 1861, viz. :

"The Expedition of Ursua and Aguirre, in search of El Dorado and Omagua, A.D. 1560-61," translated from the "Sexta Noticia historial" of Fray Pedro Simon, by W. Bollaert, Esq. ; with an Introduction by Clements R. Markham, Esq.

"The Discoveries of the World from their first original unto the year of our Lord 1555, by Antonio Galvano, Governor of Ternate, corrected, quoted, and published in English by Richard Hakluyt (1601)," now reprinted, with the original Portuguese text, and edited by Rear-Admiral Bethune.

In addition to the above works, two others have been undertaken by Editors, which will provide for the demands of the ensuing year, viz. :

"The Life and Acts of Don Alonzo de Guzman y Henriquez, written by himself," containing a Narrative of his Adventures in Germany, Italy, and other parts of Europe, as well as in South America, during the reign of Charles V. Translated from a manuscript in the National Library at Madrid, by Clements R. Markham, Esq.

"Account of the Journey of Caterino Zeno to the Empire of Persia, in the time of Uzun Hassan ; and of the Discovery of Frislanda, Eslanda, Engroenlanda, Estotilanda, and Icaria, by the two brothers Nicolo and Antonio Zeno. The Journey to Persia edited, with notes and an Introduction, by Major General Sir Henry C.

Rawlinson, K.C.B.. The discovery of Frislanda, etc., edited, with notes and an Introduction, by R. H. Major, Esq., by whom the whole is translated from the edition of Francesco Marcolini, Venice, 1558.

The following six Members retire from the Council, viz. :

SIR JOHN BOWRING, LL.D.,
LIEUT.-GENERAL C. R. FOX,
LORD WENSLEYDALE,
THE REV. W. WHEWELL, D.D.,
THE RIGHT HON. SIR DAVID DUNDAS, M.P.,
HIS EXCELLENCY THE COUNT DE LAVRADIO.

Of this number, the three following are recommended for re-election, viz. :

THE RIGHT. HON. SIR DAVID DUNDAS, M.P.,
HIS EXCELLENCY THE COUNT DE LAVRADIO,
THE REV. W. WHEWELL, D.D.

And the names of the following gentlemen are proposed for election :

CHARLES F. BEKE, Esq., Phil.D.,
T. HODGKIN, Esq., M.D.,
MAJOR-GENERAL SIR HENRY C. RAWLINSON, K.C.B.

The Council have also to report that the Honorary Secretary, Mr. Clements R. Markham, having returned from India last May, has resumed his duties.

Statement of the Accounts of the Society for the year 1860-1.

	£	s.	d.		£	s.	d.
Balance at Bankers' at last Audit	239	6	3	Mr. Richards, for Printing	219	17	0
Petty Cash	8	11	5	Mr. J. E. Richard, for Paper	53	15	0
Received by Bankers during the				Maps	22	8	0
year	273	8	0	Index	4	14	0
				Gratuity to Agent's Foreman	5	0	0
				Transcriptions	3	11	4
				Stationery, Parcels, Postage, and			
				Sundries	2	16	0
					312	1	4
				Present Balance at Bankers'	208	19	5
				Present Balance in Petty Cash	0	4	11
	£521	5	8		£521	5	8

Examined and Approved, November 11th, 1861.

CHARLES CANNON,

WILLIAM YOUNGER FLETCHER.

THE
HAKLUYT SOCIETY.

President.
SIR RODERICK IMPEY MURCHISON, G.C.St.S. F.R.S., D.C.L.
Mem. Imp. Acad. Sc. St. Petersburg, Corr. Mem. Inst. Fr., &c. &c.

Vice-Presidents.
THE MARQUIS OF LANSDOWNE.
REAR-ADMIRAL C. R. DRINKWATER BETHUNE, C.B.

Council.

THE HAKLUYT SOCIETY, which is established for the purpose of printing rare or unpublished Voyages and Travels, aims at opening by this means an easier access to the sources of a branch of knowledge, which yields to none in importance, and is superior to most in agreeable variety. The narratives of travellers and navigators make us acquainted with the earth, its inhabitants and productions; they exhibit the growth of intercourse among mankind, with its effects on civilization, and, while instructing, they at the same time awaken attention, by recounting the toils and adventures of those who first explored unknown and distant regions.

The advantage of an Association of this kind, consists not merely in its system of literary co-operation, but also in its economy. The acquirements, taste, and discrimination of a number of individuals, who feel an interest in the same pursuit, are thus brought to act in voluntary combination, and the ordinary charges of publication are also avoided, so that the volumes produced are distributed among the Members (who can alone obtain them) at little more than the cost of printing and paper. The Society expends the whole of its funds in the preparation of works for the Members; and since the cost of each copy varies inversely as the whole number of copies printed, it is obvious that the Members are gainers individually by the prosperity of the Society, and the consequent vigour of its operations.

New Members have, at present, the privilege of purchasing the complete set of the publications of the Society for previous years for ten guineas, but have not the power of selecting any particular volume.

The Members are requested to bear in mind that the power of the Council to make advantageous arrangements, will depend, in a great measure, on the prompt payment of the subscriptions, which are payable in advance on the 1st of January, and are received by MR. RICHARDS, 37, Great Queen Street, Lincoln's Inn Fields, who is the Society's agent for the delivery of its volumes. Post Office Orders should be drawn on the *Charing Cross Post Office.*

WORKS ALREADY ISSUED.

1—The Observations of Sir Richard Hawkins, Knt.
In his Voyage into the South Sea in 1593. Reprinted from the edition of 1622, and edited by Capt. C. R. DRINKWATER BETHUNE, R.N., C.B.   [*Issued for* 1847.

2—Select Letters of Columbus.
With Original Documents relating to the DISCOVERY of the NEW WORLD. Translated and Edited by R. H. MAJOR, Esq., of the British Museum.   [*Issued for* 1847.

3—The Discoverie of the Empire of Guiana,
By SIR WALTER RALEGH, KNT. Edited, with Copious Explanatory Notes, and a Biographical Memoir, by SIR ROBERT H. SCHOMBURGK, Phil. D., etc.   [*Issued for* 1848.

4—Sir Francis Drake his Voyage, 1595,
By THOMAS MAYNARDE, together with the Spanish Account of Drake's Attack on Puerto Rico, edited from the Original MSS., by W. D. COOLEY, Esq.   [*Issued for* 1848.

5—Narratives of Early Voyages
Undertaken for the Discovery of a Passage to CATHAIA and INDIA, by the Northwest, with Selections from the Records of the worshipful Fellowship of the Merchants of London, trading into the East Indies; and from MSS. in the Library of the British Museum, now first published, by THOMAS RUNDALL, Esq.   [*Issued for* 1849.

6—The Historie of Travaile into Virginia Britannia,
Expressing the Cosmographie and Commodities of the Country, together with the Manners and Customs of the people, gathered and observed as well by those who went first thither as collected by William Strachey, Gent., the first Secretary of the Colony; now first Edited from the original manuscript in the British Museum, by R. H. MAJOR, Esq., of the British Museum.   [*Issued for* 1849.

7—Divers Voyages touching the Discovery of America,
And the Islands adjacent, collected and published by RICHARD HAKLUYT, Prebendary of Bristol, in the year 1582. Edited, with Notes and an Introduction, by JOHN WINTER JONES, Esq., of the British Museum.   [*Issued for* 1850.

8—A Collection of Documents on Japan,
With a Commentary, by THOMAS RUNDALL, Esq.   [*Issued for* 1850.

9—The Discovery and Conquest of Florida,
By DON FERDINANDO DE SOTO. Translated out of Portuguese, by Richard Hakluyt; and Edited with Notes and an Introduction, by W. B. RYE, Esq., of the British Museum.   [*Issued for* 1851.

10—Notes upon Russia,
Being a Translation from the Earliest Account of that Country, entitled RERUM MOSCOVITICARUM COMMENTARII, by the Baron Sigismund von Herberstein, Ambassador from the Court of Germany to the Grand Prince Vasiley Ivanovich, in the years 1517 and 1526. Two Volumes. Translated, and Edited with Notes and an Introduction, by R. H. MAJOR, Esq., of the British Museum. Vol. 1.   [*Issued for* 1851.

11—The Geography of Hudson's Bay.
Being the Remarks of CAPTAIN W. COATS, in many Voyages to that locality, between the years 1727 and 1751. With an Appendix, containing Extracts from the Log of CAPT. MIDDLETON on his Voyage for the discovery of the North-west Passage, in H.M.S. "Furnace", in 1741-2. Edited by JOHN BARROW, Esq., F.R.S., F.S.A.   [*Issued for* 1852.

12—Notes upon Russia. Vol. 2.   [*Issued for* 1852.

13—Three Voyages by the North-east,
Towards Cathay and China, undertaken by the Dutch in the years 1594, 1595, and 1596, with their Discovery of Spitzbergen, their residence of ten months in Novaya Zemlya, and their safe return in two open boats. By GERRIT DE VEER. Edited by C. T. BEKE, Esq., Ph.D., F.S.A.   [*Issued for* 1853.

14-15—The History of the Great and Mighty Kingdom of China and the Situation Thereof.
Compiled by the Padre JUAN GONZALEZ DE MENDOZA. And now Reprinted from the Early Translation of R. PARKE. Edited by SIR GEORGE T. STAUNTON, BART. With an Introduction by R. H. MAJOR, Esq. 2 vols.   [*Issued for* 1854.

16—The World Encompassed by Sir Francis Drake,
Being his next Voyage to that to Nombre de Dios. Collated with an unpublished Manuscript of FRANCIS FLETCHER, Chaplain to the Expedition. With Appendices illustrative of the same Voyage, and Introduction, by W. S. W. VAUX, Esq., M.A.   [*Issued for* 1855.

17—The History of the Tartar Conquerors who Subdued China.
From the French of the Père D'Orleans, 1688. Translated and Edited by the EARL OF ELLESMERE. With an Introduction by R. H. MAJOR, Esq.   [*Issued for* 1855.

18—A Collection of Early Documents on Spitzbergen and Greenland,

Consisting of: a translation from the German of F. Marten's important work on Spitzbergen, now very rare; a translation from Isaac de la Peyrère's Relation de Groenland, and a rare piece entitled "God's Power and Providence showed in the miraculous preservation and deliverance of eight Englishmen, left by mischance in Greenland, anno 1630, nine moneths and twelve days, faithfully reported by Edward Pelham." Edited, with Notes, by ADAM WHITE, Esq., of the British Museum. [*Issued for* 1856.

19—The Voyage of Sir Henry Middleton to Bantam and the Maluco Islands.

From the rare Edition of 1606. Edited by BOLTON CORNEY, Esq. [*Issued for* 1856.

20—Russia at the close of the Sixteenth Century.

Comprising "The Russe Commonwealth" by Dr. GILES FLETCHER, and SIR JEROME HORSEY'S Travels, now first printed entire from his manuscript in the British Museum. Edited by E. A. BOND, ESQ., of the British Museum. [*Issued for* 1857.

21—The Travels of Girolamo Benzoni, in America, in 1542-56.

Translated and edited by ADMIRAL W. H. SMYTH, F.R.S., F.S.A. [*Issued for* 1857.

22—India in the Fifteenth Century.

Being a Collection of Narratives of Voyages to India in the century preceding the Portuguese discovery of the Cape of Good Hope; from Latin, Persian, Russian, and Italian sources, now first translated into English. Edited, with an Introduction, by R. H. MAJOR, ESQ., F.S.A. [*Issued for* 1858.

23—Narrative of a Voyage to the West Indies and Mexico.

In the Years 1599-1602, with Maps and Illustrations. By SAMUEL CHAMPLAIN. Translated from the original and unpublished Manuscript, with a Biographical Notice and Notes by ALICE WILMERE. Edited by NORTON SHAW. [*Issued for* 1858.

24—Expeditions into the Valley of the Amazons,

During the Sixteenth and Seventeenth centuries: containing the Journey of GONZALO PIZARRO, from the Royal Commentaries of Garcilasso Inca de la Vega; the Voyage of FRANCISCO DE ORELLANA, from the General History of HERRERA; and the Voyage of CRISTOVAL DE ACUNA, from an exceedingly scarce narrative written by himself, in 1641. Edited and translated by CLEMENTS R. MARKHAM, ESQ. [*Issued for* 1859.

25—Early Indications of Australia;

A Collection of Documents shewing the Early Discoveries of Australia to the time of CAPTAIN COOK. Edited by R. H. MAJOR, Esq., of the British Museum, F.S.A. [*Issued for* 1859.

26—The Embassy of Ruy Gonzalez de Clavijo to the Court of Timour, 1403-6.

Translated, for the first time, with Notes, a Preface, and an Introductory Life of Timour Beg, By CLEMENTS R. MARKHAM, ESQ., F.R.G.S. [*Issued for* 1860.

27—Henry Hudson the Navigator.

The Original Documents in which his career is recorded. Collected, partly Translated, and Annotated, with an Introduction, by GEORGE ASHER, Esq., LL.D. [*Issued for* 1860.

28—The Expedition of Ursua and Aguirre,

In search of El Dorado and Omagua, A.D. 1560-61, translated from the "Sexta Noticia historial" of Fray Pedro Simon, by W. Bollaert, Esq.; with an introduction by C. R. Markham, Esq. [*Issued for* 1861.

Other Works in Progress.

The FIFTH Letter of HERNANDO CORTES, being that describing his Voyage to Honduras in 1525-6. To be Translated and Edited by C. G. SQUIER, Esq.

The Voyage of VASCO DE GAMA round the Cape of Good Hope in 1497, now first Translated from a cotemporaneous manuscript, accompanied by other documents forming a monograph on the life of DE GAMA. To be translated and edited by RICHARD GARNETT, Esq., of the British Museum.

The DISCOVERIES OF THE WORLD from their first original unto the year of our Lord 1555, by ANTONIO GALVANO, Governor of Ternate, corrected, quoted, and published in English by RICHARD HAKLUYT (1601), now reprinted with the original Portuguese text, and edited by REAR-ADMIRAL BETHUNE.

The LIFE AND ACTS OF DON ALONZO DE GUZMAN Y HENRIQUEZ, written by himself, containing a Narrative of his Adventures in Germany, Italy, and other parts of Europe, as well as in South America, during the reign of Charles V. Translated from a manuscript in the National Library at Madrid, by CLEMENTS R. MARKHAM, Esq.

ACCOUNT OF THE JOURNEY OF CATERINO ZENO to the Empire of Persia in the time of UZUN HASSAN, and of the Discovery of Frislanda, Eslanda, Engroenlanda, Estotilanda and Icaria, by the two brothers NICOLO and ANTONIO ZENO. The Journey to Persia edited, with notes and an Introduction, by MAJOR-GENERAL SIR HENRY C. RAWLINSON, K.C.B. The Discovery of Frislanda, etc., edited, with notes and an Introduction, by R. H. MAJOR, Esq., by whom the whole is translated from the edition of Francesco Marcolini. Venice, 1558.

Works suggested to the Council for Publication.

The Discovery and Conquest of the Canary Islands, by Bethencourt, in 1402-25; and the Voyages of Mendana and Quiros in the South Seas.

Laws of the Hakluyt Society.

I. The object of this Society shall be to print, for distribution among its members, rare and valuable Voyages, Travels, Naval Expeditions, and other geographical records, from an early period to the beginning of the eighteenth century.

II. The Annual Subscription shall be One Guinea, payable in advance on the 1st January.

III. Each member of the Society, having paid his subscription, shall be entitled to a copy of every work produced by the Society, and to vote at the general meetings within the period subscribed for; and if he do not signify, before the close of the year, his wish to resign, he shall be considered as a member for the succeeding year.

IV. The management of the Society's affairs shall be vested in a Council consisting of twenty-one members, namely, a President, two Vice-Presidents, a Secretary, and seventeen ordinary members, to be elected annually; but vacancies occurring between the general meetings shall be filled up by the Council.

V. A General Meeting of the Subscribers shall be held annually, on the first Thursday in March. The Secretary's Report on the condition and proceedings of the Society shall be then read, and, along with the Auditor's Report, be submitted for approval, and finally, the Meeting shall proceed to elect the Council for the ensuing year.

VI. At each Annual Election, six of the old Council shall retire; and a list of the proposed new Council shall be printed for the subscribers previous to the general meeting.

VII. The Council shall meet ordinarily on the 2nd Monday in every month, excepting August, September, and October, for the despatch of business, three forming a quorum, and the Chairman having a casting vote.

VIII. Gentlemen preparing and editing works for the Society, shall receive twenty-five copies of such works respectively.

IX. The number of copies printed of the Society's productions shall not exceed the estimated number of Subscribers; so that after the second year, when the Society may be supposed to have reached its full growth, there shall be no extra copies.

X. The Society shall appoint Local Secretaries throughout the kingdom, empowered to enrol members, transmit subscriptions, and otherwise forward the Society's interests; and it shall make such arrangements with its correspondents in the chief provincial towns, as will insure to subscribers residing in the country the regular delivery of their volumes at moderate charges.

Rules for the Delivery of the Society's Volumes.

I. The Society's productions will be delivered without any charge, within three miles of the General Post Office.

II. They will be forwarded to any place beyond that limit, the Society paying the cost of booking, but not of carriage; nor will it be answerable in this case for any loss or damage.

III. They will be delivered by the Society's agent, Mr. THOMAS RICHARDS, 37, Great Queen Street, Lincoln's Inn Fields, to persons having written authority of subscribers to receive them.

IV. They will be sent to the Society's correspondents or agents in the principal towns throughout the kingdom; and care shall be taken that the charge for carriage be as moderate as possible.

LIST OF MEMBERS

OF

THE HAKLUYT SOCIETY.

Admiralty (The), 2 *copies*

Ainslie, Philip Barrington, Esq., St. Colme

All Souls College, Oxford

Allen, Mr. E., 12, Tavistock-row, Covent-garden

Allport, Franklin, Esq., 156, Leadenhall-st.

Alston, Lieut. A. H., H.M.S. *St. George*, West Indies

Amsterdam, de Bibliothek van het Collegie Zeemanshoop.

Antiquaries, the Society of

Arlt, Mr., Moscow

Army and Navy Club, 13, St. James's-square.

Arrowsmith, John, Esq., Hereford-square, South Kensington

Ashton, J. Y., Esq., Liverpool

Asher, A., Berlin

Athenæum Club, The, Pall Mall

Athenæum Library, Boston, U.S.

Atkinson, F. R., Esq., Oak House, Pendleton, Manchester

Dr. Baikie

Bancroft, —, Esq.

Bank of England Library and Literary Association

Baring, Hon. Francis, M.P., 16, St. James's-square

Barlersque, C., Esq., Bordeaux

Burney, Chas. Gorham, Richmond, Virginia

Barrow, J., Esq., F.R.S. F.S.A., 17, Hanover terrace, Regent's Park

Batho, J. A., Esq., 49, Upper Charlotte-street, Fitzroy-square

Becher, Captain, R.N., 13, Dorset place, Dorset-square

Beck, Dr., New York State Library, Albany

Beke, Charles T., Esq., Phil. D., Bekesbourne, Canterbury

Belcher, Captain Sir Edward, C.B., R.N., Union Club, Trafalgar-square

Bell, Reverend Thomas, Berbice

Bell, Robert, Esq., Norris Castle, East Cowes, I.W.

Belfast Library

Benzon, E. L. S., Esq., Sheffield

Berlin, The Royal Library of

Betencourt, Alonzo, Esq., Philadelphia

Bethune, Rear-Admiral C. R. Drinkwater, C.B., 4, Cromwell-road, Princes Gate

Bibliothèque Impériale, Paris

Biden, Captain

Birmingham Library (The)

Blackie, Dr. Walter G., Villafield, Glasgow

Blyth, James, Esq., 24, Hyde-park-gardens

Bois, H., Esq., 110, Fenchurch-street

Bombay Geographical Society

Bone, J. H. A., Esq., Cleveland, Ohio, U.S.

Booth, B. W., Esq., Manchester

Boston Athenæum, The

Boston Public Library, U.S.

Botfield, Beriah, Esq., Norton Hall, Northamptonshire

Bowring, Sir John, LL.D.

Bradshaw, Lieut. Lawrence, Woolwich

Brevorst, J. C., Esq., New York

Brockhaus, F. A., Esq., Leipzig

Brodhead, J. R., Esq., New York

Broome, Major A.

Broughton, Lord, 42, Berkeley-square

Brown, George, Esq., Cambridge-street, Belgrave-square

Brown, J. A., Esq., Newcastle-place, Clerkenwell

Brown, John Carter, Esq., Providence, Rhode Island

Brown, R., Esq., Sydney Mines, Cape Breton

Brown, W. H., Esq., Chester

Bruce, John, Esq., F.S.A., 5, Upper Gloucester-street, Dorset-square

Brussels, Royal Library of

Bunbury, E. H. Esq., 15, Jermyn-street

Burnett, W. F., Commander, R.N.

Cambridge University Library

Campbell, R. H. S., Esq., 5, Argyle-place, Regent-street

Canada, The Parliament Library

Cannon, Charles, Esq., British Museum

Carlton Club, Pall Mall

Chapman, Mr. John, Strand

Chapman, William, Esq., Richmond

Chauncey, Henry C., Esq., New York

Chichester, J. H. R., Esq., 49, Wimpole-street

Christie, Jonathan Henry, Esq., 9, Stanhope-street, Hyde-park-gardens

Churchill, Lord Alfred S., F.R.G.S., 16, Rutland Gate

Colledge, Dr., Lauriston House, Cheltenham

Collier, John Payne, Esq., F.S.A.
Colonial Office (The)
Congress, Library of the, United States
Cooper, Colonel E. H. 36, Hertford-street
Corney, B., Esq., M.R.S.L., Barnes-ter.
Costello, Dudley, Esq., 54, Acacia-road, St. John's Wood
Cotton, R. W., Esq., Barnstaple
Cracroft, Capt., R.N.
Cranstoun, G., Esq., Corehouse, Lanark
Crowniushield, —, Esq. (per Mr. Stevens)
Cunard, Edward, Esq., New York

Dalrymple, Arthur, Esq.
Dalton, J. Stuart, Esq., for the Liverpool Free Public Library
Deane, Charles, Esq., Boston, U.S.
Delepierre, O., Esq., 18, Gloucester-terrace, Hyde Park
Delft, Royal Academy of
Dilke, C. Wentworth, Esq., 76, Sloane-st.
Dilke, C. W., Esq., Jun., 76, Sloane-street
Drake, Samuel G., Esq., Boston, U. S.
Dry, Thos., Esq., 25, Lincoln's Inn Fields
Ducie, Earl, 30, Princes-gate
Dundas, Rt. Hon. Sir David, 13, King's Bench Walk, Temple
Dundas, George, Esq., 9, Charlotte-square, Edinburgh
Dundas, John, Esq., 25, St. Andrew's-square, Edinburgh
Duprat, M. B., Paris

Ecky, John H., Esq., Philadelphia
Ellice, Rt. Hon. Edward, M.P., 18, Arlington-street
Ellis, Sir Henry, K.H., F.R.S., 24, Bedford-square
Elphinstone, Lieut., 3, Chesham-place, Belgrave-square
Ely, Miss, Philadelphia
Emmet, Dr. Addis, New York

Flagg, Geo. W., Esq., Charleston, South Carolina
Fletcher, Wm. Younger, Esq., British Museum
Foley, Lord, 26, Grosvenor-square
Folsom, Hon. George, New York
Foote, John, Esq.
Force, Colonel Peter, Washington, U.S.
Foreign Office (The)
Forster, John, Esq., 46, Montague-square
Fox, General, Addison-road, Kensington
Franck, Mons. A., Rue Richelieu, 67, Paris
Frere, W. E., Esq.

Galignani, M., Paris
Garnett, Richard, Esq., British Museum

Gladdish, William, Esq., Gravesend
Glasgow College
Glendening, Robert, Esq., 5, Britain-st., Portsea
Grant & Farran, Messrs. 21, Ludgate-st.
Gawler, Colonel, United Service Club
Giraud, R. Hervé, Esq., Furnival's-inn
Graves, Robert Edmund, Esq., British Museum
Grey, R. W., Esq., M.P., 47, Belgrave-sq.
Grylls, Rev. W.
Guild, G. F., Esq., Boston, U.S.
Guillaume, Mr., Chester-square
Guise, W. V., Esq., Elmore-ct., Gloucester

Hale, J. H., Esq., Park-road, Stockwell-common
Harcourt, Egerton, Esq., Carlton Gardens
Harker, Turner James, Esq., 10, Northampton Park, Islington
Hawes, Sir Benjamin, 9, Queen's-square, Westminster
Hawkins, Edward, Esq., British Museum
Henderson, Dr., 6, Curzon-st., Mayfair
Hodgkin, Thomas, Esq., M.D., 35, Bedford-square
Hollond, R., Esq., M.P., 63, Portland-pl.
Holmes, James, Esq. 4, New Ormond-street, Foundling
Home Office (The)
Horner, Rev. J. S. H., Wells Park, Somersetshire
Howes, John, Esq., Chicago (per Messrs. Low)
Hull Subscription Library
Hunter, David, Esq., Blackness, Dundee

India Office, 20 *copies*

Jones, J. Winter, Esq., F.S.A., British Museum
Jones, W. Bence, Esq., Lisselan, co. Cork
Jukes, J. B., Esq., 51, Stephen's-green, Dublin
Junior United Service Club, Charles-st., St. James's

Kennedy, Robt. Lenox, Esq., New York
Kerslake, Mr. T., Bristol

Laird, John, Esq., Birkenhead
Lansdowne, the Marquis of, 54, Berkeley-square
Lavradio, His Excellency the Count de, 12, Gloucester-place, Portman-square
Law, William, Esq., 103, Piccadilly

Leicester Permanent Library
Lemon, Sir C., Bart., M.P., 46, Charles-street, Berkeley-square
Lenox, James, Esq., New York
Little and Brown, Messrs., Boston, U.S.
Liverpool Free Public Library
Logan, A. J., Esq., Singapore
London Institution, Finsbury Circus
Lott, Capt. E. P., 159, Parliament-street, Liverpool
London Library, 12, St. James's-square
Lowe, Right Hon. Robert., M.P., 34, Lowndes-square
Loyes, Edw., Esq., 33, Paternoster-row
Lyceum Library, Hull

M'Calmont, Robt., Esq., 30, Eaton-square
Mackenzie, John W., Esq., Edinburgh
Macleay, Geo., Esq., Brownhills, New South Wales
Macready, W. C., Esq., Sherborne House, Dorset
Madan, Capt. Frederick, H.C.S., 5, North-wick-terrace, St. John's Wood
Madras Literary Society
Major, R. H., Esq., F.S.A., British Museum
Malcolm, W. Elphinstone, Esq., Burnfoot, Langholm, Carlisle
Mantell, Walter, Esq., New Zealand
Markham, Clements R., Esq., 21, Eccleston-square
Marlborough, His Grace the Duke of, Blenheim
Marsh, Hon. George P., Constantinople
Massie, Captain T. L., R.N., Chester
Melbourne, Public Library of, per Mr. Guillaume
Muller, F., Esq., Amsterdam
Munich Royal Library
Murchison, Sir Roderick Impey, F.R.S. &c., 16, Belgrave-square
Murphy, Hon. C. H., Brooklyn, New York
Murray, John, Esq., Albemarle-street

Newcastle-upon-Tyne Literary and Scientific Institute
Newman, Mr. James, 13, York place, Kentish Town
New York Mercantile Library
Nicholson, Sir C. D. E. L., New South Wales
Nimmo, Thomas, Esq., Demerara
Norris, Edwin, Esq., Sec. Asiatic Society, 5, New Burlington-street
Norton, C. B., Esq., New York

Oriental Club, Hanover-square
Ouvry, F., Esq., F.S.A., 66, Lincoln's Inn Fields

Paine, W. Dunkley, Esq., Cockshutt-Hill, Reigate
Parker, J. W., Esq., West Strand
Parliament Library, Toronto
Pasley, Major-General Sir C. W., K.C.B., 12, Norfolk Crescent, Hyde Park
Peacock, George, Esq.
Peacock, Septimus, Esq., Alexandria
Pemberton, Mrs.
Pennington, John, Esq., Philadelphia
Pennsylvania, Historical Society of
Perry, Sir Erskine, M.P., Eaton-place
Petit, Rev. J. Louis, the Uplands, Shiffnal
Petit, Miss
Phillimore, Charles B., Esq., 6, Green-street, Grosvenor-square
Platt, T. Clayton, Esq., Philadelphia
Plowden, W. H. Chicheley, Esq., F.R.S.
Portland, His Grace the Duke of
Portsmouth, the Royal Naval College
Pourtales, Count Albert, Berlin
Powis, Earl of, 45, Berkeley-square
Prescott, Rear H., Admiral C.B., United Service Club
Putnam, G. R., Esq., New York

Quaritch, Mr., 15, Piccadilly

Rawlinson, Sir H., K.C.B., Athenæum Club
Reed, F. J. Esq., 34, Bedford-square
Richard, John E., Esq., Wandsworth, Surrey
Richards, Thomas, Esq., 4, St. Alban's-road, Kensington
Richardson, Sir John, M.D., F.R.S.
Richardson, Ralph, Esq., Greenfield Hall, Holywell, Flintshire
Riggs, G. W., Esq., Washington, U.S.
Robinson, Capt. Walter F., R.N., F.R.G.S., Junior United Service Club
Royal Geographical Society, 3, Waterloo-place
Royal Society, Burlington House
Roys, Thos. Wm., Esq., Southampton, Long Island, New York
Rowsell, E. P., Esq., 29, Finsbury-circus
Rumbold, C. E., Esq., 1, Eccleston-square
Rushout, Miss, Tetbury
Rye, W. B., Esq., British Museum

Scarth, J., Esq., Canton
Schomburgk, Sir Robert, Bangkok
Sedgwick, the Rev. Adam, Woodwardian Professor, Cambridge
Sheffield, Earl of, 20, Portland-place
Shillinglaw, —, Esq., Admiralty
Shrewsbury, Earl of
Simpson, Lieutenant
Singapore Library

Smith, Edmund, Esq., Hull
Smith, George, Esq., 21, Russell-square
Smith, J., Esq., 5, Cavendish-square
Somers, Earl, 33, Princes-gate, Hyde Park
Stanford, Mr. E., Charing-cross
Stanley of Alderley, Lord
Stanley, Hon. Henry E. J.
Stuart, Alexander, Esq., New York
St. Andrew's University
St. David's, the 'Right Rev. the Lord Bishop of, Abergwili, Carmarthenshire
St. Petersburg, Imperial Library of
Stevens, H., Esq., Boston, United States
Stockholm, Royal Library of (per Messrs. Longman and Co.
Stirling, Wm., Esq., of Keir, 128, Park-st.
Stubbs, Lieut., R.N., H.M.S. *Edgar*
Stuart, R. L., Esq., New York

Taunton, Lord, 27, Belgrave-square
Ternaux-Compans, Mons. H., Paris
Thompson, Thos., Esq., Solicitor, Hull
Thomas, W. A., Esq., 50, Threadneedle-street
Tolstoy, George, Esq., St. Petersburgh
Trade, the Board of, Whitehall
Travellers' Club, 106, Pall Mall
Trinity House, Tower Hill

Union Society, Oxford
United Service Institution, Scotland-yard
Upham & Beet, Messrs. 46, New Bond-st.

Victoria Library and Reading Rooms, Hong Kong
Vienna Imperial Library
Virginia State Library

Vivian, Geo., Esq., 11, Upper Grosvenor-street
Van Rÿckevorsel, H., Consul de Venezuela, Conseiller à la Régence de Rotterdam

Waite, Henry, Esq., 68, Old Broad street
Wales, George Washington, Boston, U.S.
Walker, J., Esq., 31, Keppel-street
Walker, Joshua, Esq., Jun., 59, Upper Brunswick-place, Brighton
Waters, J. S., Esq., Baltimore, U.S.
Watts, Thomas, Esq., British Museum
Weir, William, Esq., 30, Great Coram-st.
Wensleydale, the Rt. Hon. Lord, 56, Park-street, Grosvenor-square
Whewell, the Rev. W., D.D., Master of Trinity College, Cambridge
White, R., Esq., Cowes, Isle of Wight
Whiteman. J. C., Esq., Theydon Grove, Epping
Wilkinson, John, Esq., 3, Wellington-st., Strand
Willis and Sotheran, Messrs., Strand
Williams,T.,Esq.,Northumberland-house, Strand
Wilson, Edward S., Esq., Hull
Wolff, H. Drummond, Esq., 44, Half-moon-st., Piccadilly
Woodd, Basil T., Esq., Conyngham Hall, Naresborough
Wood, Lieutenant John, H.E.I.C.S., 137, Leadenhall-street
Woods, Samuel, Esq., Australia
Wright, H., Esq., Cheltenham
Wyld, James, Esq., Strand

Young, Capt. Allen, Riversdale, Twickenham
Young, G. F., Esq., 80, Cornhill

RICHARDS, PRINTER, 37, GREAT QUEEN STREET.

WORKS ISSUED BY

The Hakluyt Society.

THE EXPEDITION OF PEDRO DE URSUA

AND LOPE DE AGUIRRE.

M.DCCCLXI.

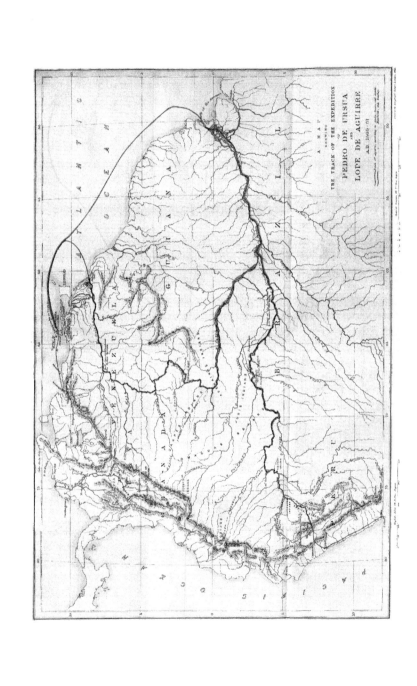

A MAP
SHEWING
THE TRACK OF THE EXPEDITION
OF
PEDRO DE URSUA
AND
LOPE DE AGUIRRE
A.D. 1560–61

THE EXPEDITION

OF

PEDRO DE URSUA & LOPE DE AGUIRRE

IN SEARCH OF

EL DORADO AND OMAGUA

IN 1560-1.

TRANSLATED FROM FRAY PEDRO SIMON'S " SIXTH HISTORICAL NOTICE OF THE
CONQUEST OF TIERRA FIRME."

BY

WILLIAM BOLLAERT, Esq., F.R.G.S.,

CORR. MEM. OF THE UNIVERSITY OF CHILE; MEMBER OF THE
ETHNOLOGICAL SOCIETY OF NEW YORK.

WITH AN INTRODUCTION

BY

CLEMENTS R. MARKHAM, ESQ.

LONDON:

PRINTED FOR THE HAKLUYT SOCIETY.

M.DCCC.LXI.

LONDON:
T. RICHARDS, 37, GREAT QUEEN STREET.

THE HAKLUYT SOCIETY.

TABLE OF CONTENTS.

INTRODUCTION i

CHAPTER I.

1. Gives a brief account of the deeds of Pedro de Ursua before his
arrival in Peru, and of his entrance into that country.—2. Certain
Brazilian Indians give information in Peru, of very rich provinces
near the river Marañon.—3. The marquis of Cañete determines to
send Pedro de Ursua to explore them, and summons him to his
presence.—4. Various opinions are formed in Peru respecting this
expedition 1

CHAPTER II.

1. Pedro de Ursua builds the brigantines for the expedition, and makes
Pedro de Ramiro his lieutenant-general.—2. Ursua leaves Lima with
his people ; he arrives at the town of Moyobamba.—3. How he con-
trives to obtain two thousand dollars from the cura or priest of the
place.—4. Ursua sends part of his people from the Motilones to other
provinces, where they provide for themselves . . . 5

CHAPTER III.

1. Arles and Frias are displeased at having Ramiro among them ;
they determine to kill him.—2. They kill Ramiro.—3. The governor
Ursua goes in person to arrest the delinquents.—4. He sends them to
Santa Cruz, where they are beheaded 8

CHAPTER IV.

1. People in Peru are fearful of mutiny in Ursua's expedition ; a friend
writes to him on the subject.—2. The governor sends two parties of
soldiers in search of provisions ; one of these, composed of thirty men,
goes down the river more than two hundred leagues.—3. Garcia del
Arze and his soldiers fortify themselves on an island against the
Indians.—4. The Spaniards are most cruel to the natives who come
peacefully to them 12

CHAPTER V.

1. Juan de Vargas commences his voyage ; arrives at the mouth of the Cocama.—2. He remains here until Ursua arrives.—3. The brigantines spring a leak when launched, which is unfortunate for the expedition. —4. Ursua descends the river with all his people, arriving at the province of the Caperuzos.—5. He sends a brigantine to advise Juan de Vargas of his coming 16

CHAPTER VI.

1. From the river Bracamoras the governor continues his voyage to that of Cocáma, where he finds Juan de Vargas with his party.—2. They continue their voyage, some of their necessities in the way of food being supplied by the *hicoteas* and their eggs.—3. They arrive at the island where Garcia del Arze and his soldiers are.—4. They find some islands lower down the river, with villages, but no inhabitants, for they had abandoned them 20

CHAPTER VII.

1. The Indians come out to see the expedition from a distance, and a chief comes with offers of peace.—2. The Indians come from the province of Carari with some provisions, which they barter for trinkets.— 3. The governor sends an officer to examine the country inland.— 4. Punishments which Pedro de Ursua inflicted on his people.— 5. Opinions entertained respecting this province, whether there were one or two 24

CHAPTER VIII.

1. Pedro de Ursua continues his course through a desert region, where his people suffer from want.—2. They establish themselves in a village, where they make up for past want by a large supply of provisions.—3. The governor, on account of the plentiful supplies, determines to encamp in the village, pass Christmas there, and make inquiries respecting the land for which they are searching.—4. Fifty Spaniards depart to assist the chief of Machiparo, against two hundred hostile Indians 29

CHAPTER IX.

1. Pedro de Ursua names a provisor or vicar-general for his fleet, believing he had power to do so.—Some grow faint hearted at the continuation of the expedition, and the governor encourages them to proceed.—3. Excuses which the mutineers make to Pedro de Ursua for their delinquencies.—4. The mutineers conspire to rid themselves of the government of Ursua, and to make Don Fernando de Guzman his successor 34

CHAPTER X.

1. The mutineers determine to kill the governor, Pedro de Ursua, and to return to Peru.—2. Mysterious warning of the death of Ursua, which was seen and heard by a knight of the order of San Juan.—3. They continue their course from this village to another lower down, of the same name. A slave of one of the mutineers discovers their design, and attempts to warn the governor.—4. The mutineers kill the governor Pedro de Ursua, and his lieutenant . . 38

CHAPTER XI.

THE CRUISE OF THE TRAITOR AGUIRRE.

1. The governor being dead, the rebels endeavour to bring all the expedition to their side.—2. They do not allow the soldiers to leave their quarters during the night, to prevent them from conferring together.—3. The murderers divide the various offices among themselves.—4. They continue the division of offices. Sancho Pizarro returns 43

CHAPTER XII.

1. The new general, Don Fernando, calls a council to discuss matters relative to the projected discovery of the new lands of the Dorado.—2. He has a document made out for their security, and orders all to sign it. Lope de Aguirre signs it, adding the word "traitor."—3. Aguirre publicly explains why he did so.—4. Juan Alonzo de la Bandera replies, saying that those who killed the governor were not traitors 47

CHAPTER XIII.

1. They leave the village (Machiparo) where they had killed Ursua, and, going down the river, arrive at another village, where they commence building brigantines.—2. They suffer so much from hunger in this village, that they are obliged to eat horses and dogs.—3. Aguirre kills Captain del Arze, because he was a friend of Uriua's, siezes Diego de Belcazar for the same cause, and has two others strangled.—4. Don Fernando takes away the office of maestro del campo from Lope de Aguirre, and gives it to Juan Alonzo de la Bandera, his lieutenant-general 51

CHAPTER XIV.

1. Don Fernando comes to an understanding with Lope de Aguirre, and promises to restore him to his post of maestro del campo.—2. The governor and Aguirre become friends, the enmity of the latter increases against Bandera.—3. Aguirre calumniates Bandera before the

governor, saying he wished to kill the governor, and rebel.—4. Aguirre kills Bandera, and one Christoval Hernandez, at the governor's house 56

CHAPTER XV.

1. The soldiers irritate the Indians, who bring provisions for them, when some Spaniards are killed.—2. Owing to these proceedings the Spaniards suffer great privations, on account of the fear the Indians have of coming near them.—3. Aguirre succeeds in gaining the confidence of Don Fernando for his own particular ends.—4. Don Fernando plans how to discover the real sentiments of the soldiers, and their devotion to him, and how he suceeeds . . 60

CHAPTER XVI.

1. Don Fernando thanks them for his new election, and makes it known that he will not force any one to follow him.—2. He asks the soldiers to take an oath to follow him, and all promise to do so, except three.—3. They all take the oath on a missal placed on an altar.—4. Difficulties that occur in consequence of the want of employment for the people, at this spot 64

CHAPTER XVII.

1. Aguirre addresses the soldiers.—2. He, together with the soldiers proclaims Fernando de Guzman Prince of Pirú.—3. Don Fernando accepts the title of Prince, and sets up an establishment accordingly —4. Don Fernando takes the office of sargento major from Sancho Pizarro (a friend of Ursua's) and gives it to Martin Perez . 68

CHAPTER XVIII.

1. Various projects regarding their journey to Pirú.—2. The plans they intend to adopt on their arrival at Nombre de Dios, Panamá, and Pirú : Don Fernando bestows titles for Encomiendas.—3. The vile doings of other traitors.—4. After three months, the brigantines being ready, they leave this village and prosecute their voyage . 73

CHAPTER XIX.

1. They arrive at an Indian village, where they pass Passion week and Easter ; Aguirre causes a soldier to be strangled.—2. They depart after Easter, and stop at another very large Indian town, where they find abundance of provisions and wine (chicha).—3. Some customs of the Indians of this place.—4. How they arranged to obtain provisions here ; and how some scruples occur to Don Fernando and his friends 77

CHAPTER XX.

1. Don Fernando calls a council, in which it is determined to kill Aguirre as it seemed necessary to do so.—2. Aguirre and his friends get more arms, taking them from the rest.—3. He divides the soldiers into companies, such an arrangement appearing to him better for his designs.—4. Aguirre arrests Gonzalo Duarte, Don Fernando's mayordomo, with the intention of killing him, but afterwards they become friends 81

CHAPTER XXI.

1. Difficulties between Captain Lorenzo Salduendo and Aguirre, as to the accommodation for Doña Ines on board the brigantines.—2. Aguirre kills Salduendo, and by his orders two soldiers kill Dona Ines.—3. Discussion between Don Fernando and Aguirre as to the death of Salduendo.—4. Aguirre pacifies Don Fernando, but, on account of an idle report which two captains repeat to Aguirre, he determines to kill Don Fernando 85

CHAPTER XXII.

1. Aguirre makes his arrangements to kill the Prince Don Fernando and others.—2. Aguirre and his companions kill two captains, and plan how the Prince is to die.—3. They go in the morning of the next day to kill the Prince.—4. Aguirre kills a priest, some captains, and the Prince Don Fernando 90

CHAPTER XXIII.

1. Aguirre explains the cause of the death of the governor and the others to the camp, and calls his soldiers the "Marañones".—2. He changes the various offices in the army, giving them to his friends.—3. They leave the town of the "Butchery", and sail through large provinces.—4. After navigating for twelve days they come to a village 93

CHAPTER XXIV.

1. They catch an Indian and send him to tell the others that they desire to be at peace with them.—2. Aguirre kills three soldiers, whilst they are putting the brigantines in order.—3. He still has tyrannical fears, although he has killed so many men.—4. The Brazilian Indian guides escape from him 99

CHAPTER XXV.

1. Going down the river, they fall in with some strongly built houses, where they find cakes of salt.—2. During the voyage they pass many islands, and on one of them they leave the greater number of Indian

servants, whom they had brought with them.—3. They continue the voyage under many difficulties. For a trifling affair Aguirre has two soldiers strangled.—4. He loses a piragua, with three Spaniards and some Indians; and others are drowned, gathering shell-fish   . 103

CHAPTER XXVI.

1. The first Spaniard who sailed out of the mouth of this river, was Captain Franciso de Orellana. Its banks are not well peopled. —2. Character, climate, and people of this river, from its sources to where it enters the sea.—3. There are more than two thousand islands near to the mouth of the river.—4. Lope de Aguirre, finding himself out at sea, sails for the island of Margarita, where he arrives and lands, having first killed two soldiers in the brigantine .   . 107

CHAPTER XXVII.

1. The maestro del campo, having received Aguirre's orders, departs, and strangles Sancho Pizarro on the road.—2. A piragua with Indians is sent from the port of Margarita, to examine the brigantines of Aguirre, and a party of soldiers visit him.—3. The Margarita people give Aguirre two bullocks, and he recompenses them.—4. The governor, on account of a letter received from Aguirre, decides upon visiting him, accompanied by some of the inhabitants of the city.—5. The governor offers him hospitality. The traitor marshals his armed men before the governor   113

CHAPTER XXVIII.

1. Aguirre makes prisoners of the governor, alcalde, and their companions.—2. All the traitors march towards the city with the governor; the maestro del campo takes possession of the city, in the name of Aguirre.—3. Aguirre enters the city, and robs the royal treasury.— 4. He continues his insolence by a thousand threats   .   . 117

CHAPTER XXIX.

1. For the love of a roving life, like that which the traitors led, some soldiers of the island join them, which causes no little detriment.—2. Aguirre sends to take a ship that was in Maracapana, belonging to the Provincial of Santo Domingo, but fails.—3. The Provincial of Santo Domingo determines to go in his ship, to the port of Burburata, and other parts, to give notice of the proceedings of Aguirre.—4. Aguirre addresses the people of the island with feigned words, and even with lies   122

CHAPTER XXX.

1. Aguirre kills one of his captains. Four of his soldiers desert.—2. Two of the deserters found; Aguirre orders them to be hung. He intends

to kill a monk of the order of Santo Domingo.—3. Aguirre informs his soldiers how he intends to proceed in his tyrannies.—4. He places his brigantines with their bows towards the shore, fearing that his soldiers might desert; and he destroys the houses and estates of an inhabitant who had fled 127

CHAPTER XXXI.

1. Aguirre kills a captain, named Juan de Turriaga, and buries him with pomp.—2. Aguirre threatens the people of Margarita with his vengeance, in case the provincial of Santo Domingo takes his men in Maracapana.—3. The provincial's ship is seen making for the island, the traitor prepares for defence.—4. Aguirre, observing that the provincial's ship had anchored, puts the inhabitants into the fort, as prisoners, and determines to kill the governor and his companions . 131

CHAPTER XXXII.

1. Aguirre arranges for the execution of the governor and his companions in captivity.—2. They kill the governor and his companions. Aguirre summons his soldiers to see the dead bodies, and makes his observations on the matter.—3. He explains, and gives his reasons for their death.—4. Aguirre orders the bodies to be buried, and sends the inhabitants back to prison. He leaves his maestro del campo in charge of the city, and then sallies forth against the governor . 136

CHAPTER XXXIII.

1. The people of the port of Burburata send tidings to the governor of Venezuela, and other cities of his government, and that of Merida, concerning the acts of the traitor.—2. Pedro Bravo de la Molina sends information to the Royal Audience of-Santa Fé, and to the other cities on the road.—3. Preparations are made by Pedro Bravo de la Molina, in the city of Merida, to resist the traitor, if necessary.— 4. The licenciate, Pablo Collado, is not unmindful of his duties, in the towns under his government 139

CHAPTER XXXIV.

1. Preparations ordered by the Royal Audience of Santa Fé, and officers appointed.—2. Orders are issued that the people of the various cities of the kingdom shall be ready for all exigencies, and what the governor Pedro Bravo de la Molina has to do in Merida.—3. The governments of Popayan, Santa Martha, and Carthagena, are ordered to collect troops, and various opinions as to sallying forth against the traitor.—4. Investigations are made, to see if there are, in the kingdom, any soldiers connected with the Peruvian mutineers. The royal seal guarded in Santa Fé 142

CHAPTER XXXV.

1. Aguirre marches with his soldiers to Punta de Piedras, whence he returns to the city. He is told unfavourable things of his maestro del campo.—2. Aguirre has his maestro del campo killed in the fortress. Some prisoners escape.—3. A horrible thing occurs to one Llamoso, relative to the body of the maestro del campo.—The Marañones and soldiers of the provincial see one another   .   .   . 147

CHAPTER XXXVI.

1. Lope de Aguirre writes to the provincial.—2. The provincial replies from his ship, and then sets sail. Aguirre hangs two soldiers.— 3. Opinions as to whether it was politic of the provincial to communicate with the traitor.—4. The opinions and objections resolved   151

CHAPTER XXXVII.

1. Aguirre prepares to leave the island, and kills a soldier.—2. He has flags made, and blessed in the church, on the feast of our Lady of Assumption.—3. Aguirre makes an oration to his captains and ensigns on giving them the flags.—4. A soldier escapes from Aguirre, on account of which he kills two others, also a woman   .   . 156

CHAPTER XXXVIII.

1. Aguirre orders an old man to be killed ; he likewise does the same to a friar of Santo Domingo. He also commands another friar to be killed, to whom he had confessed.—2. Of another who was strangled, which caused much sorrow in the town.—3. The traitor hangs an old man and a woman ; he also does ridiculous things to some soldiers.— 4. One Francisco Taxardo comes to the island of Margarita from Caraccas, with some people; with the intention of routing Aguirre 160

CHAPTER XXXIX.

1. Aguirre embarks with all his people, and, while doing so, he causes his admiral to be killed.—2. The traitor sails, but changes his route, by going to the port of Burburata.—3. He is becalmed, which retards his voyage.—4. They burn a ship they find in the port, and the inhabitants advise the governor of Venezuela of Aguirre's arrival 165

CHAPTER XL.

1. Garcia de Paredes goes from Merida to Tocuyo with some followers, sent by the governor.—2. The governor of Venezuela sends to the governor and inhabitants of Merida, to come and assist him.—3. The governor of Merida goes with twenty-five soldiers to Tocuyo.— 4. Aguirre's men find a pilot in the town of Burburata, who was one of those who had passed over to the provincial   .   .   . 169

CHAPTER XLI.

1. Aguirre is informed that some soldiers, who were friendly to him, are in that part of the country. He sends in search of them.—2. The traitor kills a soldier. He burns his vessels, and takes up his quarters in the town.—3. The soldiers look about for horses, so as to sally forth with them. The traitor declares war against the king of Castille.—4. The whole country is in a state of ferment ; the robberies of the soldiers ; they find the alcalde, and a tradesman of the town. Aguirre sends to the town of Valencia for horses . 173

CHAPTER XLII.

1. Aguirre kills a tradesman, also a soldier, in this town of Burburata. —2. Two of his soldiers desert from him. He begins his march on foot, for want of horses.—3. Aguirre leaves his camp on the road, and returns to Burburata, where he gets drunk with his companions ; three desert.—4. Disturbances in the camp whilst Aguirre was at Burburata, two soldiers are killed.—5. Opinion among the Marañones relative to the death of one. The tyrant is informed of what had happened, and returns to the camp 177

CHAPTER XLIII.

1. Aguirre marches, but with much trouble, towards Valencia. He becomes ill on the march.—2. They arrive at Valencia, and find it deserted by the inhabitants. Aguirre becomes worse, but recovers, and then kills a soldier.—3. The alcalde, Chaves, takes two soldiers in Burburata, and sends information to Aguirre ; one of them runs away. —4. The traitor manages to lay hands on the inhabitants of Valencia, and on another soldier 182

CHAPTER XLIV.

1. The traitor allows the priest of Margarita to return to his dwelling, on condition that he forwards a letter that Aguirre had written to the king.—2. The alcalde of Burburata informs the traitor, as to the preparations the governor is making to oppose him. Aguirre kills three soldiers.—3. A sentinel informs the town of Barquicimeto, that Aguirre is marching on it ; the inhabitants fly.—4. Ten of Aguirre's soldiers desert on the march, at which he becomes very wrath, and utters ten thousand blasphemies, as was his custom . . 187

CHAPTER XLV.

1. Aguirre, marching from Valencia to Barquicimeto, comes to a mining settlement, where he falls into some trouble.—2. The traitor advances to the river of the valley of Damas, where he rests a day.— 3. Here he determines to kill some of his men, but he does not do so.

One of his captains comes from Margarita to Barquicimeto, and gives information as to Aguirre's forces.—4. The maestro del campo, Diego Garcia de Paredes, reconnoitres the forces of the traitor . 197

CHAPTER XLVI.

1. The maestro del campo, in a narrow part of the road, unexpectedly finds himself in Aguirre's camp. Both parties retire.—2. The general Peña takes letters of pardon from the governor, for Aguirre and his soldiers.—3. The king's party determine to await Aguirre's attack upon the town. Aguirre writes a letter of promises and threats.—4. The traitor's party show themselves to those in the town, but no action ensues 202

CHAPTER XLVII.

1. Garcia de Paredes lays hands on some clothes and ammunition belonging to the traitor. His soldiers find the letters of pardon.— 2. Aguirre talks to them on the subject, they decide on following him. —3. Aguirre sets fire to the town. The maestro del campo fires into the enemy's camp. This vexes Aguirre.—4. Pedro Bravo de la Molina arrives with men from Merida, where the governor had made him his lieutenant-general 207

CHAPTER XLVIII.

1. Bravo accepts the posts conferred on him by the governor ; they all leave Tocuyo for the king's camp.—2. Aguirre's letter to the governor, Pablo Collado.—3. Those from Tocuyo join the king's forces, when victory over the traitor is anticipated.—4. Two of Aguirre's soldiers desert to the king's side. The maestro del campo and captain Bravo catch some Indians belonging to the Marañones . . 211

CHAPTER XLIX.

1. Aguirre sends sixty arquebusiers to fire into the king's camp at night, but without any result.—2. The traitor comes out to the aid of his men, and prepares to resist the royalists.—3. Aguirre's fire makes no impression on the royalists. Captain Diego Tirado deserts from the traitor.—4. Another soldier tries to desert to the royalists. A mounted soldier of the king's party makes the circuit of Aguirre's entrenchment 216

CHAPTER L.

1. Aguirre, having fears of the desertion of his men, retires to his entrenchment. The royalists go to their quarters, but with hopes of victory over the traitor.—2. The traitor meditates on killing the sick and those soldiers he has fears of, but is dissuaded from this.—3. He

takes their arms away from some of his soldiers, and drives away others, telling them to go and join the king's camp.—4. One of Aguirre's soldiers kills Pedro Bravo's horse. The traitor determines to return to the coast 220

CHAPTER LI.

1. The maestro del campo and captain Bravo come up towards Aguirre's entrenchment. Some soldiers go out to oppose them.—2. Captain Espindola, with a troop, deserts to the royalists, and all the rest of Aguirre's soldiers follow their example by various routes.—3. The maestro del campo sends news of the victory to the governor. Aguirre kills his daughter.—4. Aguirre is killed by two arquebuses fired at him. His head is cut off, and his hands are given to those from Merida and Valencia 224

CHAPTER LII.

1. Gives an account of the country Aguirre came from, his character and customs.—2. His occupations during the years he was in Peru. —3. An account of the depredations he committed.—4. Although the governor kept his promise of protection, with some of the Marañones, yet some were punished 230

INTRODUCTION.

THE blood-stained cruise of the " tyrant Aguirre," the translated narrative of which, from the text of the old chronicler Simon, is now printed for the first time, is by far the most extraordinary adventure in search of El Dorado on record. The dauntless hardihood of those old Spaniards and Germans, who, undismayed by the reverses and sufferings of numerous predecessors, continued to force their way for hundreds of miles into the forest covered wilds, is sufficiently astonishing; but in this cruise of Aguirre all that is wildest, most romantic, most desperate, most appalling in the annals of Spanish enterprise seems to culminate in one wild orgie of madness and blood.

The history of previous searches aft : the fabled El Dorado, which led to the expedition of Ursua and Aguirre, truthful and authentic as i· is, yet seems fitter for the pages of King Arthur's romance than for a sober narrative of facts. It is ne ¬sary, however, that these romantic expeditions sh ˒ˡ be fresh in the reader's mind, in order to und ˌrstand the objects and views of the men who followed Aguirre to destruction, and the exact position which his expedition occupies in the history of South American geographical discovery.

When the Spaniards had conquered and pillaged the civilized empires on the table lands of Mexico, Bogota, and Peru, they began to look round for new scenes of conquest, new sources of wealth; the wildest rumours were received as facts, and the forests and savannas, extending for thousands of square miles to the eastward of the cordilleras of the Andes, were covered, in imagination, with populous kingdoms, and cities filled with gold. The story of El Dorado, of a priest or king smeared with oil and then coated with gold dust, probably originated in a custom which prevailed amongst the civilized Indians of the plateau of Bogota;[1] but El Dorado was placed,

[1] "When the chief of Guatavita was independent, he made a solemn sacrifice every year, which, for its singularity, contributed to give celebrity to the lake of Guatavita, in the most distant countries, and which was the origin of the belief in El Dorado, in search of which so many years and so much wealth was employed. On the day appointed the chief smeared his body with turpentine, and then rolled in gold dust. Thus gilded and resplendent, he entered the canoe, surrounded by his nobles, whilst an immense multitude of people, with music and songs, crowded round the shores of the lake. Having reached the centre, the chief deposited his offerings of gold, emeralds, and other precious things, and then jumped in himself, to bathe. At this moment the surrounding hills echoed with the applause of the people; and, when the religious ceremony concluded, the dancing, singing, and drinking began."—*Descubrimiento de la Nueva Granada, por el Coronel J. Acosta*, p. 199.

Here we have the origin of El Dorado, and of Raleigh's lake

by the credulous adventurers, in a golden city amidst the impenetrable forests of the centre of South America, and, as search after search failed, his position was moved further and further to the eastward, in the direction of Guiana. El Dorado, the phantom god of gold and silver, appeared in many forms. The Spaniards of Bogota and Venezuela explored the head waters of the Orinoco and the Rio Negro in search of the "gilded man," or the golden "house of the sun," and no fabulous tale was too wild for their credulity. The settlers at Quito and in Northern Peru talked of the golden empire of the Omaguas, while those in Cuzco and Charcas dreamt of the wealthy cities of Paytiti and Enim, on the banks of a lake far away to the eastward of the Andes. These romantic fables, so firmly believed in those old days, led to the exploration of vast tracts of country, by the fearless adventurers of the sixteenth

of Parima, and golden city of Manoa. It is implied that the ceremony did not take place subsequent to the conquest of Guatavita by Nemequene, the Zipa of Bogota, about forty years before the appearance of the Spaniards; so that, on their arrival, traditions only existed of the gilded chief of the lake, which, in a confused and exaggerated form, seem to have originated the belief in El Dorado, and in a great city in the central plains of South America.

The people of Guatavita believed that their deity resided in the lake, and yearly sacrifices of gold and emeralds were made to him. Cochrane gives an amusing account of an attempt to drain this lake, which is only a short distance from Bogota; and several gold ornaments have been fished up, from time to time, but it is believed that millions still remain buried in the slime, at the bottom. —*Cochrane's Travels*, ii, p. 201.

century, portions of which have never been traversed since, even to this day.

The most famous searches after El Dorado were undertaken from the coast of Venezuela, and the most daring leaders of these wild adventures were German Knights.[1]

Shortly after Ojeda had discovered the coast of Venezuela, and Rodrigo de Bastidas had established a settlement at Santa Martha, the emperor Charles V made an agreement with a company of Germans to colonize these rich provinces. The Velsers of Augsburg were great merchants who traded in all parts of the world, and they agreed, through their Agents, Enrique de Alfinger and Geronimo Sailler, to found two cities and three forts within two years, to arm four ships, and take out three hundred Spaniards and fifty German miners; on condition that the emperor granted them the country extending from Cabo de la Vela to Maracapana (except the portion previously granted to one Juan de Ampuez) and without limit to the south, gave the title of Adelantado to the governor appointed by them, and allowed them to make slaves of the Indians.[2] At about the same time Bastidas, the governor of Santa Martha, had died, and it was arranged that Garcia de Lerma,

[1] The early expeditions to the river Orinoco, of Diego de Ordaz, and Geronimo de Ortal, the lying tale of Martinez concerning the city of Manoa, the advance of Sedeño towards the Meta, and the remarkable expedition of Berreo, have already been described in Sir Robert Schomburgk's copious notes to Raleigh's *Guiana*.

[2] Yet two friars were sent out, with the title of " Protectors of the Indians."

a knight of Burgos, the new governor, should go out
in the German ships to Santa Martha, and that the
Germans should then proceed to their destination.
Ambrosio de Alfinger was named governor, and
Bartolomè Sailler Lieutenant Governor, by the Vel-
sers, both Germans, and the expedition sailed from
Spain in 1528.

Having landed Lerma at Santa Martha, Ambrosio
de Alfinger, with four hundred men and fifty horses,
went to Coro, on the coast of Venezuela, which had
been founded in 1527 by Juan de Ampuez, who
afterwards retired to Curaçoa. The coast offered few
temptations to the German adventurer, and Alfinger,
leaving his lieutenant Sailler in command at Coro,
determined to make an expedition into the interior,
in 1530, in search of some fabulous golden city in the
forests far to the south. He left Coro with about
two hundred Spaniards, and several hundred unfortunate Indians, laden with provisions and stores;
and the cruelties, committed by this savage on the
poor defenceless people, were reported in Europe, and
were amongst the tales which made the blood of
Raleigh and Sir Richard Hawkins boil with generous
indignation at the very name of a Spaniard. To
prevent the laden Indians from deserting, Alfinger's soldiers fastened them to a chain, by a ring
round their necks; thus, to let one out, it was
necessary to loosen the whole row; but, to save
time, when an Indian became too tired to go on,
they cut off his head, and let the body drop out,
saying that, as it was necessary to leave him behind,

it was the same to them whether he was alive or dead, and the trouble of loosening the chain was saved.

When Alfinger reached the lagoon which the river Cesar forms, at its confluence with the Magdalena, the fame of his cruelties had preceded him, and all the natives had taken refuge on the islands in the lake; but the greedy Spaniards, seeing the glitter of their golden ornaments from a distance, spurred their horses into the lake, and swam to one of the islands, where the Indians, terrified at so strange a sight, were all killed or taken prisoners. The Indian chief of the district of Tamalameque gave himself up, and supplied the Spaniards with provisions and gold ornaments. So great was the spoil, that Alfinger sent twenty-five of his men back to Coro, with booty valued at 60,000 dollars, to buy horses and arms; and waited a whole year for their return, at the confluence of the rivers Cesar and Margarita. He waited in vain, and at length the ruthless adventurers began to follow the stream of the Magdalena, living on wild fruits and insects, and suffering from fever, and the torments of mosquitos. Their wretchedness soon became unbearable, and Alfinger led them up the mountains to the eastward, into a cold country, where they lived on land shells, and where three hundred of the naked Indians and many Spaniards were frozen to death during the nights. The wanderers then descended into the valley of Chinacota, where they were exposed to constant attacks from the wild Indians, and finally Alfinger was wounded in the neck, and died in three days. He was buried at the foot of a tree, and his epitaph was cut in the bark, by his surviving comrades.[1]

His worn out followers reached the valley of Cucuta, but, rendered fiercer and more cruel by their sufferings, they slaughtered men, women, and children in the villages on their line of march; and, in 1532, worn out and decimated by disease, they found their way back to Coro; and thus ended the first expedition of the Germans in Venezuela, and the first search for El Dorado.[2]

On the death of Alfinger, a German knight named Nicholas Fedreman went to Castille, to apply for the government of Venezuela; but it was given to another knight of the same nation, named George of Spires, and Fedreman was appointed his lieutenant-general. They raised four hundred men in Andalusia and Murcia, and reached Coro in 1534. Since the time of Alfinger, the rumours concerning great wealth to be found in the wilds, to the eastward of the Andes, had increased in number; and George of Spires resolved to make an attempt to solve the mystery which enveloped those unknown regions.[3] He left Coro with three hundred infantry and one hundred cavalry, crossed the mountains near the sources of the Tocuyo, descended to the plains, and, after

---

[1] *Castellanos*, pt. ii, el. i, canto 4.

[2] Strictly speaking, Alfinger did not search for El Dorado, as that fable was not yet in existence, but for some golden country of his own imagination.

[3] *Herrera*, Dec. v, Lib. 9, cap. v.

waiting for some months until the periodical in-
undations of those regions had subsided, began his
march to the south. The expedition of George of
Spires, which commenced in 1536, was composed of
determined men ; and they penetrated into regions
which have scarcely ever been visited since, braving
hardships and dangers which would have been in-
surmountable to men, who were not actuated by
the extraordinary enthusiasm of these early conquerors. They avoided the mountains, on account
of the great difficulty of making roads passable for
horses ; but, in doing this, they encountered great
risks in crossing the rivers, and suffered from want
of provisions, the swarms of mosquitos, the unhealthi-
ness of the climate, and the attacks of wild Indians.
During the dry season they found plenty of deer on
the plains, which supplied them with wholesome
food, but, when the rains came on, and the country
was inundated, their sole food consisted of *palmitos*
and wild roots : and the attempts they made to construct canoes, and go afloat in them, in search of
provisions, only ended in disappointment. It is also
recorded, that the jaguars were so numerous and
ferocious, that they carried off the horses in broad
daylight, and even killed a Spaniard, and several
Indians.

George continued to advance to the south, through
a country inhabited by different Indian tribes, and
found great inconvenience from the diversity of languages, which rendered interpreters useless. They
crossed the Ariari, and afterwards the Guaviare river,

where they encountered a tribe of Indians called Guayupes,[1] who painted their bodies black, and came to battle half drunk, so that it was not difficult to repulse their attacks. The extreme point reached by the knight of Spires was the margin of the river Papamene,[2] whence he returned to Coro, and a glance at the map will show the immense extent of country which he traversed, in this daring and romantic expedition. During the retreat to Coro, many officers died, and among them Murcia de Rondon, who had acted as secretary to Francis I, during his captivity in Madrid. George of Spires reached Coro in May 1538, after an absence of three years, during which time he marched upwards of one thousand five hundred miles into the interior of South America. He was a mild good man, and died peacefully as governor of Venezuela, in 1540.[3]

In the meanwhile his lieutenant, Nicholas Fedreman, followed his chief, with reinforcements and supplies, until he found himself in the vicinity of his countryman's camp, when ambition prompted him to avoid a meeting, and to continue his discoveries on

[1] The Uaupes Indians, on the head waters of the Rio Negro, of whom a very interesting account is given by Wallace, p. 482.

[2] The same as the river Caqueta, or its tributary the Rio de la Fragua, according to Humboldt; but Colonel Acosta, in his map, makes the river Papamene one of the tributaries of the Guaviare.

[3] Benzoni, however, says that he was murdered in his bed, by the Spaniards, who mangled him, by dragging his body ignominiously about, and finally throwing it into a wood. He adds that the murderers were severely punished, by order of the emperor. (*Benzoni, in Hakluyt Coll.*, p. 76.)

his own account, with about two hundred men. Fedreman is described as an active and energetic German, of middle size, with a flowing red beard; he was beloved by his soldiers, and no cruelty to the Indians is recorded of him. After leaving the track of his chief, Fedreman came to the banks of a river, where there were ruins of villages, and the Indians told him that, many years ago, a serpent with numerous heads had come out of the river, and devoured all the inhabitants. He passed the rainy season at the foot of the mountains, near the banks of the river Casanare, then crossed the Meta, and, after wandering about for three years, he finally crossed the most difficult part of the cordilleras of Sumapaz, and met the famous conquerors, Quesada and Belalcazar, on the plains of Bogota, in April 1539.

This was, in many respects, a very remarkable meeting. The great conqueror of New Granada, Don Gonzalo Ximenes de Quesada, and his colleague, the Adelantado Pedro Fernandez de Lugo, in exploring the course of the river Magdalena, had discovered the country of the civilized Chibchas, and reached the plateau of Bogota in 1537. The history of the conquest of New Granada, which is equal in interest to those of Mexico or Peru, has not yet found a Prescott; although the Chibchas were more civilized than the Aztecs, prodigious wealth was derived from the sack of their cities,[1] and the ad-

---

[1] At Tunja alone the Spaniards found 191,294 dollars worth of fine gold; 37,288 dollars of rough gold; 18,390 dollars of silver; and 1815 emeralds.

ventures of the Quesadas were as romantic as those of Cortes or Pizarro.

Sebastian de Belalcazar had marched north from Quito, conquered Popayan in 1535, and reached Bogota in 1538; while Fedreman, after wandering for three years in search of El Dorado, also joined Quesada and Belalcazar, on the heights of Bogota, in 1539. After a brief sojourn, the three discoverers proceeded down the river Magdalena together; Lugo died at Santa Martha, while Quesada proceeded to Spain, to obtain the government of his new discoveries, where he found a formidable rival in Luis, the son of Pedro Fernandez de Lugo.

Hernan Perez de Quesada, the brother of the great discoverer, was left in command at Bogota, and, excited by the narrative of Fedreman's adventures, he also became wild for the discovery of El Dorado. A party, led by Montalvo de Lugo, had arrived from Venezuela in the footsteps of Fedreman, and Quesada joined this small force with about two hundred men and some horses, and set out in search of " the house of the sun." Before departing from Bogota, however, he was guilty of the cowardly and unnecessary murder of the young Zaque of the Chibchas, in order, as he said, that he might leave the affairs of Bogota in a state of tranquillity in his rear.[1] Quesada

[1] This Quesada was a brutal adventurer. He not only murdered the innocent young Quemichua, Zaque of Bogota, on this occasion, who was much loved by the Indians; but also the chiefs of Samaca, Turmeque, Boyaca, and others, as he said, to preserve tranquillity in his rear. It was believed that his death by lightning some years afterwards, was a divine visitation for this cruelty.

appears to have marched from Tunja, and to have descended into the plains, taking the same route as George of Spires, until he reached the forests of Mocoa. His people endured the most appalling hardships, and, having eaten all the horses, they were finally reduced to feed upon an unhappy old donkey belonging to Friar Requejada, their father confessor, which, as the chronicler pathetically relates, " was brought from the hills of Santa Martha, to leave its bones amongst the affluents of the Amazons." At length Quesada gave up all hopes of finding " the house of the sun," and, having lost one half of his men, he returned to Bogota, after an absence of one year.[1] He was the first to enter the land of the Musos Indians.

While Quesada was penetrating into the central plains, from the side of Bogota, a large and important expedition in search of El Dorado was organized in Venezuela. Soon after the death of George of Spires in 1540, the Bishop, Don Rodrigo Bastidas,[2] became governor of Venezuela, and appointed a German knight named Philip von Huten to be his Lieutenant General.

Huten[3] was a relation of the Velsers, and had been

[1] Some chroniclers state that Quesada descended a second time into the plains, in search of El Dorado. He governed Bogota for his brother, for two years; and was killed by lightning, in a ship, when on his way to join the judge Armendariz at Carthagena, in 1545.

[2] *Piedrahita*, pt. i, lib. x, cap. i. Bastidas, formerly dean of St. Domingo, was appointed first bishop of Coro in 1531, and governor of Venezuela in 1541.

[3] He is called Felipe de Utre, or de Urre, by the Spaniards.

one of the companions of George of Spires in his famous expedition. He was prudent and brave, and no captain in the Indies is said to have been more humane. In July 1541 this officer organized a great expedition to search for El Dorado, in the hope of meeting with more success than had fallen to the lot of his old commander, George of Spires. Many gallant young cavaliers flocked to his standard; Pedro de Limpias was his maestro del campo; Bartolomè Velser, a youth of great promise, Sebastian de Amengua, and Pedro de Artiaga were his captains. The expedition left Coro by sea, landed at Burburata, marched thence to Barquisimeto, and, advancing into the central plains, wintered at a village called by George of Spires, of our Lady, and by Fedreman, La Fragua, where he received tidings that Quesada, with 200 men, had passed, a short time before him. After the winter, Huten reached the province of Papamene,[1] near the skirts of the cordilleras of Timana, where an Indian advised him not to follow Quesada, as he must have entered an uninhabited region, and suffered severely. The Indian offered to conduct Huten to a land rich in gold and silver, to a city called Macatoa, on the banks of the river Guaviare; and he showed him some apples made of gold and silver, which he said his brother had brought from that city. But the tales of this Indian were not sufficient to induce the German knight to desist from following on the track of Quesada,

[1] In the neighbourhood of the head waters of the river Caqueta or Japura.

and, after marching for eight days, the Indian guide escaped.

Sickness and famine now began to press hard upon the intrepid explorers. Their hunger was appeased by placing the heads of maize corn at the mouths of ant's nests, which were soon covered with ants, and this, for many days, was their only food. Some of them found a wild fruit, which proved to be unfit for food; for, on eating it, their hair, beards, and eye-brows fell off, and the horses lost their hair, and died. After wandering for a year, in this forlorn state, they found they had been moving in a circle, and came to the spot from whence they had set out full of hope, twelve months before.

The determination of the intrepid German, to con-tinue the search for El Dorado, was undiminished by this failure; he had heard of a city called Macatoa from the Indian; and he once more started with Pedro de Limpias, who was known to be brave and quick in learning languages, and forty men. After a long march they reached the banks of the river Guaviare, where Huten met with an Indian, whom he sent as an envoy to Macatoa, which he had heard was at no great distance. In a few days five canoes arrived, with the chief's son, who ferried them across the river, and supplied them with venison, fish, maize, and cassava. The explorers were then conducted to the city, which they found to consist of well-con-structed houses (or huts?), built in streets, with open spaces at intervals, containing about eight hundred inhabitants of the Guaypis, Guayupes, or Uaupes tribe of Indians. Their chief was a man about forty years of age, of middling stature, well built, with an aquiline nose, and fine countenance.

The chief of the Uaupes advised Huten not to advance against the Omaguas, a rich and powerful tribe to the southward, with so small a force; but he added that they possessed much gold and silver, which was a sufficient inducement to the explorers to brave all dangers; and Huten continued his march, with guides and provisions. This dauntless commander had now entered the country which Mr. Wallace, as late as 1853, calls "the unknown regions between the Rio Guaviare on the one side, and the Japura, on the other."[1] After marching for five days the explorers came to a village of fifty huts, inhabited by Indians appointed to guard the crops of the Omaguas. Huten and his companions, from this place, saw a town of such size that, although one part of it was very close, they could not see the other end of it; the streets were straight, with the houses touching each other; and there was an edifice of great height in the centre of the town, which, according to the Indian guides, was inhabited by Quarica, the lord of the Omaguas, and served also as a temple for many idols of gold. The guides added that further on there were other cities, larger and richer than this.

Stimulated by the stories of the Indians, Philip von Huten charged down the hill, towards the city, with his intrepid little band; but the Omaguas came

[1] Wallace, p. 502.

out of the city in great force, to the sound of drums; and Huten, having been severely wounded, was obliged to retreat, and was carried off the field in a hammock, by his friendly Indian guides. The retreating Spaniards were followed by a large army of Omaguas, who harrassed their rear until they were finally repulsed by Pedro de Limpias, but this stubborn resistance of the Omaguas put an end to the search for El Dorado. The friendly chief of the Uaupes resorted to a strange method of discovering the means of curing Huten's wound. An old slave was dressed in the German knight's armour, and placed upon his horse, and, while in this position, an Indian wounded him in the same way that the Omagua had wounded Huten. Thus, by cutting the old slave up, they discovered the direction of Huten's wound, and cured him.

The explorers now recrossed the Guaviare, and determined to return to Coro, where a melancholy fate awaited their gallant leader. During the expedition a jealousy had arisen between Pedro de Limpias, the maestro del campo, and Bartolomè Velser, the lieutenant-general; which ended in the former deserting Huten, and returning to Coro before him.

The land discovered by Philip von Huten, between the Guaviare and the Caqueta, may not improbably have been inhabited, in those days, by a very populous nation, for there is other evidence to show that the Omaguas, though now dwindled to a small tribe on the banks of the Amazons, may have been both powerful and numerous in the days of Huten, three centuries ago. The great city reported by Huten may be taken to mean a populous region studded with villages, and there is nothing improbable in the rest of the account of this remarkable expedition. Humboldt thinks it likely that the streamlets which form the rivers Uaupes and Caqueta, flowing through the region in which Huten sought for El Dorado, and where he fought the battle of Omaguas with a handful of men, may be auriferous; and he mentions that though the Indian tribes of this region have no name for silver, they all have one for gold. Be this as it may, the expedition of Philip von Huten created a great sensation throughout the New World; from that time the name of the Omaguas was coupled with that of El Dorado, as the emblem of inexhaustible wealth; and from the days of Huten to those of Humboldt only one European[1] explored the region between the Guaviare and the Caqueta.[2]

During the absence of the expedition in search of El Dorado, the government of Venezuela had been seized by one Carbajal, a brutal soldier, who

[1] Fray Francisco Pugnet, Humboldt's informant, the guardian of the convent of St. Francis, at Popayan.

[2] The expeditions of Gonzalo Pizarro to Canela, and of Orellana down the river Amazon, took place just before that of Philip von Huten. Orellana sailed down the Amazon, and heard of the Omaguas, in 1540; and Huten started from Coro in July 1541, the month previous to Orellana's arrival at the mouth of the Amazon. Humboldt remarks that " the descendants of those intrepid warriors who had pushed their conquests from Peru to the coast of New Granada, and the mouth of the Amazon, were ignorant of the roads which lead from Coro to the river Meta."

d

arrested Huten and Velser on their return to Coro, caused their hands to be tied, and their heads to be cut, or rather sawn off with a blunt *macheta*, which had been used for chopping wood. With the sad deaths of these two chivalrous knights, ended the rule of those Germans in Venezuela, who added so romantic a page to the history of South American discovery.[1] Carbajal continued to commit many excesses ; and in 1545 he founded the city of Tocuyo, in a beautiful valley, producing wheat, cotton, and sugar-cane. In the same year the Licentiate Juan Perez de Tolosa of Segovia, a learned and prudent man, was sent out by the emperor to settle the affairs of Venezuela, and in 1546 he tried and executed Carbajal.[2] The Germans were deprived of the government, owing to the numerous complaints of tyranny and disorder that were made against them, insomuch that the good Las Casas called the province " infeliz y desgraciada."

For several years the Spaniards occupied themselves more in settling the immediate neighbourhood of the coast, than in exploring expeditions. Tolosa's brother crossed the Apure, and reached the valley of Cucuta ; in 1547 Juan de Villegas discovered the lake of Tacarigua ; in 1549 Pedro Alvarez founded Burburata ; and in 1552 Villegas founded Barquisimeto. Thus the province of

---

[1] My accounts of the expeditions of Alfinger, George of Spires, Fedreman, Quesada, and Huten, are taken from Castellanos, Simon, Piedrahita, Herrera, and Oviedo y Baños.

[2] *Oviedo y Baños,* i, lib. iii, cap. iii.

Venezuela was gradually colonized, and it will only be necessary to mention one other settler, because he appears on the scene in the narrative of Aguirre's cruise.[1] This was Francisco de Taxardo, the son of a Spaniard of the island of Margarita, by an Indian princess of the Guaigueri nation. He determined to form a settlement in the country of Caraccas, and, sailing from Margarita in April 1555, in two piraguas with twenty Indians of his mother's tribe, was well received by the natives of Caraccas, and was established there when Aguirre reached Margarita in 1561.

While the Germans were searching for El Dorado from the side of Venezuela, the course of events in New Granada brings Pedro de Ursua on the scene; the principal person in the narrative which forms the subject of the present volume.

We have seen that Gonzalo Ximenes de Quesada, the great conqueror of Bogota, had sailed for Spain to obtain the government of his new discoveries. In this Quesada failed, and Don Luis Alonzo de Lugo, the son of his former comrade, was appointed Adelantado of the new kingdom of Granada; but his reign was very brief. He reached the coast in 1542, and in 1545 the Judge Don Miguel Diaz de Armendariz was sent out by the Council of the Indies, to examine into his conduct, and to take what was called a *residencia* of Carthagena, Santa Martha, and Popayan, with full powers. Immediately on landing at Carthagena, Armendariz received numerous com-

---

[1] See page 164-5 of this volume.

plaints of the tyranny of Lugo, from persons who had
been banished from Bogota; and he appointed his
young nephew, Don Pedro de Ursua, to proceed to
that city and take charge of the government, whilst
he completed his examination into the state of affairs
on the coast. Ursua was accompanied by Gonzalo
Suarez Rondon, the founder of Ronda, and other
exiles, who had been banished by Lugo, and they
proceeded up the Magdalena in light canoes. Ursua
was received at Tunja as Governor, but, during the
night, the house in which he was lodged was burnt to
the ground, and this served as a pretext for arresting
Lugo, and confining him in prison. Ursua then continued his journey to Bogota, where he administered
the government until the arrival of his uncle Armendariz, whose first act was to torture a citizen, to force
him to disclose the persons who had set fire to Ursua's
house at Tunja.

Pedro de Ursua was a knight of Navarre, and it
was considered, at the time, that he was too young
and inexperienced for the important post entrusted to
him by his uncle; yet he proved himself, during the
short period of his rule, to be equal to the best ad-
ministrators that had ever served in the Indies. He
is said to have been a youth, who united a good
education and great sweetness and amiability of
temper, to uncommon bravery and dexterity in martial exercises. Garcilasso Inca de la Vega, who
knew him in Peru, says that he was a generous and
honourable man, a perfect gentleman, and generally
liked; so that, when he was collecting supplies for

his expedition, people readily gave him all he wanted, because he was an universal favourite.[1] It was natural that a young knight of such a disposition, on hearing the accounts of the expeditions of Alfinger, George of Spires, Fedreman, Quesada, and Philip von Huten, in search of El Dorado and the Omaguas, should be inspired with a longing to emulate their chivalrous deeds, and to make a name for himself also, as an intrepid explorer of unknown regions. Accordingly, Armendariz, at his own urgent request, appointed him to the command of an expedition to search for the snowy mountains which George of Spires and Fedreman were reported to have seen from a distance, and for the rivers which flowed over sands of gold.

Ursua, and his friend Ortun de Velasco, assembled a force of 400 men, who expressed their desire to serve under so noble a youth, and in 1548 they left Tunja and directed their course to the north-eastward. The expedition crossed the river Sogamoso, and entered the land of the Laches Indians, whence they advanced to the country of the Chitareros, where Ursua founded a city, which he named after his native town in Navarre. This new Pampluna was laid out on a regular plan, with one hundred and thirty-six lots for houses, and in April 1549 the officers of the new city were nominated. It is 70 leagues N.E. of Bogota, in the eastern cordillera, the climate is cold, but suitable for the cultivation of corn, and at that time the immediate neighbourhood

[1] II, lib. viii, cap. 14.

was inhabited by 200,000 Chitareros Indians.   Ursua remained here until 1550, when he resigned the command to Ortun de Velasco, who governed the new city[1] for twenty years, and had the satisfaction of drawing and quartering the murderer of his old comrade's lady love, after the defeat and death of the monster Aguirre in 1561.[2]

While Ursua was absent on his Pampluna expedition, his uncle, Armendariz, commenced the promulgation of the new laws, which caused such excitement in the New World, and which, in Peru, led to the death of the viceroy Blasco Nuñez de Vela, and the rebellion of Gonzalo Pizarro.   Armendariz sent copies of these new laws to Sebastian de Belalcazar, with orders to publish them at Popayan, but they were as ill received by the colonists of Cauca as they had been in Peru.   Belalcazar, however, was a wiser man than the rash Gonzalo Pizarro; he represented to the people the fatal consequences of disobeying their sovereign, and advised them to send a deputation, to pray for the repeal of the obnoxious ordinances.[3]   At the same time the astute Belalcazar evaded the orders he had received, by promulgating the new laws, and on the same day suspending them

[1] The province of Pampluna extended from the river Zulia to the lake of Maracaibo; and by this route came the merchandize of Castille, until the rising of the Quiriquies Indians took place, who were many years masters of the banks of the Maracaibo Lake, and destroyed its navigation.

[2] See p. 237 (note) of this volume.

[3] For an account of these new laws, see *Prescott's Conquest of Peru*, ii, p. 231, and *Helps' Spanish Conquest of America*, iv, p. 153.

until further directions were received from Spain ; and it was at this time that the derisive saying originated, which afterwards became so common in Spanish America, " *Se obedece pero no se cumple.*"[1]

In 1549, and in the midst of these difficulties, Armendariz was superseded by a Royal Audience, consisting of lawyers, named Mercado (who died at Mompox on his way), Gongora, and Galarza. Armendariz resigned his office to the two latter, who were young and ignorant, but conciliatory and upright, and inclined to exercise the office of peacemakers ; so that when, shortly afterwards, the lawyer Zurite arrived to take a *residencia* of Armendariz, against whom complaints were not wanting, not of avarice and peculation, however, the almost invariable cry against functionaries in the Indies, but of sensuality, he was let off very easily. The complainers then wrote to the Council of the Indies, who, very unfairly sent out a severe man, named Montaño, to take another *residencia*, and Armendariz was this time sent to Spain, and so heavily fined, that the alguazils took the cloak from his back, to pay their fees. On his arrival in Spain, Armendariz became a

[1] While I was at Puno, in Southern Peru, last year, I was told an anecdote of a Spanish intendente, who imitated the conduct of Belalcazar. Gonzalez Montoya, the intendente in question, a benevolent, as well as a determined man, governed Puno towards the end of the last century. He abolished the *mitas* of Indians in his district, for the mines of Potosi, which he declared to be a system of butchery ; and, when ordered by the Spanish government to re-establish them, he, like Belalcazar, exclaimed " *Obedesco pero no cumplo.*"

presbyter, and the third governor of New Granada died a canon in Siguenza. His persecutor Montaño was, not long afterwards, beheaded for rebellion and cruelty.

The downfall of Armendariz does not appear to have immediately affected the fortunes of his nephew; for in 1549 the auditors appointed Ursua to conduct an expedition against the Musos Indians, who had recently defeated a Captain Valdez, and to search for El Dorado. Ursua's party consisted of one hundred and fifty men, and it is related that they had plenty of powder, but so little lead that they melted half the utensils in the colony to make bullets. They entered the territory of the Musos, and entrenched themselves in a strong position, but met with much resistance from the natives. At length Ursua made a truce with them, and a sort of fair was held near his camp; when he invited the chiefs to come in, and treacherously murdered them, " a felonious act," says the chronicler, " and unworthy of a soldier of honour, like Ursua." The Navarrese knight then founded a city named Tudela, and returned to Bogota for reinforcements, which he conducted to his new settlement by another road. In 1552, however, the Spaniards were so constantly attacked by the brave Musos, that they retired from their new city of Tudela, and their enemies burnt it before their eyes.

No Spaniard entered the country of the Musos for some years after this repulse; and this gallant tribe of Indians strove for their independence, with a constancy and valour worthy of better success, for, in the end, they were subjugated. They recognized no chief, but followed the bravest in war, and the oldest in council; and their chief places of worship were two high rocks, near the river Zarbi, where they offered maize, potatos, and yucas.[1]

After his return from the country of the Musos, in 1551, Pedro de Ursua was appointed justicia mayor of Santa Martha; and he immediately began to prepare for the conquest of the Tayronas, one of the most warlike of the Indian tribes, who dwelt in the mountains overhanging the town and valley. Their country was rich in gold and silver, and they made gold ornaments, in the shape of snakes, toads, eagles, deer, crescents, and bats; many of which are often dug up at the present day, closely resembling those which have been lately discovered at Chiriqui, on the isthmus of Panama. In 1552 Ursua, having collected the necessary arms and supplies, marched out of Santa Martha, and penetrated far into the mountains; but the Tayrona Indians retreated before him, harassing his outposts, and cutting off his supplies, until he was reduced to great straits. At length Ursua was attacked by fever, and commenced a retreat, when the whole tribe of Indians occupied a dangerous part of the road, with a precipice on one side, and a wall of rock on the other, called the

[1] Herrera gives a full account of the formidable Musos Indians. —Dec. v, lib. iv, cap. 3. Their territory bordered on the provinces of Bogota (whence it was twenty-four leagues distant, to the westward), Velez, and Tunja.

Pasos de Rodrigo, with the intention of disputing the passage of the invaders. The Spaniards encamped near this narrow pass, and were roused, towards morning, by the shouts of the Indians, and by the blows of their war clubs. Ursua was in his tent with the fever upon him, but he rushed out, well armed, but only half dressed, and with but one shoe on ; and found his little army surrounded by the enemy. With twelve men he led the way up the craggy rocks, to gain the head of the pass, stones were hurled down upon him from the summit, but he reached the important post, fought like a lion for three hours, and at length the Tayronas wavered, and, seizing the critical moment, the Spaniards charged and scattered them.[1]

Ursua then returned to Santa Martha, but, being evidently of a very restless disposition, and disgusted with the insufficient means at his command for conquering the Tayronas, he threw up his appointment, and sailed for Nombre de Dios, with the intention of going to Peru. At Panama he met with the Marquis of Cañete, the new viceroy of Peru, then on his way to Lima, who had already heard of his adventurous career in New Granada. At that time the isthmus of Panama was infested by large numbers of runaway negro slaves, called Cimarrones, who frequented the road from Nombre de Dios to Panama, robbing and murdering all who fell into their hands. The Marquis of Cañete recommended the Cabildo of Panama to secure the services of Pedro de Ursua,

[1] Piedrahita, Pte. i, lib. xi, cap. ix, p. 492.

to command a force for the extirpation of these marauders; and that captain soon afterwards entered the tangled forests, with a body of two hundred Spaniards. The negro chief, named Bayano, endeavoured to tire out his pursuers by long counter-marches, and sudden night attacks; the encounters were numerous, most of them hand to hand between the swords of the Spaniards and the *machetas* or wood knives of the negros; but, in the course of two years, nearly the whole of the Cimarrones were killed, and the remainder surrendered, and returned to their masters.[1] After this very toilsome, but completely successful campaign, Ursua departed from Panama, and sailed for Peru, in search of employment and distinction; and it was at Lima, in 1559, that he received, from the viceroy Marquis of Cañete, the command of the expedition in search of El Dorado, and the Omaguas, the extraordinary narrative of which forms the subject of the present volume.

The marquis of Cañete, who was viceroy of Peru from 1555 to 1561, arrived shortly after the suppression of a revolt headed by Francisco Hernandez Giron,[2] and found the country in great disorder,

[1] Piedrahita, Pte. i, lib. xii, cap. iv, p. 528-30.

[2] For a brief account of Giron's insurrection, see *Helps' Spanish Conquest of America*, vol. iv, p. 290-96. See also note at p. 232 of this volume. It was reported, while Giron was at Nasca, in the course of his rebellion, that Ursua had arrived at Piura, and declared for Giron. This shows that Ursua was a captain of some renown, and that his name was known throughout South America.—*G. de la Vega. Com. Real.*, ii, p. 429.

and infested by disbanded soldiers, and lawless cha-
racters of every description. He commenced his
administration by several acts of great severity, of
which the traitor Aguirre complained bitterly in his
letter to king Philip;[1] and the expedition of Ursua
exactly suited his policy, because it enabled him to
get rid of a great number of lawless ruffians from all
parts of Peru, who, now that the civil wars were at
an end, were prowling over the country without
employment. It is probable, however, that the
viceroy, in common with the rest of his countrymen,
also believed firmly in the tales concerning El Dorado
and the Omaguas, which were brought directly to his
notice in the following way.

It appears that on the coast of Brazil there was a
valorous Indian chief, named Viraratu, probably of
the nation of Tupinambas, who assembled a large
body of warlike men in a fleet of canoes, with arms
and food, intending to enter the river Marañon, and
conquer other lands. He was accompanied by two
Portuguese, who knew his language. After ascending
the river Marañon for some days, they came to a
great lake, in a vast plain surrounded by lofty mountains, with so many and such large villages on its
shores, that the Brazilians were astonished. The
natives collected a great fleet of canoes, and a naval
battle followed, in which the invaders were defeated.
Viraratu, therefore, returned to the river, but the
people of the lake followed him, and shot arrows
from both sides. The Brazilians continued to ascend

[1] See p. 188 of this volume.

the great river steadily, until they at length reached
Moyobamba, near the river Huallaga in Peru, a district inhabited by the Motilones Indians.[1]   Viraratu
talked to these people by signs, and related how he
had left Brazil, all that he had seen, the numerous
villages he passed on the river, and the quantities of
gold and silver which they *ought* to contain.   He was
then sent to Lima, where the marquis of Cañete heard
his story, and saw some of the gold he brought with
him ; and it was the report of Viraratu which led to
the organization of the expedition in search of El
Dorado and Omagua, under Don Pedro de Ursua,
in 1559.[2]

I will now proceed to give some account of the
authors to whom we are indebted for narratives of
the expedition of Ursua and Aguirre down the river
Marañon, the fullest and best of which, that of Fray
Pedro Simon, has been translated for the Hakluyt Society.   The career of Aguirre is certainly the
most marvellous and extraordinary in the history of
South American discovery, during that age of won-
ders, the sixteenth century ; yet the sources from
which the story has been derived, are authentic and
trustworthy.

I. The earliest account extant, of the expedition
of Ursua and Aguirre, is contained in a manuscript,

[1] They are so called because they have a custom of shaving their
heads.—*Vasquez MS.*

[2] This account of the expedition of the Brazilian Indians under
Viraratu, up the Amazon, is taken from a manuscript in the
National Library at Madrid, "*Jornada del Rio Marañon, por
Toribio de Ortiguera,*" J. 143.   The handwriting is very illegible.

now in the national library at Madrid, actually written by a soldier who accompanied them down the Amazon, and who witnessed all the horrors he relates, until he made his escape at the island of Margarita. This was the Bachiller Francisco Vasquez, one of the three loyal men who, when the mutineers foreswore allegiance to the king, boldly refused to be accomplices in their treason.[1] The other two were Juan de Cabañas, and Juan de Vargas Zapata. Cabañas was murdered by Aguirre, for some imaginary offence, soon afterwards,[2] but Vasquez effected his escape, while the traitors were detained at Margarita.[3] The prefix of Bachiller seems to show that Vasquez, though in the position of a private soldier, was a man of some education; and it would thus appear that men of all ranks crowded to these El Dorado expeditions, just as they did to the Sacramento, during the Californian gold fever.

The manuscript is entitled, " A narrative of all that happened in the expedition to Amagua and Dorado, which the governor Pedro de Ursua went to discover, with powers given him by the viceroy marquis of Cañete, president of Peru : treating also of the mutiny of Don Hernando de Guzman, Lope de Aguirre, and other tyrants." It is particularly interesting, because it is the source from which Simon obtained his information,—indeed page after page of Simon is transcribed word for word from the manuscript of Vasquez. No source of information could be more authentic. All the remarks, at page 21 of

---

[1] See page 65 of this volume.   [2] P. 101.   [3] P. 128.

this volume, on the sources of the river Cocama or Ucayali ; and at page 107 on the Marañon, are taken from Vasquez, as well as the description of Aguirre, at the end of Simon's narrative.[1]

On the last page of the manuscript, the following notice is written :—" This narrative was made by a soldier named the Bachiller Francisco Vasquez, a soldier of the tyrant Aguirre, and one of those who refused to take the oath to Don Fernando de Guzman, as prince, nor to foreswear their country, nor to deny their king and lord. Credit may be given to his account, and to all he writes, because he was an honest and upright man, and he accompanied the tyrant, who always treated him very well, both him and the others who refused to join in the rebellion.[2] For, when the rebellion commenced, the said tyrant and Don Fernando declared to all the camp that those who desired to join the rebellion of their own free will could do so, and that those who desired not to join it would not be forced to do so: therefore those who were rebels against the lord our king had no excuse, and are deserving of the severest punishment."

II. There is another contemporaneous manuscript account of the expedition of Ursua and Aguirre, in the national library at Madrid, by Don Toribio de

---

[1] Papeles MSS., originales y ineditos, en la biblioteca nacional de Madrid. J. 136 (117 pages, small 4to).

[2] This is not exactly true, for he murdered Juan de Cabañas (see p. 101), and would have done the same to Vasquez, if he could have caught him (see p. 128).

Ortiguera; entitled " Expedition down the river Marañon, with all that happened in it, and other notable events, worthy to be known, which happened in the Western Indies; dedicated to the most happy Don Philip III, our lord."[1]   Ortiguera was at Nombre de Dios in 1561, and sent some forces against Aguirre.   He remained in South America until 1585, and returned to Spain after an absence of twenty-five years.   He heard all the details of the unhappy expedition down the Marañon from many persons, and was thus enabled to write a history of it, which differs in no material point from that of Vasquez.   It consists of fifty-six short chapters, two of which relate to the expeditions of Gonzalo Pizarro and Orellana, and all the rest to Aguirre's piratical cruise.   This writer declares that, never since the civil wars in Peru, have such strange and wonderful things happened, as in this affair of the river Marañon.[2]

[1] Papeles MSS., J. 143.

[2] There is another interesting manuscript, containing information on the river Amazon, in the national library at Madrid.   It is entitled " The Discovery of the river of the Amazons, and its extensive provinces : a report sent to the most excellent Lord Don Garcia Mendoza de Haro, count of Castrillo, president of the Royal Council of the Indies; by Don Martin de Saavedra y Guzman, knight of the order of Calatrava, of his majesty's council, captain-general of the new kingdom of Granada, and president of the Royal Audience.   1639."

It is a well-written official report, in which the captain-general states that he has received a narrative respecting the river Amazon from Quito, containing geographical and other details supplied by Texeira.   There is a curious coloured map with it.—*Papeles MSS.*, Q. 196.

III. The first published account of the expedition of Ursua and Aguirre, is contained in the " *Elegias* [1] *de Illustres Varones de Indias*," by the Presbitero Juan de Castellanos. This writer was originally a soldier, and served in the conquest of New Granada, but, like many others, he changed his life and became a priest, first at Carthagena, and afterwards at Tunja, where he remained many years, writing his " Elegias" first in prose, and then turning them into verse. The first part was printed in Spain in 1588, and contained the exploits of Columbus; Ponce de Leon; Francisco de Garay in Cuba; the conquest of Trinidad, the Orinoco, and Cubagua; and finally the expedition of Ursua and Aguirre. A second part followed, but was never published until 1847, giving an account of the deeds of the German knights in Venezuela, searching for El Dorado; and a third, relating the conquest of Carthagena by Lugo, of Popayan by Belalcazar, and of Antiochia.[2] The fourth part, containing the conquest of New Granada, was never printed, and

[1] This word here means eulogies, not elegies.

[2] An edition of the three existing parts was published at Madrid in 1847, in the library of Spanish authors, edited by Don Buenaventura Carlos Aribau. The poet Alonzo de Ercilla acted as censor to the second and third parts of the work, and, in the beginning, records his opinion that many events, which he either saw or heard of when he was in the Indies, are faithfully and truthfully recorded by Castellanos, accounts of which had never before been written by any author.

Ticknor says, " The whole, except the conclusion, is written in the Italian octave stanza, and extends to nearly ninety thousand lines, in pure, fluent Castilian, which soon afterwards became rare, but in a chronicling spirit, which, though it adds to its value as a

f

is lost; but Piedrahita had the use of the original manuscript. No copy, however, has been found in modern times.

Castellanos was a patient investigator, and wrote in a clear simple style, with an extensive personal knowledge of the localities he describes. He is by far the most genial historian of Ursua's expedition.

The history of the expedition of Ursua and Aguirre is contained in *Parte* i, *Elegia* xiv, and *Cantos* ii to vii of the work of Castellanos. He gives a tolerably detailed account of all the principal events, and his information was probably derived from the same sources as that of Ortiguera, namely, from men who were actually eyewitnesses of, and, perhaps, actors in the events which they described. Castellanos' version of the bloody career of Aguirre is remarkable, because he stands up as the champion of the unfortunate lady who accompanied Ursua; while all other writers, whether they be men of the world, like Vasquez and Ortiguera, or greasy friars, like Simon and Piedrahita, unite in heaping reproaches and calumnies upon her.

Vasquez says that the lady went, against the advice of Ursua's friends, that she was said to be a person of bad character and worse manners, and that she was the principal cause of the murder of Ursua;[1]

history, takes from it all the best characteristics of poetry."— *History of Spanish Literature*, ii, p. 435.

Colonel Acosta, in his history of the discovery of New Granada, says that Castellanos is very inexact.

[1] Garcilasso de la Vega says, with reference to this poor lady, "Love has destroyed many great captains, Hannibal, and others." —II, lib. viii, cap. xiv, p. 495.

Ortiguera makes similar insinuations; and Simon[1] copies from Vasquez; but Castellanos, like the true gentleman that he evidently was, defends the memory of the poor young lady. The truth seems to have been that Dona Inez de Atienza, the beautiful young widow of a citizen of Piura, fell passionately in love with Don Pedro de Ursua, when he arrived in Peru. Pedro de Ursua was a young knight of Navarre, handsome, brave, and generous, possessed of many noble qualities, and universally liked; he had, though still young, already acquitted himself well in more than one post of great danger and responsibility, and the fame of his exploits had gone before him into Peru.[2] Inez de Atienza, a young, beautiful, and spirited

---

[1] See p. 13 of this volume; also p. 36; and, for the murder of the lady Inez, p. 87.

[2] Castellanos thus describes him:—

> " Salio buen capitan y diligente
> Para le cometer qualquier jornada
> Y ansi, por aqui daba buena cuenta
> En los negocios de mayor afrenta
> Descubrio los caminos mas rigorosos
> Allano la montaña rigorosa
> Conquistò la provincia de los Musos
> Deste reino la mas dificultosa.
> Vile hacer a la real corona
> Otros muchos servicios señalados
> Y en Santa Marta recorrio la Sierra,
> Puesto que sin victoria deste guerra."—
>
> Pte. i, Elegia xiv, Canto ii.

Piedrahita says that, in his expeditions, it was not so much Ursua's desire to amass riches, for their own sake, to which he was always indifferent, as to reap the glory of conquering new countries for his king.—Pte. i, lib. xi, cap. ix, p. 692.

woman, as both Vasquez and Simon allow, gave him
her heart; but her's was no common love; it is not
every woman, gently nurtured and accustomed to the
comforts of civilized life, who would have willingly
encountered the appalling hardships of a search for
El Dorado, and a voyage down the great river.   At
all events there is only one other instance of such
devotion on record: Inez de Atienza and Madame
Godin[1] are the two heroines of the river Amazon;
they stand alone, and their romantic stories are almost
unrivalled in the history of woman's love.   The very
sublimity of this noble creature's devotion, which no
terrors could daunt, no hardships damp, ought to
have protected her from the cowardly sneers of dirty
friars, and the calumnies of gold-seeking adventurers.
The lady Inez " forsook not her lord, in his travels,
unto death ;" and her heroism and her sorrows
almost hallow a love, which may not have been sanctioned by a priest.[2]   If she was guilty of any fault
after the death of Ursua, which Simon asserts, and
which I do not believe,[3] let it be remembered that
the poor broken-hearted girl was utterly helpless,
and in the hands of incarnate fiends, with hearts
harder than the nether mill stone.   That mad devil

---

[1] For a brief notice of the adventures of Madame Godin, see a
note at p. liv of the introduction to " The Expeditions into the
Valley of the Amazons" (Hakluyt Society's Publications, 1859).

[2] Yet even this is doubtful; for Simon allows that Ursua took
the lady Inez to Moyobamba, with the intention of marrying her,
and there is no evidence that he did not do so. See p. 13.

[3] See p. 85 of this volume. I do not believe this, because I do
not find it stated by Vasquez.

Aguirre finally caused her to be murdered, because
her mattress would take up too much room in the
boat! and Castellanos writes more like a pastoral
poet than a rhyming chronicler, when he records the
cruel deed :—" The birds mourned on the trees, the
wild beasts of the forests lamented, the waters ceased
to murmur, the fish groaned beneath them, the winds
execrated the deed, when Llamoso cut the veins of
her white neck. Wretch! art thou born of a woman?
No! What beast brought forth a son so wicked?
How is it that thou dost not die in imagining a
treason so enormous? Her two women, amidst
lamentations and grief, gathered flowers to cover her
grave, and cut her epitaph in the bark of a tree :—
' These flowers cover one whose faithfulness and
beauty were unequalled, whom cruel men slew without a cause.' "

IV. All the authorities already mentioned, namely
Vasquez, Ortiguera, and Castellanos, were contempo-
raries of Aguirre. The next chronicler of his career,
Fray Pedro Simon,[1] lived some years afterwards; but
his account has been selected for translation in preference to the others, because it is by far the fullest,
and is equally reliable and authentic. Pedro Simon
was born at Parrilla, near Cuenca, in 1574, thirteen
years after the death of Aguirre. He was educated
in the convent of San Francisco de Cartagena in
Spain, and, in 1604, was sent out to South America,

[1] "Primera Parte de las noticias historiales de las conquistas
de Tierra Firme, en las Indias Occidentales, compuesto por el
Padre Fray Pedro Simon," &c., &c.—*Cuenca*, 1627.

to teach theology and the arts, in the convent of his order at Bogota. In 1607 he accompanied Don Juan de Borja,[1] the President of the Audience, in his campaign against the Pijaos Indians, travelled through Venezuela, embarked at Coro for the Antilles, and returned to Bogota. He also made journeys to Antioquia, Carthagena, and Santa Martha, and conversed with some of the conquerors and settlers, while many of the incidents of the conquest were still fresh in their memories, before he began to write his history. He is said to have suffered severely from gout.

In 1623 Simon began to write his "*noticias historiales*," for which he had been collecting materials for many years. The first part, the only one ever printed, appeared at Cuenca in 1627; and consists of seven "*noticias*" treating of the affairs of Venezuela, and of the expedition of Ursua and Aguirre. The other two parts, also composed of seven *noticias* each, exist only in manuscript. The second relates the discoveries on the right bank of the river Magdalena, from Santa Martha; and the third relates the conquests of Carthagena, Popayan, Antioquia, and Choco; and is said, by Colonel Acosta, to be the most complete and most valuable account of the affairs of New Granada in the sixteenth century, in existence. Simon is, on the whole, a trustworthy writer; his style is simple, and without any attempt to imitate

---

[1] Grandson of the duke of Gandia (who was general of the Jesuits, and afterwards canonized), by his natural son Fernando. He was president from 1607 to 1628.

the classical historians; but a very large proportion of his first part is taken from Castellanos, and much of the remainder is copied from the manuscript of Vasquez. The time of his death is not known, but he is believed to have died in Spain.

Simon's account of the expedition of Ursua and Aguirre is contained in the fifty-two chapters of the sixth historical notice of the first part of his work; which have now been translated for the Hakluyt Society, and form the present volume. His principal authority was the manuscript of Francisco Vasquez, one of the companions of Aguirre, from whom he copies largely, and without any acknowledgment. He could not have taken his narrative from a more authentic source; and it is possible that he may have conversed with other followers of Aguirre, or with men who were engaged in the campaign which ended in the traitor's death.

V. The next author who gives an account of Aguirre's cruise, is the bishop Piedrahita. Lucas Fernandez Piedrahita was born at Bogota, in the early part of the seventeenth century, the son of Domingo Hernandez de Soto Piedrahita, by Catalina Collantes. He studied in the college of his native town, where he is said to have shown great talent for poetry, and, having been ordained, he became treasurer of the choir of Bogota in 1654, and canon of the cathedral. For several years he was the favourite preacher in that city, and, in 1669, was appointed bishop of Santa Martha, where he lived in a simple style. His clothes were often torn and ragged, so that his flesh could be seen, and he practised all the Christian virtues. In 1676 Piedrahita was appointed bishop of Panama, but, before his departure, the buccaneer, John Coxon, landed and sacked Santa Martha, burnt the church, seized the bishop, and, refusing to believe in his poverty, tortured him to make him give up his riches. The poor man only possessed one jewel, a ruby in his episcopal ring, which he was forced to surrender, and he was then carried off, and brought before Morgan, on the island of Providence.[1] That notorious buccaneer not only liberated him, but gave him some episcopal robes which he had stolen from Panama, years before; and the poor bishop at length reached his new diocese.

Piedrahita passed the last years of his life, converting the Indians of Darien, and preaching, not only in the churches, but also in the streets of Panama. He died there in 1688, aged seventy, and was buried in the college of the Jesuits, now in ruins. The materials for his history[2] were the journal of the great conqueror Gonzalo Ximenes de Quesada; the fourth part of the *Elegias* of Castellanos; and the *Noticias Historiales* of Simon. His style is pure and clear, the events are placed in chronological order, his descriptions of localities are good, and he affects

---

[1] In the Bahama Islands, a favourite resort of the buccaneers at that time.—*Burney,* iv, p. 322.

[2] Entitled "Historia General de las conquistas del nuevo Reyno de Granada, por el Doctor Don Lucas Fernandez Piedrahita, Obispo Electo de Santa Marta."

allusions to classical authors, as much as Simon
neglects or despises them; but he cites few authorities, and is inferior, in his method of narrating
events, to Simon; from whom, however, he copies
long passages almost literally, without any acknowledgment, a habit which he may have caught from
his predecessor.[1]

Piedrahita does not give any detailed account of
the proceedings of Aguirre, until he lands in Venezuela; but from that time until the traitor's death,
the account is almost as full as that of Simon; and it
is taken, he tells us, from Simon, Castellanos, and
that part of the "*Varones Illustres del Nuevo Mundo*"
which treats of Diego Garcia de Paredes.[2]

Like Garcilasso Inca de la Vega, the historian
Piedrahita was descended from the Incas of Peru;
and was thus the second native of South America
who wrote the history of his country. His ancestor,
captain Juan Muñoz de Collantes, who went out to
the Indies as captain of the guard to Garcia de
Lerma, the governor of Santa Martha in 1528, was
a native of the Alhambra, in Granada. He afterwards lived in Peru, and married Dona Francisca
Coya, an Inca princess, by whom he had a daughter
named Mencia de Collantes. Mencia married Alonzo
de Soto, and was the great grandmother of the historian Piedrahita.[3]

[1] I am indebted for the particulars of the lives of Simon and
Piedrahita, to the notices at the end of Colonel Acosta's work on
New Granada.
[2] *Piedrahita*, Pte. i, lib. xii, cap. viii, p. 566 to 586.
[3] The royal family of Mexico, as well as that of Peru, produced

g

VI. The last authentic account of the expedition of Ursua and Aguirre, was written by a native of Caraccas, and is entitled—"Historia de la conquista y poblacion de la provincia de Venezuela, descrito por Don Josè de Oviedo y Baños, vecino de la cuidad de Santiago de Leon de Caraccas. Primera Parte. Madrid. 1723." Oviedo y Baños confines his narrative of Aguirre's excesses to the part which relates to Venezuela, and his account is, for the most part, a mere abstract of Simon.[1] There is no copy of this work in the British Museum, but they have one in the library at Madrid. Mr. Southey says that he could not, after diligent inquiry, find a copy of Oviedo y Baños; yet I see that Robertson, in his *History of America*, quotes him once or twice.

None of the other old Spanish historians give more than a passing notice of the extraordinary expedition which forms the subject of the present volume. Garcilasso de la Vega, who knew both Pedro de Ursua and Fernando de Guzman personally, speaks highly of the character of Ursua, but refers the reader to Castellanos for further details.[2] Herrera says little more; and Acosta, whose sources of information were almost as good as those of Simon (for he tells us that a brother of his company, being then young, sailed with Ursua, with whom he was present at all his strange adventures, and at the pernicious acts of

a historian. This was Fernando de Alva Yxtlilxochilt, a descendant of the kings of Tezcuco, on the lake of Mexico, who wrote a history of the Chichemecs.

[1] Pte. i, lib. iv, cap. i, p. 173, to cap. ix, p. 224.

[2] *Com. Real.*, Pte. ii, lib. viii, cap. xiv.

Aguirre, from whom God delivered him to place him in the company of Jesuits), merely makes a passing allusion to the subject.

Sir Walter Raleigh, in his account of the attempts of his Spanish predecessors in the search for El Dorado, makes several mistakes when he comes to describe the cruise of Aguirre ;[1] and these mistakes have been greatly amplified by numerous modern authors. The chief offender is M. Gomberville, the French translator of Acuña's voyage down the Amazon, (Paris 1692) who interpolates an account of Aguirre's voyage, which must have been invented by himself, as it contains as many mistakes as sentences, none of which are to be found in Acuña's original narrative, where the expedition of Ursua and Aguirre is very briefly noticed.[2] Condamine, Mr. Dalton in his history of British Guiana, and other modern writers, follow M. Gomberville, who leads them far away from the truth.[3] The Ulloas, who ought to have

[1] See Raleigh's *Guiana*, edited by Sir Robert Schomburgk, for the Hakluyt Society, p. 23.

[2] See *Valley of the Amazons*, p. 48. (Hakluyt Society).

[3] It would be tedious to enumerate all M. Gomberville's errors, but amongst them are the following. He says that Aguirre and Guzman were in love with the lady Inez, for which he has no authority whatever; that her name was Agnes or Anes; that Aguirre proclaimed himself king; that he descended the river Coca into the Amazon; that, when he left Margarita, he went to Cumana; that he desolated all the coast of Caraccas; that he then went to Santa Martha, and put every one to the sword; that he entered New Granada, and was defeated there; that he was taken a prisoner to the island of Trinidad; that he had a considerable estate there; that he was executed there, his houses razed, and the sites strewn with salt. All these are pure inventions.

been better informed, give a more erroneous account than even M. Gomberville. They say that Ursua, and the greater part of his men, were killed by the Indians, in an ambuscade ; a misfortune entirely due to his own misconduct ; and that thus the expedition came to an end.[1]

Indeed the ignorance of late Spanish writers, respecting what they themselves declare to be one of the most memorable events of the time, is very remarkable. Velasco, the historian of Quito, gives an account which he must have picked up from some vague tradition.[2] He says that Ursua founded a colony, as a base for his operations, on the banks of the river Sapo, a tributary of the Huallaga, and called it Saposoa : that he started in 1559, and was murdered while navigating the Sapo by a soldier named Aguirre : that the rock overhanging the river Huallaga is still shown, where, if the day is clear, the inscription may be distinctly read, which was cut by Aguirre, after he had murdered Ursua in the Sapo : and that Saposoa was abandoned a few years afterwards.

This rock, mentioned by Velasco, is still known as " El Salto de Aguirre" (the leap of Aguirre). Soon after leaving Chasuta, going down the river Huallaga, the canoe passes " between cliffs of dark red rocks, where the river deepens to forty-two feet. On one of these rocks, appearing like a gigantic boulder of

---

[1] *Viaje de Don Jorge Juan, y Don Antonio de Ulloa*, lib. vi, cap. v.

[2] *Historia del Reino de Quito.* Quito, 1789. Tom. iii, lib. v, p. 181.

porphyry, were cut rude figures of saints and crosses, with letters which are said to express ' the leap of the traitor Aguirre.' They were too much worn by time and weather, to be made out."[1] According to the *Mercurio Peruano* there is a tradition amongst the Motilones Indians that a vulture lived on this rock, and preyed upon travellers, until a man named Aguirre killed it ; and the explanation is supposed to be that a man of that name persuaded the people to kill a pirate, or, as the author in the *Mercurio Peruano* supposes, the origin of the tradition is to be found in the murder of Ursua by Aguirre.

Another tradition respecting the cruise of Aguirre, which is mentioned in the *Mercurio Peruano*, may here be alluded to. The Mayorunas Indians are a tribe living on the right bank of the mouth of the Ucayali. They have thick beards, and comparatively white skins; and wander through the forests as hunters, without going much to the banks of the rivers. They are often called Barbudos, are very numerous, taller than most other tribes, at enmity with all their neighbours, go perfectly naked, are well formed, with straight noses, and small lips, and, alone of all the tribes in this region, are remarkable for their cleanliness.[2]

The legend is, that they are descended from some Spanish soldiers of Ursua's expedition, by native

---

[1] *Valley of the Amazon,* by Lieutenant Herndon, U.S.N., p. 169.

[2] *Velasco,* iii, p. 108; *Smyth,* p. 223; *Herndon,* p. 218.

women;[1] and it is just possible that this may be true, for two of the soldiers of Garcia del Arze's party were lost in the forests,[2] and they may have been the progenitors of the Mayorunas.[3]

It is very difficult to assign its true place, in the history of geographical discovery, to the voyage of Aguirre. It was the opinion of most of the ancient Spanish writers that the mutineers found their way to the Atlantic, either by leaving the course of the Amazon, ascending the Rio Negro, and, by the Cassiquiari canal, entering the Orinoco, and descending it to its mouth; or by making their way into some of the rivers of Guiana. If this was the case the discoveries of Aguirre were both extensive and important, but Baron Humboldt and Mr. Southey saw no reason for supposing that he ever left the course of the Amazon.[4] The arguments for and against these two conflicting opinions may be stated as follows. In favour of the Orinoco route there

---

[1] *Mercurio Peruano*, No. 76.

[2] See p. 14 of the present volume.

[3] The Jeberos, another tribe of the Amazon, are also descended from Spanish progenitors, but on the female side; their ancestors having captured a number of Spanish women, in the insurrection of 1599: so that many of them now have beards, and fair complexions.

[4] Mr. Southey originally intended to have inserted a chapter on Ursua and Aguirre, in his history of Brazil, but the subject being only slightly connected with that country, he laid his manuscript aside. He afterwards published it in the *Edinburgh Annual Register*, vol. iii, part 2, and finally reprinted it in a separate volume, which was published by Longman in 1821. Southey gives a full abstract of Simon's narrative, and also quotes Piedrahita and

are several circumstances which may be urged, and the weight of authority is decidedly on that side of the question.

After the murder of Ursua, the traitors wished to return to Peru, but at the same time Aguirre desired to avoid the supposed land of Omagua, which he believed to be lower down the stream of the Amazon; because he feared that the soldiers would land and settle there, and thus thwart his design of returning to Peru, and upsetting the government of the viceroy, whom he cordially hated. He, therefore, " made a turn out of the way of their direct route, and navigated three days and a night in a westerly direction;[1] that is, judging from the probable position of the adventurers at the time, he either began to ascend the stream of the Rio Negro, or one of the branches of the Japura, which communicate with it. Again, some days afterwards, he continues to " direct his course to the left, by a branch of the river, and navigates by branches coming from the west,"[2] evidently continuing his course up the Rio Negro, until he finds himself among the Arekainas Indians, a tribe only met with on the upper waters of the Rio Negro, or on the Putumayu.[3] All these statements seem to point to the Rio Negro as the course Aguirre was taking, and, afterwards, when mention is made of cakes of salt in an Indian village,[4]

Herrera; but he was unable to get a sight either of Castellanos or Oviedo y Baños, and he had never seen either of the contemporaneous manuscript accounts of Aguirre's career.

[1] See p. 76 of this volume.

[2] See p. 97.   [3] See p. 99, and note.   [4] See p. 104.

he may be supposed to have been approaching the mouths of the Orinoco, and that this salt was obtained by the Indians from sea water, by solar evaporation. This is all the testimony that can be obtained from Vasquez or Simon ; but Herrera, Garcia, and Acosta all believed that the traitors reached the sea by some river opposite the island of Trinidad, and the latter had his information from a man who was actually in Aguirre's expedition.[1] Acuña, also, positively states that Aguirre did not reach the sea by the mouth of the Amazon.[2]

But the strongest evidence in favour of the Orinoco route is to be found in the way many early writers confuse the rivers Orinoco and Marañon, a confusion, which, as I believe, arose from the conflicting accounts given by the men of Orellana's, and those of Aguirre's party. Orellana, having descended the main stream of the Amazon, gave a tolerably correct account of its position ; but Aguirre's men, having reached the Atlantic by descending the Orinoco, and still continuing to call all the water they had seen by the name of Marañon,[3] stated that its mouth (that is the mouth of the Orinoco) was opposite the island of

[1] See a note at page 111 of this volume.

[2] See *Valley of the Amazons*, printed for the Hakluyt Society, p. 49.

[3] The fanciful derivations of the word *Marañon*, given by Simon, Velasco, and Manuel Rodriguez, will be found in a note at p. 95 of this volume ; and Simon erroneously asserts that the word originated during Aguirre's cruise. Mr. Southey, however, in his history of Brazil, has clearly shown that the name was applied to this great river, fifty-nine years before the time of Aguirre. He

Trinidad. This especially appears in the account of the Jesuit who was Acosta's informant; and the confusion became so great at last, that Friar Simon declared that he could not tell which river was the Marañon, and that it must remain an open question, until some one writes about it with better information.[1]

On the other hand, the evidence in favour of Aguirre having entered the sea by the mouth of the Amazon, is chiefly negative. The time that is stated to have elapsed between the murder of Ursua and the arrival of Aguirre's vessels in the sea; as well as the length of the voyage from the mouth of the river to the island of Margarita; are more in favour of the Amazon than of the Orinoco theory, and it is also stated that the description of the numerous islands, and of the breadth of the mouth of the river, is better suited to the Amazon.[2] Mr. Southey thinks it very improbable that Aguirre ever left the main stream of the Amazon; and Baron Humboldt, although at one time he believed that Aguirre ascended the Japura, and reached the Atlantic by some river of Guiana; afterwards came to the conclusion that there was no evidence that the traitor did not descend the Amazon to its mouth. Neither of these two eminent writers, however, gives the grounds on which he formed this opinion.

points out that it is used by Peter Martyr in his epistles, and in the oldest account of Pinzon's voyage; and he thinks it was the name of some person in Pinzon's expedition, A.D. 1499.

[1] See p. 109 of this volume.
[2] See also the note at p. 110 of this volume.

h

It might be supposed that the frightful catastrophe
in which the expedition of Pedro de Ursua was in-
volved, would have damped the ardour of the search-
ers after El Dorado, at least for a considerable time;
but this was very far from being the case. In 1566,
only five years afterwards, one Martin de Proveda
started from Chachapoyas in Peru, close to Ursua's
point of embarkation, on a similar errand. He made
his way in a northerly direction, through dense
forests, where the great majority of his men perished,
and eventually turned up at Bogota: but there was
no result from this expedition, except a rumour that
there were rich provinces to be found still deeper in
the primeval forests. This rumour, however, vague
as it was, induced a fellow townsman of Proveda's, to
initiate another search for El Dorado.

This was Don Pedro Malaver de Silva, a native of
Xeres, who was a rich and enterprising man, married
in Chachapoyas. In 1568, in furtherance of his
object, he went to Spain, and received powers to
conquer Omaguas and El Dorado, for a space of
three hundred leagues, with the government for two
lives. At the same time Don Diego Fernando de
Cerpa received a concession from the Boca del
Drago, by the mouths of the Orinoco, to the frontier
of Silva's country. The two rival adventurers were
in Seville when news came of the insurrection of the
Moriscos, in the mountains of Granada; and Serpa
was detained to serve against them, while Silva
sailed with two ships in March 1569, accompanied
by two brothers, named Alonzo and Diego Braba.

Silva reached Burburata, and marched thence to Valencia, in Venezuela; but his forces were disunited, some went to Barquisimeto, others to Tocuyo, others hid themselves near Valencia, and the Barbas sailed for Carthagena, having first stolen all the wine which their chief had left at Burburata. At length Silva entered the plains, to the south of Venezuela, with one hundred and forty men, in July 1569.

Cerpa succeeded in getting his men away from the Morisco wars, and, sailing from Spain in 1569, with four hundred soldiers, landed on a coast inhabited by the warlike Cumanagotos Indians, at the mouth of the Rio Salado. Here he founded a city called Santiago de los Cavalleros, where he left the women of his party, intending to cross the land to the south, and discover the Orinoco. But the Indians attacked him on the march, killed him with their *macanas* or clubs, and scattered his party. Nearly all his men died of wounds or of disease, very few escaping back to Santiago; and the place was abandoned, the survivors retiring to the island of Margarita.

In the meanwhile Silva returned to Barquicimeto, quite disheartened, and, after visiting his home in Peru, proceeded to Spain with the intention of trying some other route. In 1574 he again sailed from Cadiz with one hundred and sixty men, and landed on the coast between the mouths of the Orinoco and Amazon, where all his party perished, some dying of disease, and others being killed by the Caribs. Among the sufferers were two little maidens, the daughters of Silva. Out of the whole party only one man escaped, named Juan Martin de Albujar, who was for ten years a prisoner amongst the Indians, but, after great dangers and hardships, he eventually reached the mouth of the river Esquinas, whence friendly Indians sent him in a canoe to Margarita.[1]

At this time, the great rivers and vast plains, between Guiana and the feet of the cordilleras, having been traversed by numerous explorers without any result, the fable of El Dorado and of the " Gran Laguna de Manoa" began to find a resting place amongst the periodically inundated plains between the rivers Rupununi, Essequibo, and Parima or Branco, in Guiana. The last expedition which can be said to have achieved any important geographical discovery was that of Don Antonio de Berreo, who had married the daughter of Gonzalo Ximenes de Quesada, the great conqueror of Bogota, and, with her, had inherited the duty of continuing the search for El Dorado. He started from New Granada in 1582, and, following the courses of the rivers Cassanare and Meta, reached the Orinoco ; suffering, like his predecessors, from disease and the attacks of Indians. He descended the Orinoco to its mouth, and proceeded to the island of Trinidad, of which he became governor. There were numerous other insignificant attempts, at about this time,

---

[1] *Oviedo y Baños.* Humboldt has suggested that the lying tale of the visit of Martinez to the great city of Manoa, which led to the expeditions of Domingo de Vera, Sir Walter Raleigh, and others of less note, may have been founded on the adventures of Albujar.

made by adventurers from Venezuela, Trinidad, or Margarita, but they all failed, and the expeditions of our own Sir Walter Raleigh and Captain Keymis may be said to close the long roll of searches after the fabulous El Dorado.

As the search for the philosopher's stone led to many discoveries in chemistry, so the romantic expeditions in quest of the golden city of Manoa, and the gilded chief, conduced more than any other circumstance, during the latter part of the sixteenth century, to the extension of geographical knowledge in South America. Many of these expeditions were conducted with great skill and perseverance; others are memorable for deeds of unequalled heroism; but none was so extraordinary as that which Don Pedro de Ursua led down from Peru into the great valley of the Amazon, and which ended in the sanguinary career of the mad demon Lope de Aguirre.

SIXTH

HISTORICAL NOTICE

OF THE FIRST PART OF THE

CONQUEST of TIERRA FIRME,

in the Weſtern Indies,

COMPOSED BY

FATHER FRIAR PEDRO SIMON,

Provincial of the ſeraphic order of San Franciſco, of the
New Kingdom of Granada in the Indies. Reader in ſacred theology,
native of the province of Carthagena in Caſtile, and born
at Parrilla, in the Biſhopric of Cuenca: dedicated
to our unconquerable Monarch, the greateſt
in either the old or new world,
Philip IV, in his royal and
ſupreme Council of
the Indies.

*Containing the narrative of the expedition of Pedro de
Urſua, and of the crimes of the tyrant
Lope de Aguirre.*

SIXTH HISTORICAL NOTICE

OF THE

CONQUEST OF TERRA FIRMA.

CHAP. I.

1. *Gives a brief account of the deeds of Pedro de Ursua, before his arrival in Peru ; and of his entrance into that country.—2. Certain Brazilian Indians give information in Peru, of very rich provinces near the river Marañon.—3. The Marquis of Cañete determines to send Pedro de Ursua to explore them, and summons him to his presence.—4. Various opinions are formed in Peru respecting this expedition.*

1. THE Captain Pedro de Ursua entered the city of Santa Fé, in the New Kingdom of Granada, with his uncle the licentiate Miguel Diaz de Armendariz, the first Juez de Residencia, who arrived there after the discovery of the kingdom, and settlement of the city.[1] This Pedro de Ursua was a native of the kingdom of Navarre, and of a town called Ursua, near the noble city of Pampluna. From Santa Fé he went down to settle in the town of Pampluna, in New Granada, and thence undertook the conquest of the Musos Indians, and founded the city of Tudela amongst them. He afterwards went to Santa Martha, and there performed deeds worthy of his noble descent. From thence, having returned

[1] For a brief account of the proceedings of Armendariz and Ursua, in New Granada, see the Introduction.

to Santa Fé, to give an account of what he had done, he descended the great river[1] to Carthagena, intending to go to Peru by way of Panamá. In the execution of this design he reached that city at a time when it was harassed by the incursions which certain negro Cimarrones[2] made almost every day. The people of Panamá, having heard long before of his valorous deeds, and of the conquests with which he had been charged; entrusted to him the pacification of their land, and the punishment of these revolted negroes. Having acquitted himself well in this undertaking, he continued his voyage to Peru, in search of more important work than he had yet been entrusted with; and arrived at the city of Lima in the year 1558; Don Andres Hurtado de Mendoza, Marquis of Cañete (worthy of eternal memory) being then viceroy of that city.

2. Certain rumours prevailed in those times, both in the city of Lima and throughout the provinces of Peru (which had been spread by Indians from Brazil), respecting rich provinces, which they had seen, as they said, when on their road from the coast of Brazil, whence more than 2,000 Indians had set out, with the intention of settling in other lands, which might be more agreeable to them, as their own were too crowded. Others declare that the Indians set out on this expedition to enjoy human food in those parts At length, after travelling for ten years with two Portuguese in their company, some by the river Marañon, and some by land, they reached the provinces of the Motilones[3] in Peru, by way of a famous river[4] which flows thence, and enters the Marañon. These Indians brought news respecting the

---

[1] The river Magdalena.

[2] Runaway negro slaves.

[3] A tribe of the river Huallaga, also called Lamistas. They are settled at Lamas, Mozobamba, and Tarapoto. They are industrious, employed chiefly in agriculture and the preparation of cotton, of mild disposition and friendly manners. *Poeppig Reise.*

[4] The Huallaga.

provinces of the Omaguas,[1] mentioned also by Captain Francisco de Orellana, when he descended this river Marañon after deserting Gonzalo Pizarro, in the Cinnamon country.[2]

In these provinces, of which the Indians spoke when they reached Peru, dwelt the gilded man, at least this name was spread about in the land, taking its origin in the city of Quito. It so excited the minds of those restless spirits with whom Peru was full, and who were ever ready to credit these rumours, that the viceroy thought it prudent to seek some way by which to give employment to so large a body of turbulent men.

3. Being aware of the talent of Pedro de Ursua, the Marquis thought he had found the proper man to command the contemplated expedition, which he intended to send on this discovery, and thus Ursua might add to the services which he had performed for his Majesty, especially in the pacification of the Negroes. The Marquis also hoped to relieve the provinces of Peru of much corrupt blood, by sending forth many idle people, who might otherwise cause some fresh insurrection, like those which had already placed this famous kingdom in danger; an object which ought always to be kept in view by those who govern, if they would avoid the lamentable occurrences which had formerly taken place. The Viceroy, being determined to give the command of this expedition to Pedro de Ursua, gave him the title of Governor of the Provinces which he might discover and conquer, with power to appoint officers, and to reward his companions according to their merits, recommending him to have a care of the conquered Indians, to form settlements consisting of such Spaniards as he might think proper, and to do this for the good of the church and the crown of Spain.

[1] Formerly a very extensive nation, particularly on the Marañon.
[2] See the voyage of Orellana, in the *Expeditions into the valley of the Amazons*, printed for the Hakluyt Society, p. 27.

He was promised, after having founded such settlements,
that he should be rewarded as the kings of Spain were
accustomed to reward those who had discovered and settled
new lands.

4. The voice of fame soon spread the news of this expedition throughout Peru, and many offered themselves ; but
there were others unfavourable to it, of low as well as of high
degree, who questioned the propriety of the conduct of the
Marquis in patronizing it, as well as in entrusting Pedro de
Ursua with the command ; some hoping to stop the expedition for particular ends of their own, others on account of
their envious spirit and idle disposition, wishing to prevent
the accomplishment of great undertakings. They said that this
was not the moment for the Viceroy to enter upon so large
an affair, the result of which would not be seen during his
period of office, as there was information that he was soon to
have a successor in Don Diego de Azuedo, (and it was said
that the Marquis was in no way pleased that the King was
about to remove him, in anticipation of his period of service). Such being the case, Azuedo would find it most inconvenient, when he came to discover that the Marquis had
taken a large sum of money from the treasury to defray the
expense of the expedition, and in the hope also of benefiting
himself. To these remarks others were added, having no
foundation, but which, coming to the ears of the Viceroy,
were expected to have the effect of cooling, in some degree,
his ardour in favouring Pedro de Ursua. These observations had some weight with the Viceroy, until news arrived
that Don Diego de Azuedo had died in Seville. The Marquis then became anxious for the departure of the expedition,
and also to reanimate Pedro de Ursua, who began to fear
whether he could successfully conduct so important an en-
terprize, for his most intimate friends had represented to
him the great difficulties that would arise. These were so
many presages of the unfortunate end of the expedition.

CHAP. II.

1. Pedro de Ursua builds the brigantines for the expedition, and makes Pedro Ramiro his lieutenant-general.—2. Ursua leaves Lima with his people—he arrives at the town of Moyobamba.[1]—3. How he contrived to obtain two thousand dollars from the cura or priest of this place.—4. Ursua sends part of his people from the Motilones to other provinces, where they provide for themselves.

1. While captains were sent to hunt up people for the expedition in the vicinity of Lima, early in 1559, so that they might not be detained for want of means to navigate the rivers, Ursua proposed to construct vessels. For this purpose he looked out for ship-builders, and found twenty-five, also ten negro carpenters; and, having manufactured tools and other requisites, he went to the country of the Motilones, whence, as we have already said, the Brazilians had come, who had given the information which had been the cause of the expedition.

In this province there was a Spanish town called Santa Cruz de Capacoba,[2] lately founded by Captain Pedro Ramiro, who was governing there in the name of the king.

Pedro de Ursua arrived here with his people, and having ascertained on which part of the banks he could cut good timber, he went down the river some twenty leagues, and reached the desired spot; and having given orders to his officers, among whom was Juan Corzo, his principal ship-wright, to build the number of vessels he required, and named Pedro Ramiro as his Lieutenant-General, Ursua returned to Lima, from which place he could dispatch the people and soldiers collected by his captains.

2. The funds of Pedro de Ursua were very scanty; and although the Viceroy had assisted him from the royal trea-

---

[1] Or Lamas, on the river Moyobamba, which runs into the Huallaga.
[2] Probably near to the town of Moyobamba.

sury, and money had been obtained from other sources, he had not sufficient for his expenses. This caused nearly a year's delay, which would have continued longer, if the people of Lima, and others favourable to Ursua's views, had not supplied him with more money for the equipment of his soldiers, purchase of powder, rope, muskets, horses, arms and munitions, cattle, ship-provisions, and other things.

At last Ursua left Lima, having sent on the greater number of his people, as a vanguard, and to watch that none deserted. He arrived at Moyobamba, where Pedro Portillo, the priest, had hoarded five or six thousand dollars. Portillo, hearing flattering accounts of Ursua's expedition, and seeing the great number of gallant followers, anxious also to increase his fortune and dignity, by becoming a bishop in the new lands to be discovered, offered to lend Ursua two thousand dollars, on condition that he would promise to appoint him cura and vicar of the expedition. Ursua gladly accepted the cura's proposal, and felt no difficulty in acceding to Portillo's wishes for ecclesiastical preferment.

3. But the priest soon repented his offer, and began to feel but little faith in the success of the expedition. He intimated that the loan of the two thousand dollars would be inconvenient to him; but Ursua could not do without money, for he had ordered many articles for which it was necessary to pay. Ursua, finding himself in an awkward position, called into his councils Juan de Vargas, who was afterwards his lieutenant, Fernando de Guzman, Juan Alonso de la Vandera, Pedro Alonzo Casco, and Pedro de Miranda, a mulatto, all fighting men and of elastic consciences; telling them his present trouble, and that he was most desirous that the money should be obtained from the priest. His friends saw no difficulty about the matter, even if a little violence was resorted to;—so one night they reported that Juan de Vargas (who was then quartered in the church on account of two wounds), was dying, and one of them went

for the cura Portillo, urging him to lose no time in going to
confess Vargas. On leaving his house the cura was seized
by Ursua's friends, and was forced to sign an order for two
thousand dollars on a merchant of the town, who was the
keeper of the cura's wealth. The cura went to Vargas, who
was in an apartment of the church. On his arrival fire-arms
were pointed at his breast, and, without waiting for the
morrow, they took him to the town of Santa Cruz de Capacoba. Here the greater portion of the expedition was encamped. At this place they forced from him the other
three or four thousand dollars of his fortune. This system
of things did not stop here; for during the progress of the
expedition there was much disturbance, and the turbulent
paid for their misdeeds by terrible deaths, as we shall see
further on.

4. The chief part of the expedition had reached the town
of the Motilones of Santa Cruz, when the Governor Pedro
de Ursua arrived, (he already took this title, without knowing where the country lay that he was to be governor of),
and although this province was fertile, and aided much in the
support of the people, yet as they were many, the governor
found it necessary to send a portion of his followers to a province called Tubalosas, not far distant, to remain and provide
for themselves there until he was ready to embark; assigning
to them as chiefs two of his most intimate friends, Francisco
Diaz de Arles, who had been with him in all his actions
since they left Navarre; and Diego de Frias, an attendant of
the Viceroy's, one who had been highly recommended to
him, and who was treasurer to the expedition. These two
had not been friendly to the Corregidor Pedro Ramiro,
since the time when Ursua made Ramiro his lieutenant-
general, because they had pretensions to the same post, as
they gave him to understand to his cost. Although the
governor felt satisfied with the two chiefs and soldiers, he
also sent Pedro Ramiro, who knew the country well, and

was feared by the natives. Ramiro was to go onwards to the said province, to make the officers and men friends with the chiefs and people, after which he was to return to Santa Cruz.

CHAP. III.

1. *Arles and Frias are displeased at having Ramiro with them—they determine to kill him.—2. They kill Ramiro.—3. The governor Ursua goes in person to arrest the delinquents.—4. He sends them to Santa-Cruz, where they are beheaded.*

1. Arles and Frias were very much displeased that Ramiro had been named as their leader, for they hated him in consequence of his appointment, as already stated; but it was necessary that Ramiro should lead the way for a few days on their journey, after which they determined to turn against him, and to carry their scheme into effect, when resting for the night. The devil instigated the act (for no other could have been the author). The assassins conferred with each other, and the evil genius who had inspired them gave the means also. They thought that on account of the great friendship both had with Ursua, he would defend them, or look over any guilty action they might commit. They vacillated only respecting the manner of committing an act which they had decided on. In this state of uncertainty, two soldiers, great friends of theirs, joined them. These men had separated from those who had gone onwards, and having missed Arles and Frias, had returned to look after them. One was named Grijota, the other Alonso Martin. They asked their officers why they had left the lieutenant, who replied that Ramiro had dismissed them, he remaining with the others, and intending to rebel, in order to enter certain lands of which he had information, and settle them.

They added that if Grijota and Martin would join them,
they would be doing a good service to the king and the
governor, by seizing Ramiro, and so stopping the progress
of his rebellion.

The soldiers did not then see through the intentions
of Arles and Frias, which were well cloaked with explanations, apparently true. They agreed to join them, and the
four continued on the track of Ramiro with the intention
of putting their design into execution on the first opportunity.

2. Having journeyed a few leagues, they saw Pedro Ramiro on the banks of a rapid river, over which it had been
necessary (there being only one small canoe for the passage
of the river, which was not fordable) to pass the rest of the
soldiers first. Ramiro, who had only one companion, the rest
having passed the river, saw the four approach him. The
four, taking advantage of the occasion, saluted him with
bland words, very different from the character of their intentions, and he felt assured that they were friendly; but
they laid hands upon him suddenly and disarmed him,
while Pedro de Frias ordered a slave he had with him to
strangle him, which was done, and then he cut his head off.
The youth who was with Ramiro made his escape, returning
as quickly as possible to the town of the Motilones, and
giving notice of what had happened to Pedro de Ursua,
who was much distressed at the news. The four murderers looked upon themselves as victors, and the canoe
returning to the landing place to fetch Pedro Ramiro, they
entered into it and crossed to the other side, persuading the
people that they had executed Ramiro by order of the Governor Ursua, in consequence of his being informed that
Ramiro designed to rebel and take the people with him.
This explanation sufficed. The murderers sent one of their
friends to Ursua to say that Captain Pedro Ramiro had been
arrested by their orders on the ground that he wished to
rebel and lead the people with him, but that they, as faithful

c

servants of the king and his governor, had made him prisoner, and would detain him until they were instructed how
to act further in the case.

But the truth had already come to the ears of the governor, through the young man who had been with Ramiro,
and he disbelieved the second messenger; but he dissembled, and gave no indication that he suspected Arles
and Frias.

There were not wanting men, who, reasoning seriously
on this murder of Ramiro, recommended Ursua to get all
his people together and return to Peru, particularly as
Arles and Frias had stated such to be their desire.

3. The Governor was grieved, indeed, at what had occurred; he had fears and suspicions that worse would succeed, even a mutiny amongst the soldiers against the four
murderers of Ramiro. He felt ill at ease until he decided
upon going himself with a few attendants, thus making no
show of power. He trusted also to the confidence Arles
and Frias had in him; for if they saw him come with a
large force (fearing the punishment their crime merited)
they might mutiny, and instead of depending on their safety
by reason of old friendships, there might occur most serious
tumults; thus in the King's name, who was so justly beloved by the good, and dreaded by the evil, Ursua unexpectedly arrived amongst the people and the murderers, so
that the latter had no time to tamper with the soldiers
against the Governor. The four assassins hurriedly collected
together what they could, escaping from the presence of
the Governor, on account of the shame they felt for their
great crimes.

Ursua made no show of disappointment at not finding the
murderers; his plan was to remain most tranquil. He sent
to tell them that they were unjust to themselves, being
men of such qualities and gifts, in making themselves culpable by flight, when it was notorious that they had ever

shown themselves diligent in their services to the King ; and, supposing they had overstepped the line of duty, they well knew the obligations he owed them, and that he could serve and favour them ; that it was better they should return to the camp, and so prevent their falling into the hands of any other judge, who would punish them.

4. These and other reasons were sufficient to give confidence to Arles and Frias, and they determined to present themselves before Pedro de Ursua. To assure them the more, he sent them immediately to the town of Santa Cruz, and promised to do his best that they should be set at liberty. The Governor followed them, after having put things in order among the soldiers and people, and appointed a chief over them. He arrived a few days after the prisoners, at the town of Santa Cruz, and ordered them to be arrested and secured as prisoners. The cause was tried by the assessor of the expedition, with all legal form; but as the crime was most grave, notorious, and conclusive, he condemned them to have their heads cut off.

Although the sentence was notified to them, they did not believe it would be carried into execution; for up to this point Ursua had been bland in his conduct to them. They considered that the sentence was only nominal, and merely given in conformity with his office as judge, in order that he might be feared by those he commanded; and that doubtless he would allow them to appeal to the royal audience at Lima. Many of the inhabitants of the town and others, being aware of the old friendship, and even relationship, between the culprits and the judge, thought that the condemned would not suffer.

But the Governor, putting aside everything but justice, which it was his duty to administer, without exception of persons, even of his own blood, and in order to make a proper example, commanded that there should be no appeal, and that their heads should be cut off in public, which was done.

CHAP. IV.

1. *People in Peru are fearful of mutiny in Ursua's expedition—a friend writes to him on the subject.—2. The governor sends two parties of soldiers in search of provisions. One of these, composed of thirty men, goes down the river, more than two hundred leagues.— 3. Garcia del Arze, and his soldiers, fortify themselves on an island, against the Indians.—4. The Spaniards are most cruel to the natives who come peacefully to them.*

1. The Viceroy and Oidores, as well as the inhabitants of Lima, began to entertain fears for the success of Ursua's expedition, for there were in it so many mutinous and turbulent persons, who had been in the rebellions of Gonzalo Pizarro, Francisco Hernandez Giron, Don Sebastian de Castilla, and that of Contreras; and the number of Ursua's followers was large, amounting to nearly three hundred men.

These suspicions increased daily, and were countenanced by idle and evil intentioned people, until a stop was put to them by the news of the execution of Arles and Frias by Pedro de Ursua. The Marquis and the Oidores then became more tranquil, and praised the decisive act of the execution, and the Governor's management, promising to themselves great successes on account of the expedition. There were, however, some superstitious people who said that as blood had been shed at its commencement, it would end in blood.

One Pedro de Linasco, a settler in Chachapoias, and a friend of Ursua's, accustomed to such expeditions, and well acquainted with many of those who were with Ursua, wrote him a letter, in which he notified to him the suspicions of people in Peru that many of his soldiers were turbulent and mutinous, and that they might be troublesome to him, and might even kill him; that he should have especial suspicion of Lorenzo de Salduendo, Lope de Aguirre, Juan

Alonso de la Bandera, Christoval de Chaves, a certain Don Martin, and others whom he named, telling him that for ten or twelve men more or less he was not to give up his journey, and he prayed him to separate those he had named from being his followers. Even should he have compassion on them in consequence of their poverty, such feelings should have no weight with him; that Ursua should send them to him, and he would take care of them until the Governor should discover the lands he was in search of, and when he thought it opportune, he could send for them, and do with them as he thought best.

He begged of him, as a friend, not to take Doña Inez de Atienza with him, who was the daughter of one Blas de Atienza, an inhabitant of the city of Trujillo, and widow of Pedro de Arcos, an inhabitant of Piura. Ursua had taken her, with the intention of marrying her, as she was a spirited and beautiful woman. Linasco said that it did not look well, and that it was setting a bad example to his followers; that greater evils would succeed than he could possibly suppose; and that if he determined to leave her, he would give orders that she should be taken care of; and this should be done in such a way that Doña Inez should not know who had been the cause of her remaining behind, or that Ursua had even consented to it. This friendly letter had not the desired effect on the governor; who, although a man of great ability, was young, and without much experience. Thus he did not follow the advice of his friend, excepting that he sent back Don Martin; neither did he reply to the letter, or do what was advised therein. Had he done so he might have been saved from death by the hands of those whose names had been given to him.

2. Pedro de Ursua, being now in the town of the Motilones or Santa Cruz, and all his people having arrived, sent one hundred men under Captain Juan Vargas by land, so that on their arrival at the river Cocama,[1] they might go up it

[1] The Ucayali.

with all the provisions they might have collected in the districts they had passed through, deposit them at the mouth of the river, and await the General's arrival with the rest of the people.

Ursua likewise sent one Garcia del Arze, a confidential friend, with thirty men, to a province twenty leagues down the river where the vessels were building, called Caperuzos (on account of a sort of hood worn by the natives), that he might collect provisions, deposit them on the margin of the river, and await the arrival of Captain Juan de Vargas. Both were to stop for Ursua, so that the whole of the expedition might go together down the river. Garcia del Arze started with his thirty companions on a raft, and some canoes, from the place where the vessels were being built, but, from some cause or other, he did not wait for Juan de Vargas as he had been ordered; so, having collected some provisions in the province of the Caperuzos, and from other localities, he descended the river for two hundred leagues, and having suffered much from hunger, and encountered great difficulties and risks, he arrived at a pleasant island in the river, which was named after him the island of Garcia.

Among other misfortunes that occurred during the voyage, was the loss of two of his soldiers who went on shore in search of food; they entered a deep forest, but went so far as not to be able to retrace their steps, and were left behind. Such was the scarcity of food that the party could not remain long in one place, and they were obliged to eat small alligators, which Arze shot with his arquebuse, in the use of which he was very dexterous.

3. Having arrived at the island (inhabited by warlike natives) they found some food, and for this reason commenced (in case the arrival of Pedro de Ursua with his people should be delayed), to fortify a convenient spot, with thick posts, so as to defend themselves from the continual

assaults of the Indians from the land, as well as from the river. These were in such numbers that had heaven not most miraculously guarded the Spaniards, they must have been overpowered, being only thirty in number, and badly found in offensive and defensive arms, for they only had two or three muskets, whilst the Indians numbered from two to three thousand; nevertheless the few arquebuses were sufficient, seeing what havoc they made among the natives. All their shot being expended, Garcia del Arze fired the ramrod from his cannon at the principal canoe, full of Indians, and although they made a fierce assault, the Indians were routed, and nearly the whole of them fell into the water; those who remained alive being terrified at the sight of the wounded.

On another occasion, when they were hard pressed, they struck down six Indians, who suffered more from being naked; but this was the last time they came to annoy them with their attacks. The Indians now considered it prudent to make peace with the Spaniards, so one day a number of them presented themselves, bringing food, and showing signs of friendship.

4. The Spaniards were suspicious of these signs of friendship, and thought that the Indians meditated treason, so they determined to lay hands on them, and, putting them into a hut within the stockade (nearly twenty in number) they killed them with their daggers and swords.

The news of the cruelties of the Spaniards was soon spread around, so that at the mere mention of their name the natives trembled; they fled from their habitations, leaving everything behind, when they knew that the soldiery were in search of them. Thus it was that thirty persons were able to maintain their position on this island for three months, before Pedro de Ursua joined them.

CHAP. V.

1. *Juan de Vargas commences his voyage—arrives at the mouth of the Cocáma.—2. He remains here until Ursua arrives.—3. The brigantines spring a leak when launched, which is unfortunate for the expedition.—4. Ursua descends the river with all his people, arriving at the province of the Caperuzos.—5. He sends a brigantine to advise Juan de Vargas of his coming.*

1. A few days after Garcia del Arze left the town of the Motilones, Juan de Vargas sailed with his people in one of the brigantines, and some canoes, down the river, on the 1st of July, 1560, to the province of the Caperuzos, whence he soon passed onwards, not finding Garcia del Arze there. Supposing he would be at the mouth of the river Cocáma,[1] as had been arranged, Vargas continued his course down the river to the mouth of the Cocáma, and not finding Arze there, he followed his orders to ascend this river in search of provisions, which he did in his canoes, leaving the more sickly soldiers at the mouth of the river, in charge of the brigantine.

They were twenty-two days ascending the river without meeting with habitations where they could obtain what they sought; after which they fell in with some native villages, where they found abundance of maize. From thence they took many native men and women as servants for the expedition, as well as canoes laden with maize. Vargas now descended the river to its mouth, where he found the people of the brigantine suffering much from hunger and the effects of the climate, of which three Spaniards had died, also many native men and women who were with them.

2. The arrival of Don Juan was hailed with joy, for he brought the remedy against so fearful an enemy as hunger; but this great benefit was soon forgotten, for the soldiers, during the two long months they had been detained here

---

[1] This is the river Ucayali.

without occupation, waiting for the general, considered that
the delay of Ursua was inexcusable, and began to plan how
to leave this spot, which they called the sweet sea.

There were two opinions or plans respecting a mutiny:
one, (and the greater number were of this way of thinking,) was to kill Juan de Vargas and return to Peru up the
river Cocáma; the other was to abandon Vargas and go
on new discoveries. However, neither of these plans was
carried into effect, for they were very slow about the matter;
but they were so secret, that it was a long time afterwards
before it came to the ears of Don Juan, and then it was
too late to punish the mutineers. The spirit of dissatisfaction ceased with the arrival of Pedro Galeas and some
soldiers, and then came General Ursua with the rest of the
party.

3. Ursua, during his stay in the town of the Motilones
or Santa Cruz, understood how to gain people to his side;
and its inhabitants were won over to follow him, leaving
their comforts behind. He promised to reward them largely
for their co-operation, in the countries which might be discovered. The entire population joined him, taking their cattle
and property with them.

Ursua having now collected his party, the vessels were
made ready; but on launching them, as the timbers they
were built of had not been seasoned, most of them sprang
leaks and were of but little use, excepting one brigantine
and three flat-bottomed boats. This circumstance caused a
long detention, for they had to build canoes and rafts to
hold the people; the spot also was inconvenient, provisions
were scarce, and time was an object. The expedition could
not remain to make proper arrangements for the people and
sailors, or for the transport of cattle, and the greater portion
were left behind at the ship-yard with luggage and warlike
stores. Of three hundred horses, room could only be found
for forty, and of the cattle but for few, the rest remaining to

run wild and without owners. The people were in such a state of ill-humour that they almost mutinied, and wished to return to Peru, so as to save what they had there; and this they would have done had not the governor, by his dexterous proceedings, arresting some, flattering and dissembling to others, warning and blandly admonishing the whole, put plainly before them the misery they would experience should they remain behind; adding that on the contrary, by going onwards there was hope of fortune, and the glory of being in such an expedition. He added to this, that he wished them fully to understand that his sorrow at parting with them would be greater than theirs at leaving him; still as a governor he felt it was his duty to do his best in satisfying all of them, and that God would take them safely to the land whither their chief promised to lead them.

4. These reflections had the desired effect, and no one left him. He embarked the people in the brigantine, canoes, and flat-bottomed boats, on the 26th of September, 1560, steering down the river. But the people were far from being comforted for the loss of their cattle, and the other things they could not take with them, and they feared the risks they would run in the narrow parts of the river, and the dangerous state of the vessels they were in. The size of the river also alarmed them, lest they should encounter a storm, in which they might all be lost ere they could gain the shore.

On the second day of the voyage they lost sight of the mountains and came into a flat country, and henceforth the country continued to be flat until they reached the coast of the north sea.

On the third day the brigantine ran on a bank, when she carried away a part of her keel; and her cargo would have been lost, had not the men stuffed their clothes and wool into the hole. They got the vessel on shore and repaired her. The voyage was then continued to the Province of

Caperuzos, where they found Lorenzo Salduendo, who had
been sent forward two or three days before, in floats and
canoes with some soldiers, to collect food and have it ready.

5. The governor was detained here two days, awaiting the
brigantine, which arrived, after encountering many difficulties, owing to her leaky state. There was fear that the cargo
would have to be left behind, as it was difficult to store it,
but, having done this after two days' work, and the provisions being divided among all the people that Salduendo
had collected, the governor ordered the brigantine to proceed
with all on board, under the command of Pedro Alonso
Galeas, with instructions that, having arrived at the mouth
of the Cocáma, he should inform Juan de Vargas, that
although the Governor might be delayed somewhat, he
was on his road to join him, and that Vargas should at
all events await his coming; for Ursua was doubtless aware
that Vargas was not well pleased with his long detention
there.

The brigantine got under weigh, and, arriving at the
mouth of the Cocama, found Don Juan and his men. The
arrival of the brigantine caused general content, which
was increased by the news that Ursua would shortly follow,
which he did. He slept on shore during the nights, fearing the navigation of the river in the dark on account of
banks, floating trees, falls, and other obstructions; and
finally they arrived at a river which joins its waters with
those of the Motilones, and is called Bracamoros, its head
waters being near the Motilones, in a province called Guanuco. It is named Bracamoros, because it commences to run
with some force in a province of that name (having previously received many smaller streams) near old Guanuco,
between Caxamalca and Chachapoyas. It continues to have
its powerful body of water increased by the many branches
running into it, so that when it enters into that of the Motilones it has doubled its size. These two rivers meet one

hundred and fifty leagues below the place where the brigantines were built, both having previously run a course of
thirty leagues from their sources.[1]

CHAP. VI.

1. *From the river Bracamoros, the Governor continues his voyage to that
of Cocáma, where he finds Juan de Vargas with his party.—2. They
continue their voyage, some of their necessities in the way of food
being supplied by the Hicoteas, and their eggs.—3. They arrive
at the island where Garcia del Arze and his soldiers are.—4. They
find some islands lower down the river, with villages, but no inhabitants, for they had abandoned them.*

1. The governor, being detained at the mouth of the
Bracamoros,[2] had sufficient time to go up it in search of
provisions ; but on examination it was found that even
higher up the shores were uninhabited. He therefore continued his course for a hundred leagues, arriving at the
mouth of the Cocama,[3] where they found Juan de Vargas and
his party, short of provisions, in consequence of the length of
time they had been waiting for the governor.   They were all
joyous at the meeting, and, the newly arrived party having
rested eight days, the expedition left that spot, with some
apprehensions at not having fallen in with Garcia del Arze,
or heard any tidin of him.

At a short distance, as they were leaving the mouth of this

---

[1] Padre Simon's geography is confused. The river *Motilones*, which
Ursua descended, is evidently the Huallaga. The *Bracamoros* is the
modern Marañon, flowing through the province of Jaen de Bracamoros.

[2] That is, at the junction of the Motilones (Huallaga) and the Bracamoros (Marañon).

[3] Cocama, or Cocoma, a tribe of the Marañon and Lower Huallaga ;
of the first missionary epoch, 1638-83. They built their huts round a
lake, near the mouth of the Huallaga. The river here called Cocama
is evidently the Ucayali.

river, the brigantine that had brought Vargas, in consequence of the rottenness of its timbers, began to break up,
and became useless. This obliged them to distribute the
crew and cargo amongst the canoes and boats, which,
being overloaded, were in great danger, the more particularly as they were in so large a river. The river was swelled
by the waters of the Motilones, Bracamoros, and Cocama,
whose sources, according to some, are the rivers Aporima
(Apurimac), Mancai (Abancay?), Nauca, Vilcas, Parios,
and Jauja, and many more. Others say that this great
river rises behind Chinchacocha, to the east of the Province
of Guanuco, passing by the towns of Paucartambo and Gua-
cabamba, and uniting with rivers which come from Tarama
(Tarma?) and also with many others from the mountains
of that district, as well as with those that were seen and
passed by the governor Gomes Arias, in what is called
Rupanapa (Rumipampa?). However this may be, the river
of Cocáma,[1] which they were navigating, is formed by all
these. It is one of the most celebrated rivers in the world
that has been discovered by man up to the present time
in this region, and navigated by our Conquistadores; for
when it enters the sea, it is without doubt the largest that
is known, and leaves the Danube, the Nile, the Ganges, and
the Plata far behind, as well as other rivers, celebrated in
ancient and modern times.

2. This river abounds in various species of fish great and
small, also great numbers of birds are on its shores, which
feed on the fish. There are many hicoteas and turtle, the
eggs of which are laid in large spaces on the sandy shores,
where the turtle cover them up under the sand, and the
great heat of the sun hatches them in due time.[2] The young

---

[1] Simon confuses the Ucayali (Cocáma) and Marañon (Bracamoros).
He is here, of course, speaking of the latter river.

[2] Hicotea or jicotea, called by Wafer hecatee, has been identified by
Gray with the *Emys Decussata* of Bell. Another species, termed by

go into the water, as a stone when thrown goes to its centre (admirable provision of nature) ; these animals are not viviparous, but oviparous ; and the same may be said of the caymanes (alligators), which have similar habits.   These animals afforded food for the people.

After six days' navigation down the river, from the mouth of the Cocama, they fell in with another river on the right, where some Indians were fishing, who, on seeing the expedition, left their nets and fish, and ran into the thick wood, with such celerity that none of them were caught, although they were followed ; but their canoes were taken and all that was in them, with more than a hundred turtle and hicoteas, also many eggs, which gave much sustenance to the people, who were but badly victualled.

3. Leaving these Indian fishermen and continuing the voyage, they came to the mouth of another river on the right, not less mighty than the Motilones, but there was no pilot in the expedition who knew what river it was, with certainty: some thought it was the Canela,[1] which rises in Peru, in Quijos at the back of Quito ; but afterwards it was found that it could not be the Canela, because that river came in further down, and near the island of Garcia ; thus the first mentioned river remained without a name.

Eight days after leaving Cocama, they arrived at the island of Garcia del Arze, where they found him and his companions in their fort, having nearly lost all hope of the arrival of the governor ; but at the sight of Ursua and his people they were happy indeed, as was the governor also.

Here they met with Indian towns for the first time since they left the Caperusos, for during a voyage of three hundred leagues they had not fallen in with one Indian village.

The people were allowed to go on shore for eight or ten

Gray the dark hicotee, is named by him *Emys Rugosa*. They are land tortoises. See also Markham's *Valley of the Amazons*, p. 60.

[1] The Napo.

days, so as to rest the soldiers and rowers ; and also to take the horses on shore to exercise them, for they had not been landed since they first went on board. The governor sent out parties in all directions in search of Indian towns, but none were found.

At this period orders were given to supply the place of one of the flat boats that had been built of unsound wood, for it could not go farther than this spot.

Ursua now found himself tired of the sole charge over such a mixture of people as his expedition was composed of. He had not as yet named his lieutenant-general to assist him, and he determined to confer this office on Juan de Vargas, and that of Alferez-general on Fernando de Guzman ; but they afterwards repaid these honours by taking away his life.

The name of the principal Indian in this place was Papa. The natives were tall and strong, clothed in well woven cotton shirt-like coverings, painted various colours. No gold was found, which produced dissatisfaction amongst the Spaniards, seeing that they had journeyed so far without meeting with the least sign of the precious metal. The food of the natives was mostly maize, of which they make much chicha. They also prepare chicha of the yuca, taking so much that they get drunk, the great sin of the Indians of these lands. They have batatas (sweet potatoes) and other roots ; beans and other vegetables ; but their chief food is fish. Their huts are large and square ; their arms are darts of palm wood with points of the same wood, like the Biscayan *gurguzes*, which they throw with wooden *anietos*, otherwise called *estolicas*,[1] the principal arm of the natives.

A little below this island the river enters, which is called after Francisco de Orellana, or that of the Canela, from that

[1] *Estolicas* are weapons with which the warriors of the Incas of Peru were very dexterous. These estolicas are flattened poles, a yard long and three fingers broad. In the upper end a bone is fixed, to which an

captain having described it.   As we have already said, it
rises to the east of Quito.

4.   Having increased the number of canoes and rafts to
meet their wants, for much of their cordage had already become useless, the people also embarked thirty-seven horses,
three having died there.   They began the descent by the
inner arm of the river going east, passing many islands, all
of them with habitations, although at that period the Indians
had left their homes and retired to the woods, on account of
the fear they had of their unfriendly neighbours, Garcia
del Arze and his companions, when Arze was on the island
up the river.   Thus the expedition only found maize, greens,
batatas half grown, some white cocks and hens of Castille,
also white parrots and macaws, things until then unseen, in
the plantations of the natives.   Of these they took good
quantity to supply their necessities, for they were badly off
for provisions.

CHAP. VII.

1. *The Indians come out to see the expedition from a distance, and a
chief comes with offers of peace.—2. The Indians come from the
province of Carari with some provisions, which they barter for
trinkets.—3. The governor sends an officer to examine the country
inland.—4. Punishments which Pedro de Ursua inflicted on his
people.—5. Opinions entertained respecting this province, whether
there were one or two.*

They sailed amongst these islands, taking possession of
the food which they found in the abandoned villages, until,
after several days, they suddenly came on one which was

arrow of nine *palmos* is fastened, with the point of bone or palm wood,
which, worked into the shape of a harpoon, remains like a javelin hanging from the person it wounds.—Markham's *Valley of the Amazons*, p.
80, Hakluyt Coll., 1859.

inhabited, on the mainland, on the right hand side, built on
the cliffs which overhang the river. The Indians fled from
this place, as they had done from all the other villages. It
was called Carari, which name was afterwards given to the
province.

Here the expedition rested, but, although many attempts
were made, the Spaniards could not lay hands on any of the
Indians ; for,though some were seen occasionally at a distance
on the river, who came out in their canoes to see the strange
fleet, they always remained afar off, owing to the fear which
they continued to feel. One chief appeared not to feel so
much timidity as the rest, for, after three or four days he came
peacefully, accompanied by some Indians, bringing offerings
of fish, maize, and other food, and was received by the
governor with a show of great friendship. Ursua embraced
him, and gave him a few trifling presents, such as glass
beads, knives, looking glasses, and other childish toys; intending that the Indians should, by this treatment, lose their
fear, and that the news might pass amongst them from one
to another ; seeing that the Spaniards had a bad name, owing
to the acts of Garcia del Arze. He thus hoped that their
confidence would return, and that they would supply information which would enable him to obtain some insight
into the nature of the country, for he wished to establish
peace with all the natives, along the whole course of the
river.

2. Desirous of securing these objects, the governor sent
the chief away, very well satisfied with the trifles that had
been given to him, which were sufficient to cause rumours to
spread amongst the natives and provinces lower down the
river, very different from those which had previously been
spread concerning the Spaniards. Very soon many Indians
began to come peacefully, bringing provisions, and coveting
such trinkets as the chief had shown them, some of which

they all received in exchange for their provisions (the poor people having nothing else to sell), so that no man was left unpaid, at least so far as the governor was aware. In order to prevent the knaveries which insolent soldiery are in the habit of committing on these occasions, especially in dealing with Indians, he issued an order that no soldier should traffic with the natives, excepting through him, or in his presence ; and thus he succeeded in satisfying the Indians. By acting in this way the governor endeared himself with the Indians ; and if, by chance, any soldiers bartered without the knowledge of the governor, they paid secretly for the provisions which they obtained, with some trifles. In this way they sailed down the same river for some days, through this province of Carari ; and the Indians never showed greater confidence in our people, waiting in their villages with all their property, and coming out on the river in their canoes, to these barterings.

3. The governor saw how extensive was the province which bordered the river, and, desiring to discover whether it extended far inland, and whether any tidings of what they were seeking could be found, he nominated an officer named Pedro Galeas, with a moderate number of men, to march inland and find out what he could, during a specified time, after which he was to return and report his proceedings. The rest of the expedition remained, on this occasion, at a considerable village, which they found to be larger than the others, on the steep ravines bordering on the river. Pedro de Galeas departed with his people, and marching inland, along the banks of a creek which communicated with the river, they came to a path leading into a dense forest. After following it for a short distance, they came in sight of some Indians laden with cassava and other eatables. When they saw the Spaniards, being astonished at their appearance and dress, they threw away their loads, and fled into the forest, which being very dense, and they having the start and run-

ning with all their speed, the soldiers were unable to overtake any except an Indian woman. She appeared to be of a different nation, judging by her language and dress, to those who dwelt in the ravine, and the other people whom they had met with on the river. The Spaniards, therefore, believed that she and the other Indians had come from another province, to traffic with those of the ravine. Presently they began to ask her by signs, where her country was ; and she replied, in the same way, that it was six suns off, that is, six days journey. Having now finished their provisions, Galeas determined to return with the Indian girl, to the place where the governor remained. They found him in great trouble, because a soldier named Alonzo de Montoya, a turbulent and restless man, and disaffected towards Ursua, had collected others like himself, and induced them secretly to seize several canoes, and to pull up the river, in order to return to Peru.

4. This treason was disclosed to Ursua ; and Montoya, having before attempted to desert, was imprisoned. But Ursua was naturally merciful, indeed too merciful, and at times his acts savoured of weakness. Sometimes he punished those who deserved severe castigation for their turbulence and crimes, making them row for some days in the brigantines and canoes ; when some of the soldiers took occasion (for from the commencement of the expedition some began to plot against the governor) to irritate those who were undergoing punishment, by telling them that death was far better than such disgrace. These malicious sayings were the sparks of the burning villainy which filled their breasts, and could not always be concealed. Thus the murderers of Ursua continued secretly to inflame the men (for they were the chief disseminators of this treason) in order to attract more people to their party, and obtain the object of their desires more securely.

5. It did not appear to the governor that the information

given by the Indian girl, who was captured by Pedro de
Galeas, was of sufficient importance to induce him to continue
the search in this province, for that rich country of Omagua,
the name of which was not even known to the natives. He
therefore determined to continue his course, more especially
as the fleet was badly provisioned, and there was cause to fear
that they might be in want of all supplies before arriving at
the country of which they were in search. Thus they sailed
down the river, until they arrived at a place on its banks,
more than one hundred and fifty leagues from the island of
Garcia. According to the opinion of some, this land and people are divided into two provinces, one called *Caricuri,* the
other *Manicuri.*[1] Others believed that the whole of this
district, extending for one hundred and fifty leagues, was
one single province, because all the inhabitants spoke the
same language, and wore the same dress ; besides the two
names which the soldiers had understood as *Caricuri* and
Manicuri were two villages, and not two provinces. This
region has remained until this day divided between these
two opinions, without any more accurate accounts having
become known. All agreed in one thing, which was that
there were few inhabitants, for the villages were small,
and five or six leagues from each other ; and there did not
appear to be altogether more than ten thousand or twelve
thousand Indians, which was very few for so extensive a
province, and compared to the usual population in other
parts. They found amongst them some pieces of fine gold,
which they wore round their necks, and hung from their ears
and noses ; but the Spaniards, passing so rapidly, could not
learn much concerning the customs or religion of these Indians. They only knew what they personally saw and obtained in this country, namely, much fruit, many roots and
grains, which they enjoyed ; and innumerable quantities of

[1] Somewhere between the Ucayali and the Yavari, the land of the
Ticunas ; a populous tribe of Indians, in those days.

mosquitos of many kinds, especially the sand flies, *Bozingle-ros*, and importunate *Xegenes*.

CHAP. VIII.

1. *Pedro de Ursua continues his course through a desert region, where the people suffer from want.—2. They establish themselves in a village, where they make up for passed want by a large supply of provisions. —3. The governor, on account of the plentiful supplies, determines to encamp in the village, pass Christmas there, and make inquiries respecting the land for which they are searching.—4. Fifty Spaniards depart to assist the chief of Machiparo, against two hundred hostile Indians.*

1. Our people were detained in this place longer than they had intended, because the brigantine had at last gone to the bottom, and they were obliged to use balsas and canoes for all the people and the cargo. Afterwards, not knowing whether this was the last village which they would come to, they departed from it without any supply of provisions, expecting to obtain them, as they had done down to this place, in other villages lower down the river. This carelessness was not a little inconvenient, for next day a terrible feeling of hunger began to afflict them, which continued during a voyage of nine days through a country entirely uninhabited, and during the whole time they did not meet with a single Indian. In consequence of having left the province of Carari without obtaining supplies, they had nothing to eat during all this time, except the fish which each man was able to net for himself, and a few *turtles*, *hicoteas*, *bledos*, and *verdolagos*, which they found on the banks; but in very small quantities for so large a party, and in some places they found none. This misery increased their weakness each day, and had it lasted a little longer they must all have died. The whole blame was laid on the

governor, for his improvidence; for had he informed himself of this long tract of desert, he might have laid in a
stock of provisions. The want of food was the reason which
prevented the governor from stopping to examine two
mighty rivers with turbid waters, caused by their flowing
through ravines with reddish soil. They join the main
river on the right hand, in the centre of this desert.[1] At
length they arrived at a village on the banks of the river,
where the inhabitants were quite unprepared for the arrival
of their guests.

2. But they made such good use of their time, fearing the
evils which might come upon them, at the hands of those
who were invading their land, that embarking all the property they could collect, with their household goods, as
quickly as possible in canoes, they went down the river,
leaving the fighting men in the village, with their blow-
pipes and arrows in their hands to defend their houses. The
governor, seeing this, collected together such soldiers as
were most at hand, with their arms, and went on ahead with
his arquebus, approaching the squadron of Indians in military order. He made signs to them with a white cloth
which he held in his hand (after having ordered his soldiers
to give no offence), desiring to make them understand that
no harm would be done to them. When the Indians understood this, without breaking up their ranks or moving from
their position, one man came out from among them, who appeared to be a chief, with some six or eight followers. He
came to the place where the governor stood, and took the
cloth with which the signs had been made in his hands, as a
token of friendship. He and his followers then joined the
Spaniards, and they walked together to an open space in
the village where the Indians were under arms; and stood

---

[1] There are several rivers flowing into the Amazons from the south,
between the Yavari and the mouths of the Putumayu, but none of any
considerable size.

watching each other, until the rest of the Spaniards appeared, who had disembarked behind Ursua. The governor then, by the best signs that he could make, asked the chief who had come forward to parley, to allot a part of the village, with the provisions in the houses, for lodgings for his people; when the Indians, with their women and children, might safely remain in the remaining part.

The Indians willingly agreed to this, and pointed out the principal houses to the governor, where his people might lodge; and it was agreed that they should not enter into the part retained by the Indians, nor injure them in any way on pain of death. All our people soon " took the belly of the evil year" (as they say), with the plentiful supply of eatables which they found, of maize, beans, roots, together with abundance of turtle and *hicoteas,* which the Indians kept alive in ponds near their houses, surrounded with pallisades, and it appeared to the Spaniards that there were alive, without counting those which had been recently killed for food, more than six or seven thousand. The Indians did not feel much confidence when they saw that the Spaniards were so numerous; and each one, in his own part of the village, began to take the provisions, and hide them at night by little and little. But they could not do this so secretly as to prevent the soldiers, who were mindful of their former misery, and anxious to avoid its repetition in future, from searching for the provisions which the Indians were hiding, and taking what they found to their huts. The governor, seeing that this was done in the face of fresh threats, and anxious to chastise the insolence of some soldiers, to overawe the rest, seized upon several. Among these was a half caste servant of his *Alferez General* Don Fernando de Guzman, and this circumstance was made use of afterwards by the discontented, who made it a point of honour with Don Fernando that the governor should have imprisoned his servant, telling him that it had been done as an insult, or at least that it was a want of respect; and thus they worked upon him to join their side, in which they afterwards succeeded.

3. There were two reasons for remaining some days in this village, which was called Machiparo[1] (the inhabitants being very different in their dress from those of the province of Caricuri). The first was the great abundance of eatables, so that the people had a good opportunity of making up for their former hunger; and the second was that Christmas was near, of the year 1560. Ursua also desired to make inquiries of the Indians of the village and its neighbourhood respecting the land of which they were in search. Two days after their arrival, Ursua sent the same officer as before, Pedro de Galeas, with some soldiers in canoes, to go up a creek which joined the river at a little distance from the village. Galeas entered by a small mouth, consisting of water so black that it terrified him, and seemed a presage of what afterwards happened. After navigating the creek for a short distance they came to a great lake, the size of which astonished them, for after they had sailed in it for two or three leagues, they entirely lost sight of land; and, fearing that if they went any further, they would be unable to find the opening by which they had entered (after having gone along the land for some days without finding any village, or sign of inhabitants) they determined to return.[2] While this officer was thus employed, two hundred warlike Indians

[1] *Machiparo* is mentioned as a province in Orellana's voyage, and is said to be ruled by a chief named *Aomagua* (evidently the *Omaguas*, and Orellana mistook the name of the tribe for the name of the chief). It is curious that Ursua's people should not also have heard the name, when it was the very one for which they were in search. (See *Expedition into the Valley of the Amazons*, Hakluyt Society's Publications, p. 27.) Ribeiro mentioned in 1775 that a chief of a tribe of *Juris*, on the Putumayu, was named *Machiparo*. Ursua's Machiparo was probably near one of the mouths of the Putumayu.

[2] There are many large lakes, through which some of the branches of the river Putumayu flow.

came down the river in canoes from the province of Carari, to attack those of Machiparo, with whom they had a feud of a very ancient date. They were not aware of the presence of the Spaniards, but came down with great clamour, hoping to give no time for defence, but to assault and sack the place at their ease.

4. Arriving with this intention at the banks of the river, near the village, during the night, and recognizing the strange guests, they did not dare to make an assault before daylight, when they might watch what took place in the village. In the morning they saw that all the Spaniards were there, and that their expedition had ended in nothing; so, raising great shouts, and making a noise with cornets and other instruments, they began to return up the river. Until these noises were made, the people of Machiparo had not been aware of their approach; but when it was known, the chief went to the governor and besought him, for the sake of the hospitality he had received, to give him assistance in chasing the enemy who had come to kill him, and destroy his village and lands. The governor consented with plea-sure, and, with the rapidity which the occasion required, he dispatched his lieutenant, Don Juan de Vargas, with fifty arquebusiers, in company with the chief; who em-barked with them, and some of his Indians in canoes, by another branch of the river. They went so quickly that they got in front of the two hundred, and surrounded them, without the possibility of escape. The Cararis were so encircled that they were forced to fight, believing that they had to deal with none but the Indians of Machiparo; but when, afterwards, they saw that the Spaniards had come to assist them, they began to make signs of peace. This ap-peared an untoward, nay scandalous thing to the soldiers, who thought they might thus be deprived of their spoils; so they were deaf to the prayers of the Indians, and began to discharge their arquebuses, and to do the Indians so much

F

damage, that they left their canoes and fled into the woods, which were so thick that, though the Spaniards and friendly Indians followed, they could not catch more than five or six, and, with all their canoes, they returned to Machiparo. It was understood that all the Indians would perish for want of food in the forests, or be killed by the Machiparos, having no canoes in which to return to their own country, and the road by land being very long; but the truth could never be known, on account of the few days which the Spaniards afterwards remained there.

CHAP. IX.

1. *Pedro de Ursua names a provisor or vicar-general for his fleet, believing he had power to do so.*—2. *Some grow faint hearted at the continuation of the expedition, and the governor encourages them to proceed.*—3. *Excuses which the mutineers make to Pedro de Ursua for their delinquencies.*—4. *The mutineers conspire to rid themselves of the government of Ursua, and to make Don Fernando de Guzman his successor.*

1. Pedro de Ursua conceived that this land was within his jurisdiction; as, according to the conjectures of the Brazilian Indians, and of one of their Portuguese companions, whom they took as guides, it was not distant from the land of the Omaguas. He, therefore, felt it to be necessary to regulate the affairs of his government, which he had not yet done, especially as regarded those which concerned spiritual matters. Some priests who were in the fleet, quarrelled amongst themselves for want of a chief: so he determined to nominate from among them a vicar-general, who, in spiritual affairs, should have jurisdiction over the fleet. He considered that he had powers to make such a nomination, in the same way as his majesty, whose person he represented, had to make

bishops and other dignitaries ; so he selected for this office
a priest named Alonzo Henao. This man began to exercise
the duties of his office by promulgating certain excommunications against those who did not restore to Ursua all
kinds of goods, live stock, tools, arms, and munitions which
they had taken. Those who envied the governor, publicly
said that he had nominated this man to be vicar-general, in
order that he might promulgate those excommunications,
and not from zeal for the public service ; and declared that
he had no right to name an ecclesiastical judge. All the
people in the camp were in this state of excitement when
Pedro Alonzo Galeas returned with the news which we have
related, and which caused new doubts to arise respecting
the chance of finding the land of the Omaguas.

2. Not only the Brazilian Indians, and their companion
the Spaniard[1] whom they took as a guide, but also others
who had descended this river with Captain Orellana, observed that they had now sailed for many days, that the
river was of great magnitude, and that they could neither
recognize the land, nor the place where they had encamped,
and their accounts differed one from the other. Some of
the evil intentioned among the adventurers, who had concerted a rising amongst themselves, began to spread a
rumour that all had been deceived, for that they had journeyed more than seventy leagues, and had neither met with
the rich provinces for which they were in search, nor even
found any sign by which they might ascertain in what direction to search. They declared that it would be best to
return up the river and go back to Peru, as there appeared
to be no hope of success. These arguments, and others by
which the mutineers spread their poison throughout the
camp, came to the ears of the governor ; who sent for some
of the chief malcontents to satisfy them, and insisted upon
the obligation not to lose all hope of bringing their enter-

[1] Portuguese ?

prise to a fortunate conclusion, and upon the duty of not giving up the expedition. He declared that there was no occasion for despair because the expeditions inland had led to small results; and that, of necessity, they must suffer hardships, without which no Indian province would ever have been discovered or settled. Perseverance, he said, would overcome all difficulties : and even if it was necessary to search from youth until old age, that this was a small thing in comparison with the attainment of such vast riches as rumour had reported.

3. Those who, in good faith, had undertaken this expedition, thought much of these words of the governor, which caused them to take heart again, and they determined to continue in the enterprise, and die at their posts; but others, who came with different intentions, such as the mutineers Lope de Aguirre, Montoya, Salduendo, and their allies, seeing that they were unable to attain their object by these means, sought out other ways of exasperating the army against the governor, saying that he was a harsh man, and that the mildness with which he had begun to govern had been changed to severity. They did not forget to add to this that he was so weak as to allow Doña Inez to govern the army through him, and that the soldiers were condemned to row in the boats for their crimes, solely that they might row in the canoe of Doña Inez: that he always made his hut apart from the rest of the army, when he ought to be in its centre, because he detested the company of the soldiers; that he was an enemy of giving away and a friend of receiving; that what he received, he considered to be offered as an obligation; and finally, that he was ignorant in affairs of war, as well as in those of government; sufficient reasons for all the army to hate him, especially when he had said that such should be their patience and endurance under the greatest privations, that even the boys of the expedition should grow grey in it, if necessary.

4. The principal mutineers, who went about with these sayings (desiring either to get rid of the governor by killing him, or by returning to Peru), were Alonzo de Montoya, Lope de Aguirre, Juan Alonzo de la Bandera, Lorenzo Salduendo, Miguel Serrano de Cazeres, Pedro de Mirando (a Mulatto), Martin Perez, Pedro Fernandez, Diego de Torres, Alonzo de Villena, Christoval Hernandez, Juan de Vargas, and others. They were now resolved, and it seemed to them absolutely necessary, to elect another chief to lead them in place of Ursua; yet there was no man whom the whole expedition was willing to obey, as they were all of low degree, and of little note or authority; for the few who could claim gentle origin were devoted to Ursua; and if they were aware of this treason, they would frustrate the designs of the mutineers. At length they decided upon speaking with the Alfarez-General, Don Fernando de Guzman, who was held to be of noble blood, and well disposed towards the soldiers; so, entering by the door of ambition (which is always open) they offered to put his hands into it, up to the elbows, by making him the successor of Pedro de Ursua. The mutineers whose names we have mentioned, having determined upon this, spoke with him one night, and disclosed their intentions to him, saying that they were founded in a holy zeal (there is no greater crime than that which is done under the mask of religion!) and that their designs would be for the good of the expedition, and especially for the service of God and the king. They told him that he should accept the office, for that his birth and merits were worthy of greater honours; that the miseries occasioned by the injustice of Ursua were notorious; and that if his rule continued much longer, it would be the occasion of infinite damage to the king's service. They pressed these arguments upon him, saying that he had been insulted by the arrest of his servant, without respect for his noble blood, nor for his office of Alferez-General; and that

if this scheme were successful, and he took the office of
general, with the consent of all the people, then, by his
good government and arrangements, they would discover
the land for which they were in search, and, having settled
it, his majesty would consider it a good service, and would
specially reward him.   If it should appear best to all not to
kill the governor, but to leave him in that village, with some
of his friends, it might be done, as it would not cause so
much scandal to the world, as his death.

CHAP. X.

1. *The mutineers determine to kill the governor, Pedro de Ursua, and to
   return to Peru.*—2. *Mysterious warning of the death of Ursua,
   which was seen and heard by a knight of the order of San Juan.*—
   3. *They continue their course from this village to another lower down,
   of the same name.   A slave of one of the mutineers discovers their
   design, and attempts to warn the governor.   The mutineers kill the
   governor Pedro de Ursua, and his lieutenant.*

Don Fernando did not dislike the arguments of the mutineers, nor was he deterred either by the grave embarrass-
ments which might follow, nor by the loyalty which (he
being a knight) should have bound him to protect Ursua,
after the honours he had received from him, and the consideration with which he had always been treated by him.
He believed all that had been told him by the mutineers,
and, swelled up by the wind of ambition, he gave them
thanks for what they had offered him, and assented to all
their projects ; so that it appeared to the messengers that
they now had all that was necessary, in order to put their
designs into execution.   The mutineers, and Don Fernando
among them, as their chief, conferred together, and began
to offer various opinions (children of tyranny and heresy)

respecting the mode of proceeding ; to some it seemed best to leave Pedro de Ursua, with some of his friends in that place (as had been suggested to Don Fernando) and, taking all the boats and canoes, to return up the river to Peru: others, among whom were Don Fernando, said that they would only do that which had been originally proposed, namely, return to Peru by descending the river, with the whole expedition, leaving Ursua behind : but there was a third party, among whom were those two good souls, Lope de Aguirre and Lorenzo Salduendo, who declared that all they had heard was unwise, but that the only plan was to kill Pedro de Ursua and, with all the people, return to Peru, and make Don Fernando the lord of the country. Don Fernando, giving reins to an ambition which he was already relishing, and promising to himself the enjoyment of the riches of Peru, also because it was of little avail to say anything else, gave out that the opinions of the two (Aguirre and Salduendo) appeared good to him ; and the rest consenting, it was agreed that Ursua and his lieutenant Don Juan should die. From this time they sought for an occasion to commit the deed, and busied themselves in gaining over the soldiers, that they might be on their side, when it became necessary.

2. Omens were not wanting, which might have served as warnings to Ursua; for, besides those we have mentioned, (seeing that some, with small reason, had predicted the fate of the expedition) on the same day that the mutineers resolved upon the murder, and five before it was perpetrated, being one of those of the feast of the Nativity (for in this way did these men celebrate it), a comendador of the order of San Juan, named Juan Gomez de Guevara, a great friend of Ursua's, ripe in years, of grave demeanour, and strictly honest and true, whilst he was out walking, at the second or third hour of the night, enjoying the freshness of the air near the door of his hut, which was next to that of the

governor, beheld something like a shade passing near the
governor's hut, from which a rough and unknown voice proceeded, which said—" Pedro de Ursua, governor of Omagua
and of El Dorado, God pardon thee!" The comendador
hurried to the spot where he had seen the object, and heard
the voice, but it had disappeared without leaving a trace of
what it was; he could not, however, persuade himself that what
he had seen was a human being, and he remained in a state
of astonishment and confusion. He communicated what he
had seen to some of his friends, and conferred with them on
the propriety of informing the governor; but they determined not to do so, considering that, as he was in a bad
state of health, this might aggravate his illness and cause
him to believe that his time was come.

3. The governor was more careless than he ought to have
been (while these things were passing amongst the mutineers), considering that he was not without friends who
desired to put him on his guard (though none of them
believed that things had become so serious), and that he
should always have had a guard about his person, of soldiers
and friends. He, however, did not hearken to their advice,
nor cause a guard to be in attendance, which led men to say
that he wished to be alone with Doña Inez, and without
witnesses. However that may be, either from carelessness,
or too much confidence, he never had any one, either within
or without his house, but his pages. Although the mutineers
were on the watch, without losing any opportunity, they
were unable to perpetrate the deed while they remained in
this village of Machiparo, which they left on the day after
Christmas. They sailed all day, until sunset, when they
reached another village of the same name, six or eight
leagues distant. This village had been abandoned by its
inhabitants, who had fled from the fear they had of our
people, who took up their abode there, without any obstacle
being made. The governor now became anxious, as it

appeared to him (according to the report of the Brazilian
Indians) that they must be near the place where they might
hear news of the province of the Omaguas. He was shown a
broad road which led from the village towards the interior,
(as it was said) to a large city or province; so he determined
to send a party of soldiers, under the command of one Sancho
Pizarro, to discover this new land.

4. The mutineers considered that this opportunity ought
not to be lost, when so many of the governor's friends were
absent with this expedition, and they resolved that he should
be killed without loss of time. They consulted together on
the morning of New Year's day, and determined to perpetrate the murder that evening, when the governor, on so
solemn an occasion, would be enjoying himself, and off his
guard. The movements of the mutineers were not so secret
but that a black slave of Juan Alonzo de la Bandera, called
Juan Primero (through an inspiration of heaven, or moved
by the atrocity of the meditated act, or perhaps thinking
that, by imparting the secret, he would be set free) made
an excuse to go to the lodging of the governor, to give
him an account of what was passing. But this circumstance
did not stop the blow levelled at Ursua, who was then with
Doña Ines; so that the slave could not communicate with
him personally, neither could he await the governor's
appearance, for fear of being missed by his master. Still
the slave did his best, by telling the object of his coming to
another negro, the slave of Ursua, and directing him to inform his master. The governor's slave either forgot to
deliver the message or, fearing to tell his master, the day
passed without Ursua being aware of what was going on.

5. The night arrived (the cloak to sinners), when all the
conspirators met at Don Fernando's lodging (so as to be
more secure) and sent a Mestizo servant, as an excuse, for
some oil, so that he might see who was with the governor
and what he was doing. The servant went, and having pro-

cured what he was sent for, returned and told the conspirators that the governor was alone.

It was the second hour of the night, on the day of the
Circumcision, when the rebels left the lodging of Don Fernando, with the diabolical intention of assailing the governor,
and taking his life. They were eager in their steps (to take
vengeance for the insults they said they had received from
him). Alonzo de Montoya was the first in advance, with
Christoval Hernandez de Chaves, and, entering Ursua's
house, they found him in his hammock talking to a little
page named Lorca. When they saluted the governor, he
said, " What seek ye here, caballeros, at this hour ?" the
reply was several stabs, which missed him. He then rose
from his hammock to reach his sword and buckler, which he
had at hand, when the rest of the mutineers entered, and
they all made a murderous onset on Ursua, so that he soon
fell dead, without being able to say more than " Confessio,
confessio, miserere mei Deus." The deed being done, they
sallied out of the hut, and one of them, with a loud voice,
shouted " Liberty, liberty! long live the king, the tyrant is
dead." This was heard by the lieutenant Juan de Vargas,
who lived hard by, and he hastily put on his escaupil,[1] with
his sword, shield, and rod of office, and went towards the
governor's lodging, whence he had heard the cries, and
meeting the murderers in the road, who were in search of
him, they recognized him, and attacked him, taking from
him his sword and shield and armour, so as to serve him as
they had the governor. Then, having torn away one sleeve
of the escaupil, and getting away the other, one of these
monsters of Satan, named Martin Perez, infuriated with
his diabolical intention, gave him so severe a thrust that
the sword went through and through his body, the point
wounding his companion badly, who was behind the lieu-

[1] Armour of quilted cotton, used by the natives of South America
before the conquest.

tenant, occupied in disarming him. The rest, coming up, gave Vargas more stabs than were necessary to take away life; after which some cried out, " Liberty, caballeros; long live the king! we will not be subject to those whose only occupations were their pleasures! it was not for this that we left our homes."

CHAP. XI.

THE CRUIZE OF THE TRAITOR AGUIRRE.

1. *The governor being dead, the rebels endeavour to bring all the expedition to their side.*—2. *They do not allow the soldiers to leave their quarters during the night, to prevent them from conferring together.*—3. *The murderers divide the various offices amongst themselves.*—4. *They continue the division of offices. Sancho Pizarro returns.*

1. The lieutenant being dead, the murderers returned to the governor's house, and then came the rest of the mutineers, their friends and allies, who had been instructed that when they heard a rumour they were to come armed, to assist if necessary. Many other soldiers came at the same time to learn the cause of the disturbance, whom the rebels forced into their own ranks, without their knowing who or how many composed this tyrannical junta, so that when they came to know how and in what manner the governor and his lieutenant had died, they were already incorporated with the traitors.

As soon as they had the greater portion of the expedition under their command, some of the murderers, with their friends, sallied out armed in search of those who were wanting; some they took by force, others they persuaded by threats and promises, and all were brought to the governor's house, that they might be present at the burial. A pit was dug for both the murdered men in Ursua's house, so that they might be together in death as in life; also that the expedition might know who was now to be their general, and obey him.

In the presence of all (the burial having taken place) they named for governor Fernando de Guzman, and for his maestro del campo, Lope de Aguirre; and without spending time in nominating more officers, they thought it best to sally forth and kill the friends of the late governor and of his lieutenant, which they did; for they laid hold of many, and would have killed more if Guzman had not stopped them, as he did not consider it judicious to commence office by causing so many deaths.

2. The traitors were fearful that the friends of some of the dead might take revenge, seeing that the general had not allowed such to be murdered; so they commanded, under pain of death, that no soldier should speak in a low voice, but that he should say what he had to say loudly and plainly, that what was spoken might be understood by every one, and that the traitors might be aware of anything going on against them.

Some of the soldiers were forgetful of this order, being accustomed to speak in a low tone, which placed their lives in jeopardy, and had it not been for some persons of standing who interceded with the traitors, the soldiers would have suffered. It was also ordered that no one should be absent at night from his quarters, under pain of death; the object being that the soldiers should devise no schemes against the traitors. They lost no time (that the obsequies of the dead might not pass without some demonstration) in giving out, with liberality, several jars of wine which Ursua had brought for his own drinking, as well as for the celebration of mass (for men who had now no pretension to hear mass, it was useless for this purpose); and they distributed the wine amongst the officers and soldiers, that they might pass the night in confidence and friendship.

This was the miserable end of Pedro de Ursua, after his power had lasted three months and six days; he having embarked at the ship-yard on the 26th of September, 1560, and having been killed on the 1st of January, 1561, aged thirty-five years. He was of middle size, slightly formed, but well proportioned, with the manners of a gentleman; light complexion and beard the same, courteous, and affable, fond of his soldiers, and more inclined to mercy than to justice; thus his very enemies could not complain of his having done them wrong: he was too confiding and had but little precaution, and his great goodness was the main cause which brought him to so sad an end.

3. This miserable night having passed (for indeed it was one for the dead, as well as for their friends who were living, and their murderers and enemies celebrated it joyously, because they had been successful in this bloody work of their hands, some believing that they had been concerned in a glorious action, and a marked service to the crown of their king), the rebels and their friends now asked the murderers for their reward, so that all might go on regularly, and that the army might be kept in a proper state; so, confirming the first appointment, that of general, in favour of Fernando de Guzman, and that of maestro del campo in Lope de Aguirre, they continued appointing one another to the several offices; Juan Alonso de la Bandera was made captain of the guard; Lorenzo Salduendo, Christoval Hernandez, and Miguel Serrano de Caceres, captains of infantry; Alonzo de Montoya, captain of horse; Alonso de Villena, *alferez-general* (standard bearer?); alguazil mayor del campo (high constable), Pedro de Miranda, a mulatto; and paymaster-general, Pedro Fernandez; leaving for the present without command, Martin Perez and Juan de Vargas, to whom they promised great things on the first occasion that offered, for their good services.

Not to appear too partial to themselves and their friends

in the distribution of the various offices, they made a sea captain of Sebastian Gomez, a Portuguese pilot, and supernumerary captains of infantry of the comendador (knight commander) Juan Gomez de Guevara, and Pedro Alonso Galeas ; also another captain was nominated to be in charge of the warlike stores, named Alonso Enriquez de Orellana ; their sea admiral was one Miguel Robedo. All these men saw how little they were benefited by accepting these appointments, still, had they not done so, their lives might have been endangered. One Diego de Belalcasar, whom they named as justicia mayor del campo, or chief judge (an office he considered too important, considering the love and loyalty he had for his king), said publicly at the time they offered him the staff of office, so that every one heard him : " This staff of office I take in the name of King Philip our lord, and in no other." This touched the mutineers severely, so they watched him narrowly, and for this saying he afterwards lost his life ; but at that time no one dared to reply to him, in consequence of the general discord that reigned in the expedition.

Sancho Pizarro had not as yet returned from the search Ursua had sent him on, neither did he know of the governor's death, nor what was passing in the camp. The mutineers being fearful that, should he get only partial information, he might make some demonstration against them, with the people he had under his command, to avenge the death of his friends ; sent spies out in the direction he was to return, to prevent any others from going out to advise him of what had occurred. Sancho Pizarro came into the camp two days afterwards, without discovering what had been going on, until he was within, when the mutineers informed him of what had happened, persuading him to believe how necessary it had been to act so, and that such was the feeling of the whole camp.

Sancho Pizarro, who was a sagacious man, feigned to be

pleased with the present state of things ; the mutineers also
said that they had not forgotten him when they shared out
the various offices, for that they had kept for him the post
of sargento mayor del campo, which he accepted, giving
them his thanks. Sancho Pizarro only discovered two empty
villages whilst he was away, by keeping on the track that
led from the camp.

CHAP. XII.

1. *The new general, Don Fernando, calls a council to discuss matters
relative to the projected discovery of the new lands of the Dorado.—
2. He has a document made out for their security, and orders all to
sign it. Lope de Aguirre signs it, adding the word " Traitor."—
3. Aguirre publicly explains why he did so.—4. Juan Alonso de la
Bandera replies, saying that they who killed the governor were not
traitors.*

1. The various offices had been distributed, when Don
Fernando, by virtue of his office, called a council of the
officers, soldiers, and principal people of the camp to confer
as to how they were to proceed in the discovery of the pretended Dorado they were in search of, so as to have their
opinions signed with their names, and that they might take
that course which seemed most convenient to all. He signed
his name first as the commander of the expedition, and gave
his opinion as follows: that they ought to continue the search
for the lands concerning which Ursua had information, and
that, should they be as rich as fame had blazoned, the king
not only would consider the discovery a great service, but
would pardon them the death of Ursua and Vargas ; still it
would be well, in the discharge of their duty, that he and all
the rest should draw up a document stating why the governor
Ursua had been deprived of life, inasmuch as he had been

most negligent and unmindful in his search after the new lands, that he had not taken the necessary steps, and that he had no intention to settle even if he should find them; that he was intolerant and severe to the soldiers, and that to preserve the men in the service of the king, as well as to discover the unknown lands, his death was a necessary act; for had he been allowed to govern them much longer, without doubt there would have been a general mutiny; that the brigantines would have been violently taken away from him, and that the people would have returned to Christian lands (Peru), leaving him on the river, without discovering the vast provinces which were before them.

2. To these he added other frivolous ideas, which he said were well founded. Alonso de Montoya and Juan de la Bandera agreed with him; but the Biscayan, Lope de Aguirre, was opposed to the new governor's views, because he (Aguirre) from the commencement of the expedition wished to return to Peru, without occupying himself in the discovery of new lands, that he might excite a rebellion in that kingdom, in which plan he had many adherents.

Aguirre and others did not deem it prudent to contradict Don Fernando by words, but their silence showed what their feelings were. This silence was understood by many, and the rest said nothing; so, as no one spoke or gave any opinion, the council was dissolved.

Don Fernando determined, however, with some of his friends, that a document should be drawn up against Ursua. This was done, and, that it might carry weight, Don Fernando ordered that it should be signed by the whole camp, for he said that it was for their mutual good. The men being present, the governor signed it first, and it was then Lope de Aguirre's turn to sign, as maestro del campo; but he withdrew the mask, and signed " Lope de Aguirre, the traitor." There was a general murmur at seeing this, particularly from those who were not so corrupted; they said that it was

an insult to his person and office thus to sign himself; but
Lope de Aguirre observing this, insolent man as he was,
and that he was but little esteemed for having signed himself as he had done, wished to give an explanation, and
spoke thus:

3. "Caballeros, what madness and gross ignorance is this
into which some of us have fallen, which, certes, looks more
like a pastime than an affair of such importance. You have
killed the king's governor, one who represented his royal
person, one who was clothed with royal powers; and do
you pretend that with documents concocted by ourselves,
we shall be held blameless? think you that the king and the
judges will not understand how such papers were got up?
This is madness; and well is it known to all, that if those
who sign it should be asked questions against themselves,
it will go against them, if they have said so much in their
own favour. Yes, we have all killed the governor, and
the whole of us have rejoiced at the act; and if not, let
each man lay his hand upon his heart, and say what he
thinks. We have all been traitors, we have all been a party
to this mutiny, and have agreed that the country (in search
of which we are) shall be sought for, found, and settled.
Now should it be ten times richer than Pirú, and more populous than New Spain (Mexico), and should the king draw
more profit from it than from all the Indies together, yet as
soon as the first bachiller or letradillo[1] comes with powers
from his majesty to take up his residence amongst us, and
to take note of what has been done by us, I tell you it will
cost us all our heads: thus our exertions and services will
have been in vain, and fruitless, for ourselves and successors.
My opinion is (and I hold it to be more to the point than
what you have conceived), that we should abandon these intentions of searching for these new lands; for if we discover

[1] Bachiller in this case is one who has obtained the first degree in the
sciences and liberal arts. Letradillo is a pettifogger.

them and people them, our lives will be sacrificed. Let us
therefore anticipate the evil time, and let us settle ourselves
well in a good land known to you all, which is Pirú. There
all are friendly to us, and, on hearing that we are approaching, they will come out and meet us. They, having the same
views as ourselves, will open their arms, and will assist us
with their lives. This is (I repeat) what we ought to do,
and this is the reason why I signed myself ' traitor.' "

In confirmation of Aguirre's opinion, Alonzo de Villena
started up (the Alferez general, and one of those who
went to kill the governor) and, said " What the Señor Lope
de Aguirre, maestro del campo, has spoken, appears to me
to be the best to be done, and must suit all, and I confirm it
with my vote ; and I believe that his reasons are good, and
any one who counsels the Señor general otherwise, is no
friend of his, but wishes his ruin and that of the expedition,
and is his enemy."

4. Juan Alonso de la Bandera, seeing that no one moved
to reply and contradict the speciousness of Lope de Aguirre,
or to second the governor, said that the death of Ursua was
no treason, neither had any crime been committed, and that
what had been done was a necessary act, because Ursua had
other intentions than those which were suited to the king's
service, who had commanded that Ursua should discover
and settle the lands of the Dorado ; and thus his majesty was
better served by the death of the governor, than that through
him so many people should perish in an expedition, wherein
so much money had been spent ; that the king would hold
it as good service that the lands should be discovered and
peopled, and that he would overlook what had been done,
and would even reward them with his royal hand : concluding, " and he who says that I am a traitor in this matter, I tell him that he lies, and I will make good my words,
and I now dare him to mortal combat."

These words so roused Aguirre and some of his friends,

that they wished to reply in the same strain, and even to
resort at once to arms; as they would have done, had not
the general and his captains put themselves between the
angry parties; but Juan Alonso, wishing to satisfy many
that what he had said was not for fear that the king would
cut his head off, again spoke, saying, " Do as you please;
and that you may not think that what I have said is from
any fear that I have of death or to save my life, I will act
like the rest, and let it be understood that I have as good
a neck as any one here." With this the disturbance ceased
for a time, and the council was dissolved; but Aguirre and
his friends henceforward incited all those they possibly
could to side with them in going up the river to Pirú, of
which way of thinking there were many.

CHAP. XIII.

1. *They leave the village (Machiparo) where they had killed Ursua, and
going down the river, arrive at another village, where they commence building brigantines.—2. They suffer so much from hunger
in this village, that they are obliged to eat horses and dogs.—
3. Aguirre kills Captain del Arze, because he was a friend of Ursua's,
seizes Diego de Belcazar for the same cause, and has two others
strangled.—4. Don Fernando takes away the office of maestro del
campo from Lope de Aguirre, and gives it to Juan Alonzo de la
Bandera his lieutenant-general.*

1. Five days after the death of Ursua, the expedition proceeded down the river, the mutineers disagreeing, some
wanting to go back to Pirú, and others to go in search of the
new lands. They arrived, on the same day that they left
Machiparo (Ursua's sepulchre) at another village on the cliffs
of the river, and so totally abandoned, that they did not
even find earthen vessels to cook their food in.

They stopped here because the greater number desired it. Lope de Aguirre, and those of his opinion, were for returning to Pirú, not by the river, but by sea,[1] and as it appeared to them that this locality was most suitable for the cutting of timber to build large vessels, so that they might go out to sea, they bored holes in one of the flat-bottomed boats, in which the horses came, to sink them as they had done to others at the village they had left; for they found themselves obliged to build brigantines and other craft of a larger sort than they had brought with them to this spot.

We shall now call Aguirre's party by the name of Marañones, as they generally called themselves. Don Fernando, finding himself with canoes only, and these not fit for the transport of horses nor for the quantity of cargo he had, ordered large brigantines to be built, and seeing that he had tools, pitch, and cordage, which Ursua had brought for such purposes, as well as from four to six ship-carpenters and twenty negros to assist; he added some soldiers to help in the building of the vessels, in which labour they spent three months, during which time several occurrences took place, as we shall explain.

2. The first, and not the least important, was a fearful famine, from which none escaped. Their principal sustenance was the wild yuca, from which they procured cassaba. They themselves had to go to the other side of the river to collect it, which was a league broad; and they had to prepare the cassaba from which they made the bread, for nearly all the Indians, male and female, who had come with them from Pirú, were dead. Neither was there much fish found in this portion of the river (all things seemed conspiring to punish them for their sins), for with the greatest trouble they only took a few; so they had to support themselves

---

[1] Namely, to proceed down the river to its mouth in the Atlantic, then coast along Terra Firma to the Isthmus of Darien, thence to Peru by the Pacific.

with a little cassaba bread and wild strawberries, which were in reasonable abundance; caymitos,[1] dates, guayavas,[2] and some other fruits, sustenance more suited for monkeys than for men. The Aguirres, in consequence of this visitation of famine (their wish daily increasing to go back to Pirú), began to eat their horses and dogs. This was not unpleasing to Aguirre, for in this case the others would find it impossible, being without horses and dogs, to commence their conquests by land. They also consumed all their poultry, without leaving any for the new settlements it was pretended they were to form, in the provinces they were to discover.

3. Those of Aguirre's opinions (a few days after arriving at this village) sought how to obtain the friendship of the greater portion of the soldiers; commencing with the first step, namely, that of liberty of conscience (the touchstone of the damned), promising them abundance of riches, lands, and appointments in that wonderful country Pirú, which they firmly believed they would conquer with ease. By such means Aguirre increased his followers, so that he was in a better position to take measures to obtain the end he desired; and his nature being inclined to the shedding of human blood, he looked around to see whom he should begin with, in the exercise of his office. He commenced with Garcia del Arze, who was a great friend of Ursua's, and of long standing. He caused him to be arrested, and informed the General how important it was for the safety of his person, and that of the camp, that Arze should not be in it; so he was strangled without more ado. In order that this small affair (as it appeared to Aguirre) might not horrify the army, he determined to kill Diego de Balcasar (of whom we have said that when they made him justicia mayor del campo, and he took the staff of office, he declared

[1] Chrysophyllum carimito.—*Seeman.*
[2] Probably the Inga spectabilis.—*Seeman.*

that he did it in the name of the king) for it was manifest to
Aguirre that a man who had spoken in such a manner was
to be feared, seeing that he might interfere with the more
mutinous in the camp. Having had his staff of office taken
from him, Aguirre went one night, with some companions,
to his lodgings, and found him in bed. He was dragged
out, with the intention of taking him to another place to
strangle him ; but Balcasar, understanding this, escaped
from them, crying out: " Long live the king, long live the
king !" with a view to alarm and obstruct his pursuers, and
also to incite others to come out and protect him. However,
seeing that his shouts did neither one thing nor the other, he
threw himself into the river, and although he hurt himself
badly, he escaped, owing to the obscurity of the night. The
governor was made aware of what had happened, and in the
morning sent men to search for Balcasar, and assure him of
his life. He consented to return, and did not die this time.

Now the powerful hand of Heaven (although it consents
to the commission of evil, by its secret judgments, does not
leave it without a punishment, which is always less than its
due), began to show its divine justice against the principal
mutineers and assassins of Ursua, causing some to be the
executioners of others, as we shall see, for in these days a
rumour ran through the camp, without it being known who
had originated it (because men so impious as they were, are not
particular in crediting rumours and saddling them on any
one they please), that Pedro Miranda Mulatto, as we have said,
who was one of the principal mutineers and alguazil mayor
of the camp, and Pedro Hernandez, the paymaster-general,
both of whom were present at the death of Ursua, meditated
the death of the General Don Fernando, as well as of certain
captains. When this came to the ears of Aguirre, without
ascertaining if there was any truth in the report (for bad
men do not scruple to act wickedly), and palliating his acts
under the shadow of apparent zeal for the safety of the life

of the General and his friends, he arrested both without further notice, put them into prison and strangled them, giving their posts to two of the mutineers; that of alguazil to one Juan Lopez Cerrato, and that of paymaster to Juan Lopez de Ayala. This gave umbrage to the rest, and then followed discords, dissensions, and deaths, because the devil had prepared their hearts, ready for his work.

4. Don Fernando de Guzman's power appeared in the ascendant, and he was principally occupied in rewarding his friends, being pleased that they should thrive through his bounty and appointments; for he felt that they would be grateful to him.

His first act was in favour of Juan Alonso de la Bandera, from whom the General had received good service on many occasions. He named him his lieutenant-general, and he, having accepted the office, commenced the exercise of its functions by opposing the doings of the maestro del campo Aguirre; they had opposed each other since the meeting of the council, when Lope de Aguirre, in the document made out by Don Fernando, signed himself, "Aguirre the traitor." Now their ill will began to show itself in earnest, and it was increased since Bandera had become lieutenant-general, because he attended well to the duties of his office, which was not agreeable to Aguirre. At last opinions were expressed by the soldiers and captains as to which of the two officers was the superior, and which of the two was to be obeyed in preference to the other. The friends of Aguirre defended the post of maestro del campo, saying that it was the superior. Those of Juan Alonso were of a contrary opinion; and soon the two parties withdrew the mask, and treated openly of their old enmities, which until then had been kept down.

The General sought to stop these dissensions, for he had not forgotten what he owed to Bandera, and he knew him to be a better friend than Aguirre. He therefore took from Aguirre his post of maestro del campo, and gave it to

Bandera, so that he now held the two offices. . This tended
to increase the flame of discord, and manifold were the
difficulties that followed; not that the governor put Aguirre
quite out of favour, for the latter could make himself
popular or rebellious; but he made him captain of horse,
and Lorenzo de Salduendo captain of the guard, which
post was previously held by Bandera.

CHAP. XIV.

1. *Don Fernando comes to an understanding with Lope de Aguirre, and
promises to restore him to his post of maestro del campo.—2. The
governor and Aguirre become friends, the enmity of the latter increases against Bandera.—3. Aguirre calumniates Bandera before
the governor, saying that he wished to kill the governor, and rebel.—
4. Aguirre kills Bandera, and one Christoval Hernandez, at the
governor's house.*

1. Lope de Aguirre did not think that this was the proper
time to show resentment for the loss of his office, but left it
to the future, contenting himself with his captaincy of horse.
At this time some of the governor's friends told him that
it was not to his interest to have Aguirre so much by his
side, for that they knew him of old to be a restless and
revengeful fellow, and that doubtless he was storing up such
feelings for an occasion when least expected. They firmly
believed that, for the security of Don Fernando's person, the
best thing to do was to kill Aguirre; and, if the governor did not wish to do it, they offered to do the deed,
with his permission. But the good feeling of the General
(which, at times, was more than requisite for the post he
held) did not allow him to kill Aguirre, or consent to his
death, although the mutineer had deserved such an end, on
too many occasions. The governor tried to appease the
anger which Aguirre might feel against him, for his removal

from the post of maestro del campo, by making him great
promises, saying, that he pledged him his faith and word
that he should have his old command before they entered
Pirú, and that he would marry a brother of his (who had remained there, named Martin de Guzman) with his mestiza
daughter, who was with her father, Lope de Aguirre.

Aguirre acted the part of a vile scoundrel, and with
smiles on his false face, accepted the honour of the prof-
fered marriage, and the promises of restoration to his old
office ; appearing to consider what the governor had offered
to be far above his deserts.

2. The General shortly afterwards paid a visit to the
daughter of Lope de Aguirre, to compliment her on the
projected marriage and relationship, taking with him, as a
present, a robe of rich silk, which had belonged to Pedro
de Ursua. He gave her the title of Doña, which she had
not received previously, and henceforth treated her as his
sister-in-law. Now as Aguirre was so wicked a man, and,
on that account, had so many friends of the same stamp,
who went about murmuring that he had been displaced, and
who might have excited rebellion, this projected marriage
was intended to appease them.

Dissembling for awhile, Lope de Aguirre again treated
Don Fernando with his former friendship, but his ill-will
towards Bandera, fanned by envy, increased hourly. The
sight of his rival placed above him, caused Aguirre to
revolve in his astute mind, how Bandera was to be hurled
from his high position. This state of things was not hidden
from Bandera, and he was informed of it by his friends,
who advised, for his own safety, that Aguirre should be
killed. With this intent they often went in search of him,
but without effect, for Aguirre was always well on his guard,
and never alone. He was armed day and night ; and even
when asleep, neither he, nor his partizans, were without
their arms.

I

The two offices held by Juan Alonso de la Bandera had produced in him a haughty and proud demeanour, which, independently of causing many of his old friends to separate from him, had rendered him obnoxious to many others, particularly to Lorenzo de Salduendo, the captain of the guard, because both pretended to the favour of Doña Inez. Salduendo was confederated with Aguirre, and rested not in devising the means to get Bandera removed from his office, and even to take away his life.

No better plan suggested itself, than to have it bruited in the camp that Bandera, not contented with the two offices he held, was ambitious to be the general of the expedition, and that it was his intention to kill Don Fernando and succeed him. This rumour having been made public (the author of it was believed to be Aguirre), the traitor went with some of his friends to Don Fernando, reporting to him what had been said, namely, that Bandera sought to kill him, and take his place. However, Don Fernando was incredulous, because he knew that Aguirre was a sworn foe to Juan Alonso, and he said that the report had more of enmity than truth in it, and that it was a mere suspicion thrown out by an unknown author.

Evil designs never want sponsors to foment them, as occurred in this case ; for Salduendo was present at this interview, and, urged on by his love for Doña Ines, he certified to Don Fernando that what Aguirre had said was true, for that he had heard it publicly asserted as a fixed project, and he affirmed that it was so, by a thousand oaths. Don Fernando then began to give some credit to Aguirre, and also to the report that Bandera had promised to one Christoval Hernandez the post of maestro del campo, when he (Bandera) became governor.

4. Without further examination into the truth of this report, the governor consulted with Aguirre how Hernandez and Juan Alonso should be killed, believing that this was

the best way to get rid of the fears which soon took possession of him (legitimate offspring of treason), and that if he
did not kill them they would kill him. It was not easy to
find the time and occasion for the deed, owing to the precautions taken by Juan Alonso, who was always accompanied
by numerous friends, although the most wary plans were
laid to consummate this wickedness.

At last Don Fernando threw the victims somewhat off
their guard, by inviting them to play at cards at his lodging; designing that, while Juan Alonso and Hernandez
were at play, Lope de Aguirre and his partizans should
come in and kill both. As it was planned, so was it executed, and, during the height of play, Don Fernando sent
for Aguirre, who came instantly with his armed followers,
and, approaching the players on one side, whilst others,
until then hidden by Don Fernando, appeared with muskets, lances, and daggers on the other, gave a cruel death
to Bandera and Hernandez, as they had done to Ursua.

This crime having been committed, Aguirre at once asked
to be paid for his services, and was again made maestro del
campo, and replaced in all his previous honours: and as two
posts were vacant by the death of the two victims, one of
whom was captain of infantry and lieutenant-general, Guzman
gave that post to one Gonzalo Guiral de Fuentes, his great
friend, and the other to one of his most intimate friends.
Thus he considered that his person and camp would now be
in security.

CHAP. XV.

1. *The soldiers irritate the Indians, who bring provisions for them, when some Spaniards are killed.*—2. *Owing to these proceedings the Spaniards suffer great privations, on account of the fear the Indians have of coming near them.*—3. *Aguirre succeeds in gaining the confidence of Don Fernnndo, for his own particular ends.*—4. *Don Fernando plans how to discover the real sentiments of the soldiers, and their devotion to him; and how he succeeds.*

1. The Indians of the vicinity were not well affected towards the Spaniards, though at times they brought some provisions to the camp, in exchange for beads and bells. The Indians would have continued to do this, if the soldiers had treated them properly, but there was no one to keep the soldiers within bounds, and they treated the Indians badly, which made them refrain from coming with provisions to the camp, and of this the stomachs of the Spaniards soon began to bear painful witness.

One day a number of Indians came with provisions, wishing to have things from the Spaniards in exchange; when a party of the most murderous of the soldiers enticed them out of their canoes, made them prisoners, shut them up in a hut, and took possession of their canoes. This was seen by other Indians, who had remained on the river in their canoes, and who fled, and were never more seen, for the fear they had of the Spaniards. Those who had been imprisoned, although they feared the white men, were also exasperated against them when they returned to their homes, having escaped after a few days confinement. Not long afterwards the soldiers suffered severely for what they had done; for trusting to the terms of friendship they were on with the Indians (not believing that the natives were so incensed against them), four or six Spaniards went into the interior, without taking any precaution for their safety, to collect the yuca plant, to make cassava bread, when a large number of Indians, who had been lying in wait for them, rushed out furiously on their foes, and, before they could collect themselves, and use their arms, they were all killed. Their names were Sebastian Gomez, a sea captain, one Molina, Villarial, Pedro Diaz, Mendoza, and one Anton Rodriguez.

2. This was a salutary lesson for the rest of the soldiers, so that they did not make more excursions, nor enter the Indian country ; and as no natives came to the camp, the want of food was most severely felt. It was thought that the Indians, after this success, would be emboldened and come by night and steal away the canoes, which were secured to the cliff, for they were of the greatest use to them, to go up or down the river in quest of food. But it was suspected that Lope de Aguirre, actuated by his evil disposition, caused some of the canoes to be secured to the shore at night, and allowed others purposely to float away down the river, so that the discontented soldiers might not have the opportunity of taking them, and deserting. This suspicion against Aguirre was increased, when it was given out that the Indians had taken them. However it might really have been, there was the fact, that out of more than one hundred and fifty canoes, scarcely twenty remained, and these were the worst and smallest.

3. Aguirre, finding himself with a smaller number of enemies, since the death of Juan Alonso de la Bandera and Christoval Hernandez, and also being reinstated in his old office (which made him the second person in the camp, and about to be related to the governor by the projected marriage of his daughter), was most anxious to have it believed on all occasions, that a sincere friendship existed between Don Fernando and himself ; wishing by this means to have it known in the camp, that, in consequence of his influence, what he ordered must be done. Thus the number of his adherents increased. Don Fernando thought that Aguirre

was much attached to him, being of too easy a nature, and believing all he heard from the maestro del campo, who had the art to persuade him that all he did was for the success of the expedition.   But it is one of the greatest errors that can happen, in the government of a people, that they should know the real character of their governor, for in that case they will generally take advantage of his weakness, as happens to birds, animals, and fish, for which men lay snares according to their natural habits, which are known, and taken advantage of.

The cautious Aguirre, knowing how to mould the plastic nature of Don Fernando, and that he was fond of show and ceremony, approached him one day by his weak side, saying that it was requisite, in order that he might know the people and soldiers he had with him, and their intentions as to continuing in the expedition, that he should call them together, try them, and ask them if they were satisfied that he should be their general; and if not, to elect whom they pleased; and to call upon those, who did not wish to follow the war into Peru, to declare themselves, and thus he would see who were devoted to him, and who were not.

4. As Aguirre had suggested, so did the general act, and, calling together all the people one day, in the open space in front of his lodging, he sallied out with a partisan (a kind of pike or halberd), accompanied by his friends, and Lope de Aguirre with his, and spoke thus :—

" Cavaliers and noble soldiers, for days past I have desired to speak with you, the more particularly as I have heard that some of you are not satisfied, in consequence of not having taken part in my election as general. My intention has never been to offend those who belong to this expedition, and if I accepted the office of general, it was because I believed I was administering to the general good. I was also warmly solicited by many, and rather against my own wishes; for you well know how difficult it is to act so as to content all, and the great care necessary in all things, particularly in warlike affairs; thus it is well that the general, who has to govern a camp, such as this, wherein there are so many cavaliers and good soldiers, should be elected by general consent, so that all may work willingly in war, being commanded by one whom they have chosen. It is for this that I have summoned you, for it is my desire that you should look around this camp, and see if you cannot find any one more eligible than myself, who, by reason of his greater sagacity and prudence, might take upon himself this office of general. I wish you to look well around, and to elect whom you please. You have entire liberty to do this, and that you may have greater freedom of action, I promise to give up and resign my office to any one you may elect, and I will obey him cheerfully, as a soldier in the ranks. In token of this resignation and renunciation, I place this partisan upright in the ground, as if it were the staff of justice." So he left the partisan standing in the ground, and, uncovering his head, he retired to those who had accompanied him, adding, " The same renunciation of their posts is made by these officers of the camp, so that you may dispose of them as seems fit and proper."

At these words the officers went through the same ceremony as Don Fernando had done, with the instruments and arms of office they had in their hands.

The soldiers and others of the camp, having listened in silence, being aware of the studied character of these proceedings, and seeing that even if they thought differently, it would be of little importance, and that the result would be against them, replied, and were followed by the friends of Don Fernando and Aguirre in the same strain. They proclaimed that the election of general, in the person of Don Fernando, had been made with the consent of all, and the same was said as regarded the other functionaries ; and they added that, if it were deemed necessary,

they would re-elect and name Don Fernando for their general, considering that they were fortunate in having so excellent and generous a cavalier to command them; and thus
they supplicated him to retain his command, and continue
it as heretofore.

CHAP. XVI.

1. *Don Fernando thanks them for his new election, and makes it known
that he will not force any one to follow him.—2. He asks the soldiers
to take oath to follow him, and all promise to do so, except three.—
3. They all take the oath on a missal placed on an altar.—4. Difficulties that occur in consequence of the want of employment for the
people, at this spot.*

1. By this proceeding Don Fernando thought that he had
arrived at a knowledge of the views of his soldiers, and he
returned to the spot where he had left the partisan, taking
it again in his hands. In order to show that he was grateful for his re-election as general, he gave the soldiers
feigned thanks, saying that he was under great obligations
to them; and that he would do his best to merit their
favour. He then gave thanks to God for what had been
decided on, declaring that justice should be done to all, and
that affairs should be managed in such a way that all might
thrive in riches and honours, for that there was more than
sufficient for all to lay their hands upon, in the broad and
rich lands of Pirú, whither they were bound, with the
intention of becoming lords of the soil. But all the camp
knew that in this war, which was made against the king of
Castille and the Indies, some engaged in it of their own
free will, and some were forced into it. Don Fernando,
however, said that his intention in this rebellion against
his king, was not to force any one to follow him, but that

each man should declare his intention, and that he who wished to follow him, should receive land, and riches; but that he who thought differently, and believed that the expedition was not a legal one, and did not wish to continue with it, if there were enough of them to remain behind, secure in some Indian village, and settle there, that he the governor would leave behind a superior officer (any one they might select), and that he would share with them all that he had of arms, munitions, and other things ; and that if they were not in sufficient number to do what had been proposed, he would take them with him as so many brothers, and leave them in the first friendly village, whence they might dispose of themselves as they best pleased. That they should have no fears of declaring what they wished, for, from this moment, he gave them his word of honour, that whatever their views were, their persons should be safe, and that he would punctually comply with what he had promised.

2. Don Fernando moreover added, that those who intended to go with him should sign their names, and solemnly swear that they would maintain the war against the lands of Pirú by fire and sword, and that they would obey their general and captains in all things, also that amongst themselves there should be order and unanimity.

The soldiery replied that they were ready to follow Don Fernando, and that they would take the oath, and sign as he had suggested.

Only three soldiers, named Francisco Vasquez, Juan de Cabañas, and Juan de Vargas Zapata, boldly said to Don Fernando de Guzman and his friends, that they would not follow them in war against his majesty, whom they recognized as their king and lord: and that on this account they wished to be excused from taking the oath, and signing.

The traitors put on an appearance of calmness at this announcement, but soon the venom of their souls was shown (for what they had said was feigned), and they replied,

K

that as it was not the intention of the three to join the war, they had no occasion for their arms; and so their arms were taken from them; and they were killed, as we shall explain. They knew what would be their doom, and they said so ere they determined how they would act, but death was preferable to a life of treason to their king.

3. It being too late, on the day of the meeting, it was left for the morrow to take the oaths and signatures; so on the following day, early in the morning, all the soldiers in the camp were brought together, and Don Fernando ordered an altar to be prepared, so that mass might be said in sight of all: and, calling Padre Alonso Henao (whom Pedro de Ursua had made chaplain and vicar of the army), he told him to robe and say mass, which he did. The effect which the traitors wished to produce by this celebration of the mass was apparent. When mass was over (which was heard by the traitors in a spirit allied to their depraved intentions), Don Fernando, without allowing the priest to unrobe, told the assembled soldiers that he had brought them together to assist at that ceremony, that there might be greater unanimity and friendship, and that they might have true faith in each other: for which object it was necessary that the oath he had suggested should be taken by all, in the most solemn manner in use among Christians. He then ordered the priest (robed as he was) to hold the consecrated host in his hands and receive the oaths from all, as they came up to him, they touching the host and missal with their hands. Don Fernando commenced, then Lope de Aguirre and the rest of the officers; then came the rest, according to their rank, who touched the host and missal, and swore by God, and Santa Maria, his most glorious mother, by those holy works of the Evangelists, and by the consecrated host, that they would be unanimous in the matter of the war that they were about to prosecute against the kingdoms of Pirú, that, between them, there should be

no difference of opinion, and that, if necessary, they would even die in the enterprise. They also swore faithfully to aid each other, without considering feelings of affection, relationship, loyalty, or any other matter that might retard or disturb the fixed plan of operations; and that in all that appertained to this war, they would have for their general Don Fernando de Guzman, obeying him and doing all he and his ministers commanded, under the penalty of being perjurers and infamous men.

After this sacrilegious and wicked oath had been taken, Don Fernando caused the document to be signed, he being the first, then Aguirre and the rest of the officers in their order, who also signed the document as to the fresh election of Don Fernando as general. Some, however, did not sign, with the design that by not doing so, they might be considered exempt from the oath; but, as there were so many crowding together, there were some who did not sign, and some were fearful that they could not write well enough. There were doubtless some who, by not signing, thought that they would be free from crime, or absolved from punishment, if the royal authorities did not find their names on the list.

The proceedings having terminated, it soon appeared that the principal object for taking the oath, was to unite the friends of Juan Alonso de la Bandera (who were soured in consequence of Bandera's death) with Aguirre and his followers, that henceforward there might be no more discord nor quarrels.

Peace appeared to be established; but, being so unjust, Heaven did not allow it to continue, for there soon occurred many misfortunes, dissensions, and seditions; and they killed each other, as we shall see.

4. The delay in building the brigantines caused much inconvenience, which hourly increased in consequence of the idle lives of the soldiers (a nest in which many evils are hatched, and the principal cause of what happened here).

Lope de Aguirre, with his sanguinary character (enemy to the human race), was always craftily employed in deceiving the soldiers, and placing so many snares in their way, that they could scarcely extricate themselves from them.

Day and night was Aguirre immersed in wicked designs. He brought forward one as base as it was dangerous, namely, to raise Don Fernando to such a height of power, that his fall would be the more certain ; and, having discussed his views with Don Fernando, and some of his friends, so that the latter might communicate the same to the soldiers, he ordered them to repair to the same place where Don Fernando's lodging stood, and, all being assembled, with Aguirre amongst them, armed as was his custom, and accompanied by his followers, he thus addressed them.

CHAP. XVII.

1. *Aguirre addresses the soldiers.*—2. *He, together with the soldiers, proclaims Fernando de Guzman Prince of Pirú.*—3. *Don Fernando accepts the title of Prince, and sets up an establishment accordingly.*—4. *Don Fernando takes the office of sargento mayor from Sancho Pizarro (a friend of Ursua's), and gives it to Martin Perez.*

1. " Cavaliers, we have not forgotten, for it is not many days since, that we named for our Captain-general Don Fernando de Guzman, of our own free will, and without any force, for all were duly informed that full liberty was given to elect whom they considered most fit ; and, after the election, the General repeated to all that they might select the road that best pleased them, to follow or not the war in Pirú, and those who did not wish to do so, have not on that account been slighted, as is well known ; and we who determined to do so, promised, on oath, to comply with our vow ; but since that time some may have changed their

minds, and determined to do something that appears to them better, or some may have had the oath forced upon them, and may say that they are compelled to follow this war, against their inclination. From this moment, I, in the name of the General my lord, and as his maestro del campo, make known and exhort every one of you to examine into what you have done and sworn to, and if you feel you have not the wish to comply, from this moment you shall be released from your oath, and permission shall be given to you (without your incurring any pain) to declare and follow what may appear best to you ; for which I give my word and honour, and promise to keep it with all, as has been kept with those cavaliers, who said that they did not wish to follow the war, nor fight against the king ; whom we have treated as bro-thers, dividing with them what they required."

2. Some who were present, and were devoted to Don Fernando and Aguirre, in the name of the rest, replied that they were not the men to fall back from their word, or break the oath they had given, particularly in so important a matter. They were persuaded that the enterprise would be successful, they were constant and firm to follow the war, already commenced, and which they had sworn to prose-cute.

Aguirre seized upon this opportunity, and said : " Yes, I perceive you are indeed firm in your views, and that such valiant souls are not only able to subject Pirú (for it is only a single province), but all the provinces of these Indies, which cannot have a good and proper government without a king at their head to govern ; it having been the custom in them (since they have been discovered and conquered), that the lands should belong to him who conquered and sub-jected them. For this object we have elected Don Fernando de Guzman our General and lord, to whom by right these kingdoms belong (and when we arrive in Pirú, we will give him the kingly crown, which will so well suit his brow), and from henceforth we will hold, recognize, and obey him as our Prince and lawful lord: to which end it is absolutely necessary that we forswear our allegiance to the kingdoms of Spain, our birthplace; and declare that we will not obey the king Don Philip; for it is clear that no one can serve two masters. In order that there may be no delay in such an important matter, and for the benefit of all, I will commence, and I say that I denaturalize myself from the kingdoms of Spain, where I was born; and if I have any rights there in consequence of my parents being Spaniards, and vassals of the king Don Philip, I give up all my rights, and I deny that he is my king and lord; and I repeat that I know him not, neither do I wish to know him, nor obey him as such; but rather, being in possession of my own liberty, I elect from this time for my prince, king, and natural lord, Don Fernando de Guzman; and I swear and promise to be his faithful vassal and to die in his defence, as he is my lord and king; and in sign of my recognition, and of the obedience I owe to him, I now go to kiss his hand, with all those who choose to follow and approve what I have said in this election of Don Fernando de Guzman, as Prince and King of all Tierra Firme; and he who does not do this, will clearly show that his thoughts are not like his words and oath."

So saying Lope de Aguirre went (with measured steps, followed by the captains and soldiers of the camp) to the lodging of Don Fernando, and said to him:—

" All these cavaliers and myself, have elected Your Excellency to be our Prince and King; and as such we come to tender you our obedience, and to kiss your hand, supplicating your acquiescence."

Don Fernando accepted the honours pressed upon him with many thanks. He would not give them his hand to kiss, but went to embrace them, beginning with Aguirre. They all called him Your Excellency, which was the title he had for the rest of his short life.

From this moment Don Fernando became proud and haughty, with the hope of seeing himself crowned as king. He became grave and severe, for such appeared to him necessary for one who in a short time was to be invested with royal honours. He ordered that his habitation, service, and servants should correspond with that of other princes; so he appointed his gentleman server, major domo, carver, pages, and gentlemen, to whom he assigned large salaries, of from ten to twelve thousand dollars and more, to be paid out of the royal treasury, in the kingdoms of Pirú. He also gave higher grades to the captains and other officers, and increased their pay. All men began to hold him in such veneration and esteem, that they not only took off their hats to his person, but also whenever a decree was read despatched by his hand, which was always headed thus: "Don Fernando de Guzman, by the grace of God, Prince of Tierra Firme, and of Peru," etc. He always dined alone, and he was served at table with all ceremonies, like unto a king; and this proud prince was so puffed up in his representation of majesty, that it looked like a comedy, or child's play; and though all this was feigned, I verily believe that had he wished to have been adored as a god, they would have done so, and he would have consented; to such a point had the wickedness of these men arrived.

4. Meanwhile Aguirre appeared to have forgotten his Christian duties and obligations, and, as a lost man, instead of repenting him of previous crimes, he committed greater ones, taking life away, and becoming a king maker and a deposer of kings. The same occurred in Castille, during the period of the factions of the commonalties,[1] with the Cura Medina and Palomero Davila; for when the communeros passed the cura's house, he treated them politely, and praised

---

[1] These were the cities of Castille, which, at the beginning of the reign of Charles V, rose against his government, in support of Spanish liberty.

them in his sermons and conversations, saying that it was just and reasonable to follow them ; but when they offended him, by taking his property and servants, he turned over another leaf with them, and instructed his parishioners to do the same; and thus the kingdom was at one time for Don Juan de Padilla, at another for the king Don Carlos. So Aguirre had the dexterity to elect as Prince of the Indies this vain hidalgo, and in a few days had the infamy to take away from him more than he had given.

A few days after Don Fernando was raised to regal power, he made Martin Perez sargento mayor del campo. He was one of those who had been without office, and who had been concerned in the death of the governor Ursua. This man well understood the office of a rebel and mutineer, and was the first to attack Juan de Vargas, Ursua's lieutenant, with such fury that his sword passed through Vargas, wounding his companion on the other side. In order to give him this office, Don Fernando took it from Sancho Pizarro, making the latter captain of horse.

CHAP. XVIII.

1. *Various projects regarding their journey to Pirú.—*2. *The plans they intend to adopt on their arrival at Nombre de Dios, Panamá, and Pirú. Don Fernando bestows titles for Encomiendas.*[1]*—*3. *The vile doings of other traitors.—*4. *After three months, the brigantines being ready, they leave this village, and prosecute their voyage.*

1. All being now arranged, as regarded the government of the expedition, the next thing to settle was, the best and readiest means of entering Pirú. Their hopes of success hourly increased, and nothing could persuade them to the contrary. After having held many councils, and weighed

[1] These were very large tracts of land, with the Indians on them.

their measures in a thousand ways, they resolved that
when the brigantines were ready (which were to be built
of larger dimensions than the old vessels), they would
adopt measures to get out to sea; and as to the victual-
ling, they resolved to go to the island of Margarita, where,
owing to the slight resistance the few inhabitants of that
place could make, in a few days they would be able to
lay in provisions, such as bread, meat, and water, which
they were to procure in four days, and if there were any
people there who wished to join them, they determined to
take them in the brigantines, and (without stopping at any
other place) to make for the port of Nombre de Dios, and,
landing at a river hard by, at night, the people being well
armed, to march straight to the town of Nombre de Dios
with such caution that, before they were perceived, they
would be masters of the place, as well as of the Sierra of
Capira (in which was the pass to the city of Panamá), for
having possession of this pass, no communication could be
made with Panamá; then to march onwards (leaving the
pass guarded) with the rest of the people and their Prince,
until they secretly arrived upon the city of Nombre de Dios,
to kill the ministers and officers of the king, and such inhabitants as they considered unfavourable to them, to plunder
and burn the place down, leaving it in such a state, that
those who had been spared by flight, would not be able to
fortify themselves there, nor offer opposition. They were
then, without any unnecessary detention, to take with them
the friends they had there, and march upon Panamá, prac-
tising the same cruelties and plunderings; but above all
things to make themselves masters of the ships in the port,
so that no information about them could be taken to Pirú.

2. This being done, they were to collect all the artillery
from Nombre de Dios, adding it to that of Panamá, and to
fortify themselves at the latter place; to build a galley and
other vessels; and, whilst so employed in Panamá, they hoped

L

to be joined by people from Veragua, Nicaragua, and other parts, as well as by more than a thousand run-away negros, who, desirous of their liberty, would be glad indeed to be with them, and to enjoy freedom; and arming all with the arms that had been plundered from the two cities, they would be able to go on to Pirú with so large a force, that, should those of Pirú be advised of their coming, and be under arms, their forces would be less than those of the invaders. Besides being well found in warlike stores, people, and arms, they hoped that the numerous friends they had in Pirú would join them, so that there could be no doubt, that in a short time they would be in possession of that kingdom. Then they could, at their leisure, divide its great riches amongst themselves; and they would then take away from its inhabitants their wives and daughters, each one naming which woman should be his, for they knew them all. Even the negros were not to be forgotten; and in this arrangement, should any one say, " I wish to have Doña So and So," another should reply, " I was thinking of taking the same, but as you have chosen her, there will not be wanting another for me," particularly as there were many Chapetonas,[1] coming from Spain.

As a wind up to such iniquitous projects, these tyrants flattered themselves (independently of the gifts in gold their Prince had promised them, from his royal treasury in Pirú), that they would be given titles to estates in that land, and the receivers of such titles disposed of such estates (as if they were really in possession), without for a moment considering that such wickedness would lead to punishment, as it did.

3. They might have called to mind the miserable end of Gonzalo Pizarro in Pirú, when, with similar intentions, he

---

[1] Chapetona, female; Chapeton, male. This term, and Polizon also, was given in America to Spaniards who went by stealth there, or without a passport.

rebelled against his king; and although during his rebellion he had a large and well armed force, and was victorious over some of the loyal vassals of the emperor, as when he conquered and killed the viceroy Blasco Nuñez, with the greater portion of his army; which made him proud indeed with his short prosperity; yet in the end he was made prisoner, his army routed at the battle of Xaquixaguana by the president Pedro de la Gasca, and his death was a miserable one. A similar fate befel Francisco Hernandez Giron, who rebelled against his king, and, with only three hundred followers, defeated the royal army one thousand two hundred strong, in the battle of Chuquinga. He gained other victories, and was better found in all ways than our Don Fernando de Guzman; yet he was beaten by Gomez de Solis. They might have had many other examples before their eyes (if their eyes had been open) of others who had risen in these Indies with the same objects, in which many of the followers of Don Fernando had been engaged; yet all these mutinous projects had had a bad end. The recollection of the wild life they had led during their participation in various revolts, spurred them on the more in the present disloyal enterprise, without for one moment anticipating the miserable results that must follow.

4. In these and other visionary schemes they passed the three months during which the two brigantines were building, and getting ready for sea. The brigantines had no upper works nor decks, but such strong hulls, that they might have been armed as vessels of war of three hundred tons.

The whole of the people embarked in them, and some new canoes. They left this place, which they called that " *of the Brigantines*," and, navigating the river downwards, came the same day to another village of the same province of Machiparo on the right hand, where they slept that night, starting with early morn the next day, and by a bend entered an arm of the river to the left, by Aguirre's orders,

who feared, if they went to the right (for it was in that direction some hoped to come upon the rich lands they had been
in quest of, according to the information of the Brazilian
Indians) that they would remain in those lands, and that
dissensions would arise as to settling them. It had come to
Aguirre's knowledge that there were many soldiers, who
would rather have remained in any moderately fair province, than go upon the present mutinous expedition. So
Aguirre arranged to make a turn out of the way of their
direct route, and, having navigated three days and one
night in this westerly direction, they came to a few empty
huts (for the inhabitants had fled), in a miserable wet country and partially flooded, where the air was filled with
mosquitos, which preyed dreadfully on the people.

The huts were square, and, being covered with straw,
rather astonished them ; for they had not seen, in the long distance they had left behind, any but such as were thatched
with palms, nor had they seen the grassy plains whence the
straw could have been procured, to thatch the huts. Those
soldiers who wished to be satisfied on this point, dared not
ask some Indians, who were too old to fly, where the lands
were whence they got the straw, for fear the friends of
Aguirre, observing them ask questions, should think they
were inquiring about the rich lands they had originally set
out in search of.[1]

[1] Aguirre seems to have entered some mouth of the Japura, and, by
going up one of the branches which communicate with the Rio Negro,
to have finally reached the latter river.

CHAP. XIX.

1. *They arrive at this Indian village, where they pass Passion week and Easter ; Aguirre causes a soldier to be strangled.*—2. *They depart after Easter, and stop at another very large Indian town, where they find abundance of provisions and wine (chicha).*—3. *Some customs of the Indians of this place.*—4. *How they arranged to obtain provisions here ; and how some scruples occur to Don Fernando and his friends.*

1. Before they arrived at this village, Alonzo de Montoya went with a party in canoes, in search of provisions, up a small branch of the river. Montoya found, at a small settlement, dried fish and some maize, which the Indians had not had time to take away when they fled. The Prince Don Fernando determined to remain eight days to celebrate Passion week, which had already commenced, and to depart after Easter. This would allow of time to rest, and to search for provisions. The fish caught by the soldiers, as well as more brought by the Indians, and bartered, was of great use ; and the love of barter brought the Indians peacefully from their hiding places, to treat with the Spaniards.

They were quite naked, they used the same weapons, and spoke the same language as those higher up the river ; so it was presumed they were of the same nation.

It happened on one of the days of Easter, that a soldier named Pedro Alonso Casto, who had been alguazil to Pedro de Ursua, in talking to another man named Villatoro, complained of the small consideration the mutineers had shown in regard to him, and that they had not given him a particular post he desired ; and, laying hold of his beard with his hand, repeated the following lines from Virgil: "Audaces fortuna juvat, timidosque repellit"—Fortune aids the bold, but overthrows the timid. There was not wanting one (who had not the fear of God before him) who made this speech known to Aguirre, and it was noticed that he was growing

morose, because many days had elapsed since an occasion
had offered to kill any one; and in order that Easter might
not pass without glutting his infernal appetite for human
blood, he had both these soldiers arrested, intending to
strangle them for what they had said. Don Fernando, being
advised that the men were seized (and well knowing the
desire of Aguirre to execute them), sent to say that they
were not to be killed; but when the messenger arrived,
Pedro Alonso Casto had been garotted, and the other was
on the point of suffering; so, by order of the Prince, his
death was delayed for some days. At the same time the
office of alferez-general, which had been given to Alonso
de Villena (he was one of the assassins of Ursua), was taken
from him, because it was considered too important a post
for one of his low blood; but, that he might not be altogether out of humour, he was made gentleman server,
and a considerable salary was assigned to him, to be paid
out of the royal treasury of Pirú; and to prevent any
bickerings as to who should have his former office, it was
not filled up.

2. The feast of Easter being passed, the next morning, at
daylight, they left that village, and in the evening came to a
larger one on the banks of the river; where there was abun-
ance of provisions in the houses, but the inhabitants had
hurriedly fled, fearing the Spaniards. They had not had
time to hide the maize and other eatables, and probably the
natives thought that the Spaniards would remain there long,
being so near the previous resting place, where they had
remained a long time.

This village was on the cliffs above the river, on a narrow
island, bounded on one side by the waters of the river, and
on the other by a marsh. The island was not broader than
a shot from a cross-bow would reach, but its length was
nearly two leagues, and it was lined with habitations.

A sort of wine, made from many things, and of a pasty

substance, was found here, which was kept in large jars, holding about five hundred weight. It was left for a certain time to ferment, as if it were juice of the grape, and then put into other vessels. When it was ready for drinking, it was first mixed with water, for its strength was such that drinking it pure would have caused drunkenness, more so than wine from grapes.[1]

The Indians had large buildings stored with this liquor, and if the Spaniards had remained, they would have emptied them, for they liked the drink.

3. The Spaniards did their best to be friendly with the Indians, in which there was no difficulty, as the soldiers bartered for what they wanted, and these natives were fond of trading, and, being pleased with what the soldiers gave them in exchange, they would not leave the camp, but rather hired themselves to row canoes, grind corn, make bread and wine, and render other services. They were useful, and kind, and although some of the soldiers used them ill, they did not discontinue their bartering, nor did they make much ado when the cruel Spaniards killed some of them.

They became crafty in their barterings, and they would come at night and steal from the heads of the beds of the Spaniards, clothes, arms, and whatever they could lay their hands on, without fearing severe chastisement for what they had done. It appeared that thieving was not considered a crime by them. Sometimes the Spaniards would imprison them for these thefts, when their companions would come and ransom them, bringing manatees (cow-fish), turtle, hicoteas, fish, and other food, but the pilferers were not let off without having first received some slight punishment.

They were a well disposed people, quite naked; and used the same arms, darts, and macanas (a sort of club), as those

---

[1] This is the *chicha*, or fermented liquor, used by the Indians : made from maize, yucas, etc.

of Machiparo. Their houses were large and square, and covered with palms leaves, which were abundant.[1]

The Indians had stored a quantity of large cedar timber in their village, brought down by the river, from which they made their canoes, and built their houses. The mutineers considered this a good place to finish building the brigantines, on account of the quantity of timber here, as well as the abundance of food.

4. They encamped as follows. In the lower portion of the Indian town, the Prince took up his quarters with his officers, gentlemen, and some captains; above him, and nearly in the centre, was Lope de Aguirre, and, as he was always meditating some diabolical act or other, he caused the brigantines to be moored near to his lodging, saying that he would thus have them under his own eye, in order to quicken the work. But he had another object, for, being in the centre of the camp, he could thus command more of it than his Prince. They began to finish the vessels, building them higher, and putting decks to them, so that they might hold more people, be better ballasted, and safer at sea.

For this object all the Spanish and negro workmen, who understood ship-building, lost no time, and some soldiers also assisted, but it took a month to conclude the work. During this time, in consequence of the want of occupation of the soldiers, difficulties occurred; some caused by feelings of conscience on the part of Don Fernando de Guzman and his friends, who became troubled in mind with the cruel and unjust death of Ursua. Then they considered the small power they had to carry into effect their idea of taking Pirú, into which plot Aguirre had thrust them. There also

---

[1] These Indians may have been the Uaupes of the Rio Negro, described by Wallace; or more probably the Juris. The latter dwell between the rivers Putumayu and Japura, and are also found on the Rio Negro. Their huts are thatched with palm leaves. In 1775 they were ruled by a chief named Machiparo.—Southey's *Brazil*, iii, p. 721; *Wallace*, p. 510.

fell upon them the fear of human as well as of divine chastisement, which comes whence it is least expected, to take that vengeance on such grave crimes, as they had been guilty of, which they already began to see was approaching.

These thoughts, and the sparks of the Christianity in which they had been brought up, caused them to waver. They thought amongst themselves that they would be lost and ruined by following the projected plan of war with Pirú; and that the only way of escape was to retrace their steps, hand themselves over to the ministers of justice, and be punished, as they deserved. By acting thus, much that they had done would be forgotten, if they now went in search of the rich lands they had started to discover, and settled in them; and they hoped that, although the king might punish them, it would not be with great severity, after adding to the riches of his dominions.

CHAP. XX.

1. *Don Fernando calls a council, in which it is determined to kill Aguirre, as it appeared necessary to do so.—2. Aguirre and his friends get more arms, taking them from the rest.—3. He divides the soldiers into companies, such an arrangement appearing to him better for his designs.—4. Aguirre arrests Gonzalo Duarte, Don Fernando's mayordomo, with the intention of killing him, but afterwards they become friends.*

1. Don Fernando considered it necessary to call his friends, and the less evil intentioned soldiers in the camp together to hold a council, without letting Aguirre know of it, whom he hated much more than his own sins; the object being to countermand the return to Pirú. They all met in the house of Don Fernando, that each might give his opinion as to whether the expedition should return to Pirú, or go in

M

search of the land of the Omaguas. The last measure was considered by the council to be the wisest; but there was a great difficulty to surmount, namely, the opposite views entertained by Aguirre. As long as he and his familiars opposed, nothing could be done, for they were more in numbers, and the most daring. The council then agreed to remove this great obstacle, by taking Aguirre's life, and this was to be done by sending for him at once. It was expected that he would come unprepared, not being aware of his danger, and when he came before them, they intended to kill him; for if he was not got rid of thus briefly, it would be impossible to prevent his becoming aware of their intentions, and then they could not be carried into effect.

They were all agreed; when the devil, who is always ready, God willing, to favour his own, and sustain them for some time, to commit greater sins, prompted Alonso de Montoya, one of the council, to say, that it was not prudent at that moment to kill Aguirre. He said that if they sent for him, he would come, but accompanied by some of his friends, and, instead of their killing him, he might kill some of them; so it would be better to put off his death, until they were on their voyage down the river, when Aguirre might be sent for to come on board the Prince's brigantine, to speak to him alone, and thus, without doing harm to others, they could kill Aguirre.

2. Don Fernando considered this a good plan, for he was of a kind disposition, and an enemy to severity and death; so he approved of this course, and it was to be effected in the manner which had been last proposed. The council were of the same opinion, because it was the will of their Prince, although against their own views; for it was certain that if they did not get rid of Aguirre at once, as had been at first resolved, greater troubles would succeed, and that he would get rid of all those who had conspired against him; as did occur, for during the course of his tyranny not one

of these escaped his vengeance, from the Prince downwards.

Not a day passed that Aguirre did not draw more followers to his side, from amongst those who resembled him in atrocity, intention, and ambition; whom he managed to supply with the best arms in the camp, taking such from those he was not sure of, on the pretext that they were not mindful of warlike affairs, and that they did not take such care of their arms as was required of them; and, as if indignant on this matter, he took the arms from them and gave them to others, who, he said, would take better care of them. In this manner he and his followers became possessed of the best armour and arms in the camp; not only of those who died, or whom he killed (whose property was under his control), but of those who were living; and thus the only useful arms were in the hands of his party.

3. It appeared convenient to Aguirre that the soldiers should be divided into companies of equal numbers, so that one captain should not have more men than another; and he determined to divide them into as many companies as possible, of forty men each, he himself naming some of his friends as captains of some of the companies; and in some of the other companies he put those soldiers who were devoted to him, so that he might have assistance from all sides, when required. The Prince's guard consisted of forty soldiers, and amongst these he introduced some of his partizans. He was now the leading hand in disposing of affairs, and he favoured his allies; his power increased, his wish to command was greater than that of his Prince, and he was more readily obeyed; thus it was not difficult to foresee that this state of things would end in trouble.

One Gonzalo Duarte, mayordomo mayor to Don Fernando, fearing what might happen to him, from the high hand Aguirre was taking, also recollecting that he had once conspired with Aguirre, and thinking that what the Prince com-

manded would be obeyed, obtained a promise from him,
that no judge or captain of the camp should have any jurisdiction whatever over him, but that he should be, in all
things, amenable only to the Prince, for any matter, however atrocious, he might be concerned in.

4. It was not long before this arrangement came to Aguirre's
ears, and, knowing why Duarte had put himself in this position, and wishing to show him that he could not escape him,
Aguirre went and made him his prisoner, intending to
strangle him at once, as he would have done, if Don Fernando (hearing that his mayordomo was arrested) had not
gone in person, and taken him out of prison. Aguirre's
diabolical rage knew no bounds, when he was informed that
his prey had escaped his hands ; he rushed to Don Fernando's dwelling, and, with ferocious language, throwing
himself on the ground before him, fire flashing from his eyes,
and foam from his mouth, supplicated that the prisoner
might be given up to him, for that he wanted to punish him
for many atrocious crimes he had committed in the service,
and that he would not rise from where he was, until he
had with his own sword (which he drew from the scabbard)
cut his head off.

Don Fernando begged him to rise and be calm ; and promised that he would examine, and see what Duarte had
done, and that he would punish him if he had been culpable.
The officers present also became mediators, pacifying the
infernal fury of Aguirre, and doing their best to make them
friends, seeing that in this they would please Don Fernando.

Duarte now explained that Aguirre should be considerate
to him, adding that he had no cause to treat him so, for
Aguirre well knew that when, in the village of the Motilones,
he had conspired and wished to kill Pedro de Ursua, and to
make Don Martin General (he whom we have said Ursua
sent back to Pirú, in consequence of what Pedro de Añasco
told him), that Aguirre was to be maestro del campo, and

he, Duarte, captain, and that they were to go back to Pirú.
A long time had passed, and, although he had been so intimate a friend of Ursua's, he had never breathed a word of
this conspiracy to any one, and he never could have supposed that Aguirre would repay his silence by taking his
life. Aguirre (as one who cared but little for his wickedness being brought to light) replied that what Duarte had
said was true, and that he was now mindful how Duarte
had befriended him, and that he was ready to serve him if
he required it ; so Aguirre became calm, and they (at the
request of the others) embraced each other, and became
friends for the time; but soon afterwards Duarte paid dearly
for this friendship, by becoming his victim.

CHAP. XXI.

1. *Difficulties between Captain Lorenzo Salduendo and Aguirre, as to the
   accommodation for Doña Ines on board the brigantines.*—2. *Aguirre
   kills Salduendo, and by his orders two soldiers kill Doña Ines.*—
   3. *Discussion between Don Fernando and Aguirre as to the death of
   Salduendo.*—4. *Aguirre pacifies Don Fernando, but, on account of
   an idle report which two captains repeat to Aguirre, he determines to
   kill Don Fernando.*

1. Doña Inez de Atienza had not left the evil ways she
had continued in since she left Pirú (although she had witnessed so many violent deaths, which Providence had placed
before her), and was living as the mistress of Lorenzo Salduendo, captain of Don Fernando's guard. Doña Inez had
with her, as a companion, a Doña Maria de Soto, a mestiza,
who was the mistress of another man in the expedition. All
being ready to start, Salduendo busied himself in arranging
how the females and their baggage could be accommodated
in the brigantines ; and, that they might repose comfortably

at night, he wished to send some mattresses on board for them. Aguirre (either because he did not like the women, or that he was jealous that any one should have a female companion), told Salduendo that the mattresses could not go in the brigantines, as they took up too much room, inasmuch as there were a great many people, and other more important things, which it was absolutely necessary to take. Thus Aguirre excused himself, and Salduendo went away in an angry mood, returning to his lodging, where he found the two women awaiting a favourable reply from Aguirre; and, having told them what had passed, and the angry way in which he had been refused, in an offended spirit he flung away from him a lance he had in his hands, saying, " Am I to beg for favours from Lope de Aguirre at these my years ?"

These words were repeated to Aguirre, with others that Doña Inez had uttered the previous day, whilst burying a mestiza servant of hers, when she exclaimed weeping, "God pardon thee, my child; but ere many days thou wilt have many companions with thee in the grave."

2. When Aguirre was told these words, uttered by Salduendo, his suspicious soul easily interpreted the meaning he intended they should have, that Salduendo meditated some evil against him, or even to kill him ; so he determined to collect some friends, and go and kill Salduendo ; who, being advised of his proceedings, and guessing that the result might be fatal, went to the Prince and told him his fears, as to Aguirre's intention of killing him. Don Fernando told him not to fear, and that he would settle the matter; and, calling Gonzalo Guiral de Fuentes, one of his captains, he told him to go to Aguirre and say, in his name, that he must look to it that Salduendo was not molested, for that he was in fear of his life; and also to do his best to calm Aguirre's anger.

Gonzalo Guiral went on his mission as quickly as possible, but as Aguirre was most active in his diabolical actions,

Guiral met him on the road with his troop of murderous followers, who were proceeding with hurried steps to kill Salduendo. Guiral gave Aguirre the message from Don Fernando, who took as little notice of it, as of the Prince whom he had placed in power; and, without stopping, he went onwards until he arrived at Don Fernando's house, when he and his partizans attacked Salduendo with swords and lances. Don Fernando tried to defend the victim, he commanded and begged that they would not kill Salduendo; but it was too late, he was soon a murdered man, like unto Pedro de Ursua his governor, whom he had assisted to slay.

The cruel beast Aguirre, now bathed in the blood of Salduendo, longed to shed that of Doña Inez, and, calling to mind his distaste for her, and some threats of hers, he determined that she should suffer a similar punishment; so he ordered one of his sergeants, called Anton Llamoso, and one Francisco Carrion, a mestizo, to go and kill her wherever they might find her. These men had already been accustomed to slaughter, and this murder of a woman rendered them more hardened for such offices in future.

No sooner was the sanguinary command given, than the murderers went to where Doña Inez lodged, and rushing upon her with drawn swords, took her life in such a barbarous manner that after her death, even the most hardened men in the camp, at sight of the mangled victim, were broken-hearted, for this was the most cruel act that had been perpetrated.

Her property, which was of considerable value, was seized, and without calling in the notary to take an inventory (desiring to be paid for their bloody work), the cruel butchers divided it between them.

3. Whilst these assassins were killing Doña Inez, Don Fernando had the lifeless body of Salduendo before his eyes. He upbraided Aguirre with want of respect for his person,

and for not heeding him when he had sent to him, praying
that he would not kill the captain of his guard; that he had
come with cruelty as well as insolence to commit the murder
in his presence, and this he told him in a bitter tone.
Aguirre, valuing the help he had from his followers more
than any favour the Prince could show him, addressed Don
Fernando in an arrogant and insulting manner. Amongst
other things, he said that Don Fernando did not understand
or know how to govern in affairs appertaining to war, and
if he (Aguirre) were wise, and wished to manage things
well, he ought not to put his trust in a Sevillano, for he
knew their character for double-dealing. Now, as Don
Fernando was a native of Seville, this was a terrible thrust
at him. He added that he should be cautious and look to
his person, as he (Aguirre) should do to his, for men in
the position of his Excellency, should have more care of
themselves than he had; and, for the future, when he
wished to have a council of war, he would advise him to
have fifty well-armed friends in his train prepared for
whatever might happen; and that it was better for him
to partake of the pebble-stones of Pariacaca, than of the
pancakes given to him by Duarte his majordomo;[1] and
he added many other observations of the same kind. He
then left his Prince, returning to his quarters with his
friends.

4. Aguirre had not been long in his quarters when he determined to return to the Prince, and give him apparently peaceful explanations, telling his Excellency that he ought not to
complain that Salduendo had been slain before his eyes, for
he intended to have killed him, Aguirre, who was one of the
Prince's most faithful and loyal servants; so if he had lost one
friend, a better friend had been spared; that he would guard
him with more fidelity than any other in the camp, for that he

---

[1] "Fuera muy mas a proposito gustar de los guijarros de Pariacaca,
que de los buñuelos que le dava Gonzalo Duarte su mayordomo mayor."

was a man to defend and assist him, and more determined in risking his life in Don Fernando's defence, than
many in whom he had put too much confidence, and that
some day the Prince would discover his mistake. With
these and other false assertions Aguirre pacified his Prince,
who could not by words show that he felt the reverse; for,
taking into consideration what Aguirre had lately done and
said, and the little respect he had for his position, he was
very suspicious of what might happen to him; this feeling
increased daily, and he became fearful and changed in his
appearance; but he did not protect his person with more
care, nor take Aguirre's life, nor did he seek to rally more
friends round him for protection; for he had become so
timid and listless that for the care of his own life he took
but little note.

Aguirre, on the other hand, was guarded at every point;
he had in his train, day and night, more than sixty men
well armed and ready to commit any crime; and he caused
it to be bruited about that he had this number of men to
guard and protect Don Fernando. This was said to deceive those who suspected that Aguirre meditated the
Prince's death.

Gonzalo Guiral de Fuentes, Don Fernando's captain, and
Alonzo de Villana (both of whom had been in the council
when Aguirre's death was determined on), seeing what had
passed between Don Fernando and Aguirre, and that no
good would result to one or the other, determined to join
Aguirre's party, which was the strongest in followers and
arms (for it is the fate of tyrants, to be served by unfaithful
ministers), so they went to Aguirre, and recounted to him
all that had passed in the council, and how it was that
he was not a dead man, in consequence of Alonzo Montoya
delaying his death for some more fitting occasion. With
this information Aguirre immediately determined within
himself (without making it known to any one) to kill Don

N

Fernando, and the whole of the council, and to make himself master of the expedition. He sent for Don Fernando to be present at a certain council, who replied (fearing he was to be killed there) that the present was not the time for councils, nor to call him to them, and he begged to be excused.

CHAP. XXII.

1. *Aguirre makes his arrangements to kill the Prince Don Fernando and others.*—2. *Aguirre and his companions kill two captains, and plan how the Prince is to die.*—3. *They go in the morning of the next day to kill the Prince.*—4. *Aguirre kills a priest, some captains, and the Prince Don Fernando.*

1. Aguirre was rather astonished when he heard of the scheme planned by the council for his assassination, so he determined to lose no time in murdering those who had sentenced him. He secretly prepared his friends for action, but only made known to two of them his intention of killing the Prince, for these two had promised Aguirre to do so two days before, when the brigantines should be on the point of sailing.

As we have already said, the island on which they were encamped was narrow. In one part of it Don Fernando was lodged, Montoya and other captains were at the other end, whilst Aguirre and his friends were in the centre.

The first thing Aguirre did was to issue an order that all the canoes, above and below the brigantines, should be brought up to them; that without his express order not one should be used, to prevent information from being carried from one part of the camp to the other; and that his friends should send their baggage secretly on board the brigantines, so that, in case their plans became known, and they were ordered to be arrested, they might embark and set sail.

2. The night arrived, and Aguirre collected his followers together, placing guards on the road to the Prince's quarters (which he could easily do as the island was so narrow), so that no one could pass and warn him of what was going on. All his friends being in his house, he told them it was necessary that he should punish certain captains and soldiers who had rebelled against their prince, and for this purpose he prayed they would accompany and assist him, as they were bound to do. Having equipped and armed them, they proceeded with him direct to the quarters of Montoya, and that of the admiral Miguel Robedo, in the upper part of the island, who were unprepared for Aguirre's plot. Aguirre, with his host of ruffians, entered the huts of both of his victims, killing them with sword and lance, unperceived by any one. Hence they proceeded on their way to do the same with Don Fernando, before any one could inform him of what was meditated against him. Aguirre was the first to inform his party that it was necessary to kill other captains and soldiers who were quartered near to Don Fernando, stating who were to die; that parties of ten of his people were to rush upon each individual, naming who were to be the murderers, and who the victims. He charged them to have a care in fulfilling his orders effectually, and promised to be in the thick of the fight with them; but they observed that it was not the most favourable hour, being so late and the night so dark, and that in the affray they might kill one another.

3. Aguirre considered the observation was not ill-founded, so he delayed proceeding until the first dawn of day, increasing the number of his followers with soldiers in whom he could confide; so that no information of what was going on might transpire in the lower part of the island. But he

did not consider it prudent to remain on shore during the rest of the night, and he therefore went on board the brigantines with his band. They were very watchful, and intended, in case the Prince should suspect what they were about, to cut the cables of the brigantines, and go down the river, leaving the Prince and the rest of the people there to perish.

The day began to dawn, and stillness reigned throughout the camp (for the two deaths they had already committed had not been discovered). Aguirre came on shore with his followers, but no one knew that they were about to kill the Prince, excepting Juan de Aguirre and Martin Perez, the Sargento mayor, his confidential friends, whom he had begged, under promise of great gifts, not to fail in killing Don Fernando de Guzman. A strong guard having been left on board the brigantines, Aguirre advanced with his men to the Prince's quarters, collecting all the soldiers they met on the road, telling them they were going to chastise some mutineers, and adding that they should be ever mindful of their Prince and lord, to reverence him and to see that he did not endanger his person; and, although some of the mutineers might fly to his side for protection, to be most careful not to harm the Prince, for it was probable, as his Excellency was of so kind a disposition (being ignorant of the treason against his person on the part of the captains they were going to kill), that he might try to save them, but they were not to be left alive.

4. Aguirre, having fully instructed his band, and approaching the hut of Padre Alonso Henao (who had said the mass, and had taken the oaths of rebellion against the king), commenced his butchery by sacrilegiously taking the life of the priest, by the sword. Some said that this deed was accidental, and that Aguirre did not kill him, but a soldier called Alonzo Navarro. Whoever committed the act, the priest was murdered. They then proceeded to the Prince's quarters, and found him on his couch, quite unprepared to be hurried out of the

world. Don Fernando arose, on hearing the noise made by the entry of the soldiers, and, on seeing Lope de Aguirre amongst them, said, " What is all this, my father ?" for this was the way the Prince generally addressed Aguirre, who replied, " Do not be alarmed, your Excellency," and, passing onwards with some followers, went to where Captain Miguel Serrano, Duarte, and Baltasar Cortes Cano were, killing them with swords, lances, and arquebuzes.

Martin Perez and Juan de Aguirre had not forgotten Aguirre's instructions, and, perceiving that the opportunity had arrived by reason of the confusion in the house, and steeling their hearts for the act, they approached Don Fernando, and fired their arquebuses at him. They afterwards attacked him with their swords, and thus he fell dead at their feet, bringing his rebellion to an end, a fate which he might have averted had he taken proper precautions. He was scarcely twenty-six years of age, of good stature, well formed and strong of limb, with the manners of a gentleman, fine face and beard, slow to action, more kind than otherwise, and born in the city of Seville.

CHAP. XXIII.

1. *Aguirre explains the cause of the death of the governor and the others to the camp, and calls his soldiers the "* Maranoñes.*"—2. He changes the various offices in the army, giving them to his friends.—3. They leave the town of the "* Butchery,*" and sail through large provinces. —4. After navigating for twelve days, they come to a village.*

1. The bloody work being over, and the day advancing, Lope de Aguirre called the people together in an open place, from whence he could be heard by all. He was armed from head to foot, and surrounded by eighty of his

best fighting friends, fully armed. He then gave an account of the late severity, adding that they ought not to be surprised, nor be tumultuous on account of the deaths they had witnessed, because such were the natural consequences brought on by wars, and that war could not be called by that name if such acts did not take place ; that their Prince, and the rest who had fallen, had been thus treated, because they did not know how to govern, nor to direct the expedition to the favourable end they all desired ; that for the safety of the army, the death of Don Fernando was most necessary ; for had he been allowed to live, they would all have perished through his bad government, which fact must be so manifest to all, that he would not trouble them further on the matter, but that henceforth they should consider him as their friend and companion, and be well assured that for the future, the war would be prosecuted to the satisfaction of all ; that they would not be sorry for having chosen him for their General, for that they could scarcely conceive the extent of the desire he felt to administer to their pleasure and contentment. He thus ended his speech, and remained with the title of General ; although some say that he was not called General, but the " Powerful Chief," and his men Maranoñes (a name they gave themselves), which for days past they had had the idea of taking, owing to the entanglements and plots (*marañas*) that daily occurred in that expedition, with so much danger to all, as we have seen ; and from this came the name of the river Marañon, without there being any other reason to call it so. We have observed that each province on the margins of the rivers that entered the Marañon had their various names. It has been said that a small branch of this river was called Marañon, from which the whole river took its name. But the truth is as we have said, and the name was never heard before, although many Spaniards had navigated near to its mouths (in the Atlantic), and the Captain Francisco de Orellana had descended it, and given it the name of Amazonas, on account of having met with women, who fought against him; and the river took that name also.[1]

2. Aguirre was now anxious to commence the exercise of his supreme power and office, as General over the expedition (which he had taken by his own will, and without other right than that obtained by the murders which he had committed). He began by giving new posts to those particular friends who had been most ready to second his designs. To Martin Perez, who had been his sergeant, and one of the murderers of Don Fernando, he gave the post of maestro del campo; one Juan Lopez (a ship's caulker) was appointed admiral; Juan Gonzalo (a carpenter) sargento mayor. The commander, Juan de Guevara, was deprived of his office of captain, given to him by the Prince, and promised that, if all arrived safely at Nombre de Dios, he should be given twenty thousand dollars and sent to Spain, for Aguirre was well aware that the commander was not cut out for a soldier.

[1] Velasco has an interesting chapter on the river Marañon (*Hist. of Quito*, 1789, i, 16.) He observes that the name of the first Spaniard who saw the river was Marañon; and that he exclaimed on beholding the vast expanse of waters, " *Hic mare an non ?*" " *Marañon*" is in reality derived from the Spanish word *Maraña*, one of the meanings of which, is a place rendered impassable by brambles and briers; and such impediments would have been encountered by the first explorers of the river. In this chapter, however, it is distinctly stated that the river took its name of *Marañon* from the " *Marañas*," or entanglements and plots which daily occurred in Aguirre's expedition. Orellana entered this great river from the mouth of the Napo, and it should retain his name of " *Amazonas*" from that point to the Atlantic ; while the name of " *Marañon*" may justly be given to the river from its source in the lake of Laurioche in Peru, to its junction with the Napo.

Manuel Rodriguez says, " A vista de los enredos y *marañas* que passaron, andando por aquel rio, y sus vueltas, le llamaron *Rio de Marañas*, y por significarlas grandes, passò à llamarse *Marañon*. Y aun solo por si, pudieron darle el nombre, por sus muchas vueltas entre islas, y montes, que le descaminan ; y por sus brazos, saltos, y despeños, llamandole Marañon de aguas, enredo y laberinto confuso de corrientes."—*Marañon y Amazonas*, lib. i, cap. v.

The office of *conducto*[1] was given to Diego de Trujello, who had been alferez to Aguirre; Diego Tirado was made captain of horse; some say that he was obliged to accept the post, or that otherwise he would have been killed, although I think it was not so, for we shall see what he did afterwards. Aguirre made Nicolas de Susaya his captain of the guard. He was a Biscayan, and a very little mean fellow, but he was soon removed. The staff of office of alguazil mayor of the camp he gave to Carrion, a mestizo, the husband of an Indian woman in Pirú, which staff was taken from Juan Lopez Carreto; but in order not to change all the captains and old officers (as also to please some of his friends, who begged him not to do so), he left Sancho Pizarro and Pedro Alonzo Galeas, in the posts given to them by Don Fernando.

3. Aguirre presently considered how he could best prevent any difficulties that might occur (being so crafty and wicked a man, he judged the world by himself), so he issued a proclamation, under pain of death, that henceforward no one should speak in private with his companions, that the soldiers should not go about in bodies, and that, when in his presence, no man should put his hand to his sword or other arms.

Not considering himself quite safe, even with these severe orders, he thought he and his friends would be better in the brigantines than on shore, (during the two days they were detained in that place, after the death of Don Fernando); so they embarked, and when there was any necessity for their coming on shore, it was done with such care and caution, and so many of them came well armed, that even if the others had sought to molest them, they would not have succeeded, seeing that they had but few arms, and that those they had were very inferior, (for as we have said,

---

[1] Conducto or Conductor—usher, or one whose business it is to introduce ambassadors.

Aguirre had for some time past appropriated the best, for himself, and his friends) and would have been of little use.

After these two days, having embarked all the people in the two brigantines and some canoes, he left the town of the "Butchery," (for so they called it), and directed his course to the left, by a branch of the river, his intention being not to sight any village or people on the right side, having received information that the Omaguas dwelt in that direction; but, navigating by this and other branches coming from the west, they soon saw some low mountains to the east, with open savannahs, whence they discerned, during the day, much smoke, and at night many fires, a sure sign that they were near a large village; but as no one was allowed to make any observation, or talk about what they saw under pain of death, they could only look and be silent.[1] The Brazilian Indian guides said clearly that those were the lands and people of the Omaguas whom they were in search of, so, to stop any investigation on this head, Aguirre immediately issued an order, under pain of death, that no one should talk with the Brazilian guides, or speak of the lands of the Omaguas.

4. They discovered other bare-looking low mountains on the left hand, which were nearly opposite to those on the right, but they did not appear so populous. These two ranges caused the river to be somewhat narrower, but not so much so as to prevent it from being very wide even here.

For eight days and seven nights the Marañones were navigating, going always to the left, and passing many islands, peopled by naked Indians with bows and arrows. They were the first they had seen on the river, who had piraguas (large boats). They landed at one of the villages in search of provisions, where they found a great number of iguanas in the huts, tied by the neck, ready to be eaten.

---

[1] Aguirre appears to have been working his way up the Rio Negro, in the direction of the Cassiquiari Canal, which connects it with the Orinoco.

At length they came near a large Indian settlement, on the right, situated on a very high cliff, at sight of which Aguirre sent thirty armed men in canoes and piraguas, with orders to lay hands on some of the Indians, who did not fly from the Spaniards, but waited, looking at them from the cliff, apparently with peaceful intentions. The soldiers gave them to understand that they were friendly also; but, as the latter were so used to the shedding of human blood, particularly that of the natives, and in this case much against their own interests, they began to fire their muskets, wounding some of the Indians, and causing the rest to fly, leaving all they had in their huts.

The soldiers went after the Indians, but could only catch a man and a woman.

Wishing to ascertain whether the plant they rubbed on their arrows was poisonous, one Juan Gonzales Serrato took one of the arrows from an Indian, and pricked him in the leg with it, drawing blood. On the following day the Indian died, so it was seen that the poison used here was most powerful.

The brigantines now came to the village, where the Spaniards disembarked, plundering the Indian huts of provisions and other things. The Indians, having placed their wives and children in safety, appeared occasionally in the distance, on land, and on the river in their canoes and piraguas, but they did not attack the Spaniards.

CHAP. XXIV.

1. *They catch an Indian, and send him to tell the others that they desire to be at peace with them.—2. Aguirre kills three soldiers, whilst they are putting the brigantines in order.—3. He still has tyrannical fears, although he has killed so many men.—4. The Brazilian Indian guides escape from him.*

1. They were anxious to lay hands on one of the Indians who were in sight, which they did; and Aguirre (giving him some hatchets and other things) made him understand by signs that he was to go to his companions, and tell them to come into the camp, and that no harm should come to them. So the Indian went, and shortly afterwards they sent two messengers, one was lame in the foot, the other in the hand, and his body bent on one side; and these, by signs, made known that the whole of the Indians would come in, and be friends.

But Aguirre's thoughts ran more upon Pirú, than upon making peace with these Indians; so he did not think it worth while to await their coming, or else he considered that they had not been prudent in sending the two Indians away, who would report what they had seen, and the natives in large numbers might come and attack them; for all around was a high plain free from marshes, being an open savanna, surrounded by a forest of cork-trees (*alcornocales claros*).

The Indians here are naked, and they use the bow and arrow with dexterity. They are Caribs, and voracious for human flesh, and are called the Arnaquinas.[1] They have temples for sacrifice, and worship the sun and moon, as the Span-

---

[1] *Arnaquinas.* These Indians may have been the *Arekainas* of *Wallace*, p. 508; a tribe on the Rio Negro, and on the upper waters of some of its tributaries; who make war against other tribes, as Padre Simon says, to obtain prisoners for food. Von Spix mentions a tribe called *Arequenas*, on the Putumayu (probably the same), *Spix und Martius*, iii, p. 1136. These Indians, like their neighbours the Uaúpes, have sorcerers, but do not believe in a God.

iards discovered, by what they saw at the doors of their sanctuaries ; for on one side, there was a large plank on which was cut the figure of the sun and that of a man. From this it was understood that they sacrificed men. On the other side was another plank, with the moon and a female engraved on it, and here they sacrificed women. Both these spots were very full of blood, which, doubtless, was human (although this could not be distinctly learnt from the Indians, as the Spaniards were ignorant of their language).

2. The Indian houses were in confusion; in one a piece of the guard of a sword was found, in others nails, and in others little things made of iron. Their food was the ordinary food of the Indians, viz., maize, which was found in quantities in their houses ; and many roots of ñame (yam), and yucas were in the ground, from which they made cassava. There was much fish in the river, and plenty of fruit on land.

Already at this spot, on the river (in consequence of the great distance they had navigated, and because the water was seen to ebb and flow, and by other signs), the pilots and others conjectured they were not far from the sea, so Aguirre determined to ship the masts of the brigantines, and to rig them, particularly as there was plenty of provisions here, to last them for the time they were occupied about the vessels. There were also large quantities of cabuyas, figues, and cacuyza, from which they made rope ;[1] also large spars for masts, jars of a good earth for holding water, much cassava, and other things.

They hurried affairs on, making sails of some cotton mantles and sheets they collected from amongst themselves, and they were ready in twelve days, which appeared to Aguirre as so much lost time, for he had not shed any blood; and that he might not forget how to do it (for his office was that of a murderer), he laid a snare for a soldier named

---

[1] Varieties of the Agave Americana.

Monteverde, saying he thought it very shameful in him to be so lukewarm in warlike affairs, and that he was of no use to him. One night he caused him to be strangled, with an inscription placed on his body as follows, " amotinadorcillo," a poor little mutineer. Some, to put a gloss over what Aguirre had done, justified the death of Monteverde, because he was a Lutheran; but let this be as it may, he did not kill him from zeal for the Catholic faith (about which he did not care), but because he thought he was not sufficiently devoted to him. Because Aguirre's wickedness was increasing, or because he wished Monteverde to have a companion, he killed Juan de Cabañas (one of the three already alluded to, who would not follow Don Fernando de Guzman, or sign anything against the King of Spain), because Aguirre considered he ought not to continue in such an opinion, although he had been permitted to act as he did. Aguirre then killed Captain Diego de Trujillo and Juan Gonzales, then Sargento Mayor, to whom he had given these posts after Don Fernando's death; and, that no one might say that they had been executed without cause, he had it reported that these men wanted to mutiny and kill him: however, the truth was that he had got rid of them out of this life because they were looked upon as good and kind men, and because many came about them as friends. Aguirre feared and believed that at some time or other this party would kill him and his band.

3. He soon gave the offices of the dead men to others: that of captain to one Cristoval Garcia, a caulker; that of serjeant to one Juan Tello. So many were the fears that disturbed the wicked conscience of Aguirre, although he had killed those whom he in any way feared, that he never felt himself secure from the survivors: so, not believing himself safe, either by day or night, on land, during the greater portion of the twelve days he and his friends lived on board one of the brigantines, and Martin Perez on board the

other, not allowing any of the soldiers, of whom he had the
least suspicion, to enter them.

There were two soldiers—one called Madrigal, the other
Juan Lopez Serrato. The latter had been alguazil mayor to
Don Fernando; they were on unfriendly terms in consequence of some affront Serrato had put on Madrigal, who
wished to have satisfaction, and with Aguirre's permission,
watching an opportunity, he, one day, and in Aguirre's
presence, came behind Serrato, and with a lance wounded
him dangerously. Aguirre pretended that he would have
him arrested and punished for this ; true he was arrested,
but never punished, because Serrato got the better of his
wounds; but Aguirre did not think it fit that Serrato should
be cured, and have his life saved, so he commanded those
who were attending on him to put poison into his wounds.
The surgeons did this, so that what they put into the wounds
soon killed him.

After some days, and when provisions had been taken in,
the Brazilian Indian guides, who had come with the expedition from Pirú, seeing that they had missed the opportunity of entering the country of the Omaguas, ran away and
fled one night ; and it was presumed that their country was
not far off, otherwise they would not have fled, because they
would have had to enter the country of the Cannibals (the
Arnaquinas), already mentioned.

4. As soon as the brigantines were ready, and stored with
maize, cassava, and water,—Aguirre embarked his people,
and, before they set sail, he disarmed all the soldiers he had
any suspicion of, bound and put them into confinement in the
fore part of the vessels, ordering that no one should go near
them, excepting his tried friends. He did the same with the
suspected soldiers who were in the other brigantine, in which
was his maestro del campo, Martin Perez.

This being done they set sail; and as the magnitude of the
river was increasing, the winds began to show their power.

They had only been out a short time, when Aguirre began to overflow with cruelty. In order not to forget his habits, he recurred to them (without waiting for any causes whatever), and determined to kill the commander, Juan de Guevara, ordering one Anton Llamoso, his serjeant, to do the deed. Llamoso went to Guevara (who was on board, and unprepared thus to die), and began to wound him with an old broken sword. Guevara prayed that he would not kill him so cruelly, and with such a sword, when the serjeant took Guevara's dagger, giving him many stabs, and, before he was dead, he threw him into the river, where, surrounded by the drowning waves, and the agonies of death, he was heard to say, " confession, confession." Aguirre gave out that he had suffered for having been concerned in the mutiny of Diego de Villanueva and Juan Gonzales, who had been executed at the last village they were at, called by them that of the *Xarcia* (Village of Ropes).

Aguirre was so overjoyed at this cruel death of the comendador, that, glorying in his infernal wickedness, he came alongside the other brigantine, in which was his maestro del campo, and told him of it, laughing most heartily. Both enjoyed the death of Guevara to their hearts' content.

CHAP. XXV.

1. *Going down the river, they fall in with some strongly built houses, where they find cakes of salt.*—2. *During the voyage they pass many islands ; and on one of them they leave the greater number of Indian servants, whom they had brought with them.*—3. *They continue the voyage under many difficulties. For a trifling affair Aguirre has two Spaniards strangled.*—4. *He loses a piragua, with three Spaniards and some Indians; and others are drowned, gathering shell-fish.*

1. After six days sailing, from the village of the Xarcia,

they came to some strong houses, on the margin of the river,
built by the Indians, on the tops of high timbers, with their
barbacoas[1] above, and surrounded below with strong planks
of palm wood, with loopholes for shooting out their arrows.
The traitor Aguirre sent one of his captains, with some soldiers, to one of these buildings, but the Indians made so
good a show of resistance, that, without receiving any harm
from the arquebuses, they dangerously wounded four Spaniards, and made the rest retreat. The Spaniards then tried
to get to the rear of the building by a creek, but, having got
to the spot, they found it empty, for the Indians had fled.
They did not find any provisions, either in this house or the
others, nor any signs of cultivation around them; so it was
presumed that the Indians lived on fish, and what they procured by bartering these fish with other Indians. They only
found some salt in cakes, prepared by boiling. They had
not met with any salt before on this river, neither did the
Indians (they had seen) know what it was.[2]

From the Caperuzas to this point, according to the opinion
of all, they had navigated one thousand three hundred leagues,
including the various bends in the river. The expedition
stayed here three days, making the necessary arrangements
for sea, when they should get out of the river.

Afterwards, there appeared on the river more than a
hundred canoes and piraguas, with a multitude of armed
Indians. The Spaniards prepared to receive them, and
defend themselves, thinking the Indians intended to
attack them when they were out of the river; but nothing
of the sort took place, for the brigantines had so much the
advantage of the canoes and piraguas, that the Indians
became terrified, and rapidly disappeared, hiding themselves
as they best could, or running away.

[1] This must mean the sleeping places of the Indians.
[2] Aguirre must have been in the head waters of the Orinoco, when he
found this salt.

2. They continued their voyage, and got amongst a large number of islands, which confused them. They now had to row, particularly as the coming in of the tide made the waters contrary for them; and when the tide fell, which it did so strongly that they did not know where they were going on that waste of waters, the pilots were confused, having no knowledge of the river and its tides. Before them they saw some points of land on the continent, or on rather high islands, and Aguirre sent certain pilots in piraguas to see how they were to proceed with their navigation; and having done so, they became the more puzzled in consequence of the difference of opinion amongst them as to which course they ought to take: so they at last determined to proceed as God pleased to let them, until they came to a small Indian village on the cliffs of the river, on one of the islands, whence the natives came peacefully to barter food with them. The Indians were naked, but on the soles of their feet they had pieces of deer skin, fastened like the sandals worn in Pirú, and as I have seen worn in the provinces of the government of Venezuela. Their hair was cut in round lines, beginning from the top.

Here Aguirre committed one of his greatest cruelties; for he left amongst these barbarous and sanguinary Indians those male and female natives who had become Christians, (some of whom they had brought from Pirú, and others from the river,) saying there was no room for them in the brigantines, and that they were a burden to him, as he had but little food for so many. It was certain that these poor creatures would soon perish by the hands of the other Indians, or by the maladies of this humid and unhealthy country.

3. The abandonment of these Indians, who served the Spaniards, was the occasion of the death of two Spaniards named Pedro Guiterrez and Diego Palomo; for, as they

P

were conversing together, they were heard to say, that it appeared that as their servants were left here, it would be as well to do at once what had to be done. This was overheard by a negro, who told it to Aguirre, and he took it to be sufficient cause for executing the two Spaniards, who were, therefore, ordered to be strangled. Diego Palomo begged hard that he might be left amongst the Indians to teach them to be Christians, but this was not what Aguirre wanted; religion might be taught by those whose profession it was, but he did not care to do good to any one.

They left this village, and a few leagues further on they found themselves near to the mouth of the river, which is nearly eighty leagues wide. Here they were in great danger, by reason of the fearful weather, and were a thousand times being nearly lost. On the left hand side, which is to the west, towards the "Cordillera," they saw that the land was well peopled, from the quantity of smoke they observed; but they did not visit the people, that not being their intention, and because there were very many shoals, which the brigantines often touched; and if the shoals had not been of soft sand, the vessels would have been knocked to pieces.

4. It happened in these waters that three Spaniards and some Indians went out in a piragua, when the (macareo) high waves of the sea or of the river upset the boat with such violence that the brigantines could not go to their assistance; and they were driven so far away, that they were soon lost sight of, and it was not known whether they were drowned, or had fallen into the hands of the natives.

It sometimes happened, that when the tide was out, islands were discovered, when the Indians they had in their service, and who were famishing with hunger, would go in canoes to look for shell-fish. Busy in this search, the tide would set in with such velocity, and with such huge rollers,

¹ In that direction was the Sierras of Coussaris and Tumucucuraque.

that they found it impossible to return to the vessels, and perished miserably. With these and other innumerable troubles, they sailed into the Sea of the North, on the 1st of July of the year 1561.

CHAP. XXVI.

1. *The first Spaniard who sailed out of the mouth of this river, was Captain Francisco de Orellana. Its banks are not well peopled.— 2. Character, climate, and people of this river, from its sources to where it enters the sea.—3. There are more than two thousand islands near to the mouths of the river.—4. Lope de Aguirre, finding himself out at sea, sails for the Island of Margarita, where he arrives and lands, having first killed two soldiers in the brigantine.*

Previous to the voyage of the Maranoñcs down this river, its first navigator was Captain Francisco de Orellana, who came from the river Canela (which, as we have said, rises in the provinces at the back of Quito). Orellana having met, during his voyage, with women of fair stature, who defended themselves from him and his soldiers, and opposed his advance, he gave them the name of Amazons, because they were like similar women of Scythia, who lived on the banks of the great river Tanais, whence they first moved to another river called Thermodon, and conquered by their arms the greater portion of Asia. These Amazons had the great Penthesilea for their queen and commander, and they are mentioned by Zachary Lilio, who says that they burnt the right breast off, that it might not hinder them in the management of arms, for the chase, or in war. Orellana had some reason for calling the women he met with Amazons, on account of their having fought against the Spaniards; yet in many provinces of these Indies, women have done the same : nor do we see why this river should be called the Amazons only on account of this occurrence. The most prevalent custom is to call it Marañon, as before stated. Its magnitude is such as to entitle it to the name of the gulf of sweet water, for, independent of its great size at its mouth, it, at times, when it rises, covers a hundred leagues of land with so much water that canoes and piraguas sail over the inundated land.

The banks of the river are not well peopled, and it is a matter of wonder how the Indians live, by reason of the myriads of mosquitos, which they call noisy zancudos, and it appears that nature has created these animals to punish and torment sinful man.

2. From the time the expedition left the dock where the vessels were built, at the Motilones (which was on the 26th of September of the past year, 1560), until they arrived at the village of Tortugas, in the month of December, very little rain fell, from which circumstance they concluded that it was the summer of this part of the world (because in all the lands of this New World, there is no other rule to know the winter and summer, but by the rainy or dry season). From December it rained much, with very heavy storms of wind, lightning, and thunder, causing great danger to the brigantines and canoes, the waves of the river being like to those of the sea in a tempest.

Some were of opinion that the risings or freshets occurred all the year round, for, from its source until it falls into the sea, its length is more than one thousand six hundred leagues (4,800 miles); thus it is necessary to pass through very many provinces, and under various constellations, so that when in one part the winter is over, it begins in another; and when the freshets cease in one part, they commence in another, particularly as each locality has its annual winter (or rainy season). All the land by which the river flows is very hot indeed and sickly, which explains why there are so few villages, and why it is so thinly inhabited.

The earthen jars of the natives were much prized, being curious and well made. No gold was found amongst the natives of the river, except what was seen in the provinces of Carari and Marari, where the Indians had a few ear-rings, but in other parts they had none; and when the soldiers showed them pieces of gold, and asked them if they had such in their country, they appeared to prize it more than any other object, and the same with silver; so it was presumed that they were acquainted with the precious metals, and that they obtained gold from other people, who found it in the streams of their country. They found innumerable quantities of turtle, and large nests of their eggs, and other river animals.

3. A short distance before entering the sea, the river has so many islands, that it is said they number over two thousand, when it is low water; but when the river rises it covers the greater portion, or nearly all of them, and when the sea has its spring tides, no islands are seen; and such is the force and bellowing of the beating waves, that it is said that the great noise is heard at a distance of four leagues.

I find so much difference of opinion amongst authors and others, as to why this river was called Marañon, or the other we have already treated largely of, the Orinoco,[1] that I cannot clearly determine which of the two is the Marañon, so it must remain unsettled until some one writes about the matter with better information; and this is the reason why I likewise call the Orinoco, Marañon.

From the time the expedition left the Motilones until they entered the sea, they navigated for ninety-four days, counting the nights, and the rest of the time they spent in resting, building the brigantines, and other occupations.

4. Lope de Aguirre, finding himself with his band upon the waters of the ocean, ordered the vessels to steer for the

---

[1] In another of Padre Simon's "Noticias historiales."

island of Margarita, with intentions already stated; but
desiring (and what sort of fears were those that must have
been always tormenting this traitor, for his vile conscience
was his executioner) that those in the other brigantine,
wherein was his maestro del campo and the rest of the
people, might not be in a position to take another course,
but of necessity follow him, he took away their compass and
the cross-staff used for taking the sun's altitude, commanding that they should follow his brigantine during the day,
and his lantern at night. So they navigated in this order,
being permitted by the secret ways of Providence. They
had a steady sea, and fair wind, and they did not separate
from one another in the seventeen days they took to cross
that gulf from the mouth of the river to the island of Margarita.[1]   If the voyage had been longer, they must all have
died of hunger and thirst; for in these days, so extreme

---

[1] It is exceedingly difficult to make out the course taken by Aguirre;
and he certainly did not know it himself, as, in his letter to king Philip,
he says, " God knows how we got through that great mass of waters."

Acuña says, " God did not permit that Aguirre should discover the
principal mouth by which this great river empties itself into the ocean;
but he came out on the coast, opposite the island of Trinidad." Humboldt, after carefully reading Simon's narrative, could see nothing to
indicate that Aguirre ever went out of the bed of the Amazons ; and, as
the current runs strongly to the north-west at its mouth, he might easily
have reached Margarita in seventeen days. Orellana, in 1541, left the
mouth of the Amazons on the 26th of August, and reached Cubagua
(between Margarita and the main land) on the 11th of September, sailing through the Gulf of Paria.

Padre Simon, however, distinctly states that, in order to avoid the
country of the Omaguas, which he believed to be lower down the main
stream, Aguirre altered his course to the west ; that is, he made his way
up one of the great rivers which flow into the Amazons from the north
and west, probably the Rio Negro. This view of the case is confirmed
by the mention of the cannibal *Arekainas* Indians, who certainly dwell
near the head waters of the Putumayu and Rio Negro. He thus reached
the ocean, either by ascending the Rio Negro, and the Cassiquiari, into
the Orinoco, which seems most probable : or by "a communication of
the rivers of Guiana."

was their suffering from both (particularly those who were
not great friends of Aguirre, for the latter had the additional
food which the others wanted) that the rations given to each
soldier daily were scanty indeed; the grains of maize were
counted, and they were allowed the fourth part of a quar-
tillo of water. This want of provisions made them so ill,
that when they arrived in sight of the island of Margarita, they thought more of dying than of landing on its
shore.

When they were in a position to land, the pilots, not
knowing the port of Pampatar, which is the principal one,
coasted along with care, but without fear, as these vessels
drew so little water, and the weather was favourable. But
as they were nearing the island, the brigantines were
separated by a mareta[1] (a wind that rises by degrees and
blows violently), which took them into different ports, that of

It has also been suggested that Aguirre ascended the Rio Negro, and
its tributary the Rio Branco, and, by a short "portage", crossed to the
Rupununi, a tributary of the Essequibo, which river he followed to the
Atlantic. A careful perusal of the narrative, however, will show that
this was not possible.

Acosta says, "The great river called by some the river of Amazons,
by others Marañon, and by others the river Orellana, flows from the
mountains of Peru, from whence it receives a great abundance of water,
both of rain and of rivers; then, passing by the great plains of Paytiti,
Dorado, and the Amazons, in the end it falls into the ocean, almost right
against the islands of Margarita and Trinidad."

"A brother of our Company, being then young, sailed it in the company of Pedro de Ursua, with whom he was present at all the adventures
of this strange entry and discovery, and at the seditions and pernicious
acts of that wicked Diego(?) de Aguirre, from the which God delivered
him, to place him in our Company."—Acosta, lib. ii, cap. 6.

It will be observed that Acosta here says that the mouth of the Marañon is "almost right against the islands of Margarita and Trinidad."
He obtained this information from one who was with Aguirre; and this
assertion must be considered as very strong additional evidence that the
traitors made their way to the sea, by the Rio Negro, Cassiquiari, and
Orinoco.

[1] This name is also given to a peculiar commotion of the sea.

Aguirre into one then known as Paraguache, now called the
Tyrant's Port,[1] four leagues from Pampatar, and that of
Martin Perez into another, to the north, two leagues dis-
tant from Aguirre, and four from the town.

No sooner had Aguirre got into port than he was seized
with terrible suspicions and fears of Gonzalo de Fuentes,
who had been one of Don Fernando's captains, and of a
soldier named Diego de Alcaraz, who had been justicia
mayor of the mutineers. He had no guarantee that when they
had the opportunity, they would not join any people whom
they found loyal to their king, and leave him. So, to quiet
his suspicions, that infernal man, before any one went on
shore, ordered them to be strangled, without confession, for
this tyrant took pleasure in killing both body and soul.
The intention of those who thus desired confession could be
of little value, being a sacrament of desire, which theologians
call *en voto*. Gonzalo Guiral, before he was made away
with, prayed most earnestly to be shriven. This the traitor
would not listen to, and so, without losing any time, he
choked him. While they were putting the cord round his
throat he began to cry out, begging for confession, and the
traitors, fearing that some one on shore might hear his cries,
stabbed him to death.

Shortly afterwards Lope de Aguirre went on shore with
some of his friends. This was on Monday, in the evening,
the 20th of July, 1561. He sent orders to the other vessel,
by a soldier named Rodriguez, his confidant, for the people
to join him. Rodriguez went with certain Indians of
the island, who were in the port, and served as guides, to
find where the maestro del campo had been driven to, and to
tell him early that night to come with all his people and

---

[1] The port of Paraguache still bears the name of the " *Tyrant's Port:*"
and when the people of Cumana, and the island of Margarita, pronounce
the words "*El Tirano*," it is always to denote the infamous Lope de
Aguirre.—*Humboldt, Narr.*, ii, p. 213 (note).

join Aguirre. Rodriguez had orders to strangle Sancho Pizarro on the road, for Aguirre was suspicious of him. The traitor then sent his captain of horse, Diego Tirado, with two or three friends, to the city of Margarita, to say that they had missed their way in sailing out of the Marañon, and were in great want of provisions, and to pray the inhabitants, in his name, to provide them with some. This embassy was accomplished by Tirado, with all care and punctuality.

CHAP. XXVII.

1. The maestro del campo, having received Aguirre's orders, departs, and strangles Sancho Pizarro on the road.—2. A piragua with Indians is sent from the port of Margarita, to examine the brigantines of Aguirre, and a party of soldiers visit him.—3. The Margarita people give Aguirre two bullocks, and he recompenses them.—4. The governor, on account of a letter received from Aguirre, decides upon visiting him, accompanied by some of the inhabitants of the city.—5. The governor offers him hospitality. The traitor marshals his armed men before the governor.

1. Rodriguez went quickly to Martin Perez, who had sent one Diego Lucero, with a guide, to inform Aguirre of his arrival, and to ask what he was to do. The maestro del campo, having received Aguirre's message, disembarked his people ; but he was obliged to delay a little for Roberto de Susaya, a barber, and Francisco Hernandez, a pilot, whom he had sent with some negro slaves to some farms half a league off, in search of food. They returned at midnight, when they all commenced their march, and they did not forget to strangle Sancho Pizarro on the way.

Aguirre sent one Juan Gomez, a caulker, his admiral, and some soldiers in search of food at the farms, who lost their way and suffered great privations. They met with some Spaniards, but did them no harm, awaiting a more favourable opportunity. They merely pressed upon them the necessity of letting them have provisions, which they did.

2. Great was the surprise of the inhabitants of the port of Margarita, when the vessels first hove in sight, for they believed them to be French; but they were somewhat quieted when they discovered that they were but small vessels, probably concerned in a similar occupation to their own, that of pearl fishing; and, as they did not make direct for the port, it was concluded that they were strangers to the coast, and a piragua with some Indians was sent out to see what vessels they were, but they did not come alongside until Aguirre's ship was at anchor. He got hold of the Indians, and would not let them return, keeping them for guides. However, when the people of the city knew that the brigantine had anchored, they sent some Spaniards by land to ascertain who their guests were, and, although these soldiers met with Diego Tirado and others on the road, they could not ascertain exactly who they were, or what was their object, for the tyrants were most careful in what they said, only stating that they had been thrown on the coast by contrary winds, and were in great want of provisions. The soldiers of Margarita continued their march to the port where Aguirre was, with a few of his friends, who were not ill, the rest being hid below decks on board the vessel. They saluted each other, when Aguirre told them that he had come from Pirú in consequence of having heard of great discoveries to be made on the lower part of the Marañon, and, having lost himself through adverse circumstances, it had pleased God that he should arrive at this island, so that he might not perish, as he and his people would have done (the sick, whom he showed, as well as the healthy), if his voyage had continued much longer. He begged of them, for the love of God, to do him the favour to send some meat and other provisions to meet the present necessities, that .

money was ready to pay what they might further require, and that they should soon sail for Nombre de Dios, on their way back to Pirú.

3. The citizens condoled with them on their sufferings, which Aguirre well knew how to represent. They ordered two bullocks to be killed (the first they could lay hands on), and expressed a wish that they had more to offer to Aguirre, who, blandly accepted the offering, made them presents in return, giving to one Gaspar Hernandez a scarlet cloak trimmed with gold lace ; thus commencing the treachery he intended to him and to the rest, letting him know that they came rich from Pirú, that they were frank and liberal, and that others from the town should come and see them.

Aguirre, having discovered the good disposition of the messengers to forward his schemes, added to the present of the cloak, a silver-gilt cup. They were so pleased and satisfied, that they made up their minds to remain there that night. They, therefore, sent a letter to the city, informing Don Juan de Villandrando, the governor of the island, what had passed, telling him who the people were that had come, that they came from Pirú having lost their way, that they only wished to purchase provisions and return to Pirú, and that it appeared that they had much money and other riches, as he would see by the scarlet cloak, and the large silver cup that had been given them.

4. Although Diego Tirado and other soldiers had reached the town, the people had not considered it necessary to give them any particular welcome, until the letter arrived, when they at once believed what Tirado had said (he being very quiet as to their real object).

The governor and cabildo gave instant orders (spurred on by the reward of good pay) to send provisions to them, and many of the inhabitants wished to make a visit to the new comers ; but it was thought more prudent that a few only should go. The governor, one alguazil, named Manuel

Rodriguez, one regidor, Andres de Salamanca, and three or four of the more important inhabitants of the city, determined to visit Aguirre.

They set off a little after midnight, so as not to travel in the very hot sun, which is always oppressive in that island, and journeyed to the port where Aguirre was. They were followed and joined by more people on the road than was at first arranged, who desired to see the strangers, and they all arrived at their destination at daybreak. Aguirre had his troops well armed and below decks, on board the brigantine, so that they were not seen that night.

When the governor and his party arrived, Aguirre, with some attendants, went out to meet him. When the governor dismounted, Aguirre approached, showing him the greatest respect and submission, and if the governor had permitted him to kiss his feet, he would readily have done so. The soldiers did the same to the citizens, and took charge of their horses, with great reverence, taking them to tie up under some trees, rather distant, so that, when the governor and his friends needed them, they could not be readily got.

5. The governor embraced Aguirre, when he knew he was the commanding officer, and with other courteous intimations offered him his personal services, his house, and all in it, for himself and his soldiers. Aguirre replied with honied words and courtly thanks, in which some time was passed, standing. Aguirre considered he was losing valuable time in what he intended to do, so, leaving the governor and the inhabitants occupied with his soldiers, he left the party, saying that he had occasion to go on board the brigantine, where he ordered the soldiers to be in readiness, the moment he ordered them to come on shore. He then returned to the shore, and joined the governor, to whom he showed great apparent devotion and friendship, and, when he found a proper occasion, he said, " Señor, the soldiers from Peru, who are so much attached to a martial life, and inter-

ested in these Indian campaigns, are more desirous of being
well armed than of dressing in fine clothing, although they
always have more than they want; so I beseech you to
allow them to come on shore with their arms and arquebusses
to exercise, and at the same time they can purchase some
things they require from your people."

The governor was a young man, and desiring to see
them and their firearms, he replied that he granted the
request; and had he been an old one and used to arms, he
would have done the same, if only for curiosity's sake.
But, in truth, when he gave his consent, it was of but little
importance, for he was surrounded by the traitors; and had
he had any suspicion of their designs, and desired to escape,
he could not have done it, or have done otherwise than
Aguirre chose. So, with the governor's permission, the traitor
went on board again, and said to the Marañones, " Mark me
well, my Marañones, sharpen your swords, and clean the
arquebusses, for they must be damp, from being at sea. You
have the governor's permission to go on shore armed, and if
he had not given it, you might have taken it."

The soldiers then came on deck and saluted the governor,
by firing their arquebusses, and showing that their arms consisted of lances, halberds, and arquebusses, more than they
had in their hands.

CHAP. XXVIII.

1. *Aguirre makes prisoners of the governor, alcalde, and their companions.*
—2. All the traitors march towards the city with the governor; the
maestro del campo takes possession of the city in the name of Aguirre.
—3. Aguirre enters the city, and robs the royal treasury.—4. He
continues his insolence, by a thousand threats.

1. This being done, Aguirre returned on shore to the
governor, to thank him on the part of the soldiers for the

permission he had given them to land, when he shortly returned on board (for the volcano of his treasons, which
burned within his breast, prevented him from being in repose for a moment anywhere), to tell the soldiers what they
had to do.

It did not appear to the governor to be prudent to allow
so many armed men to be there ; so he stepped on one side
with his followers, and debated how they might disarm
them, being really ignorant of Aguirre's intentions, for they
were not accustomed to tumultuous or mutinous people.
Whether this discussion of the governor's as to disarming,
proceeded from covetousness, or from fear, we cannot say,
but we think it was more likely the latter.

The traitor Aguirre caused his men to land well armed,
and in order of battle, and marched to where the governor
and his friends stood.   He then changed the tone and
manner he had previously used, and said, " We, Señores,
as already stated, are returning to Pirú, where tumults and
wars are not wanting, and we are informed, that you have the
idea that we do not go to serve the king, and that you wish
to stay our voyage and take our arms from us, also that it is
certain you do not intend to treat us with hospitality ; so,
Señores, you will consider yourselves our prisoners ; but you
must be active (you being our prisoners) in ordering all we
may require to be given to us, for our voyage."

This caused a tumult amongst the governor's party, and
they went back a few paces, saying, " What is all this ?
what is all this ?" putting their hands to their swords, as if in
defence ; but this was in vain, for the traitors surrounded
them, presented lances, partisans, and arquebusses to their
breasts, and thus they were made prisoners ; when Aguirre,
his captains and soldiers, advanced and disarmed them,
taking also their staves of office, and their horses.   They
then mounted, and took possession of the passes, and roads,
so that no one could go to the city, and give information of

what had been done ; and if they met with any inhabitants, they disarmed them, robbed them of their horses, and brought them in on foot.

2. Aguirre then ordered (so that himself or soldiers might lose no time) the march to the city. He mounted the governor's horse, inviting him, if he pleased, to get up behind ; but the governor was so disconcerted and angry at seeing himself in such a position, that he refused the offer. Aguirre, seeing this, dismounted, saying : " Well, then, we will all go on foot;" and, having walked a short distance, they met his maestro del campo, and all the people of the other brigantine, who were on their march to join the traitor Aguirre. He was pleased to receive this addition to his own men, assuring himself the more that he would succeed in his designs. The two bands complimented each other on having imprisoned the authorities, and continued their way together to the town. While on the road (for he was tired of walking), Aguirre mounted the governor's horse, and invited him to get up behind. The governor, seeing he got nothing by being angry, and feeling the pain of going on foot, chose the least evil, and got up behind, Aguirre being in the saddle ; and so they travelled, disarming all the people they met, and taking their horses, thus obliging them to return on foot.

Martin Perez, who was well mounted, went in advance, with a chosen party, to take possession of the city in Aguirre's name, which he did on St. Magdalen's day, on a Monday (a bitter one for the inhabitants) at noon, the soldiers shouting, " Long live Aguirre! liberty, liberty! long live Aguirre!" They were highly excited, and running through the streets, went to the fort, which was open, and which they took possession of. Some of them went in parties about the streets, taking arms from all who had them, and treating the people with great insolence.

3. Thus were these ministers of Satan occupied, and the

city was in a fearful tumult, when Aguirre entered with his prisoners, and went straight to the fort, leaving the prisoners under a strong guard. He presently came out, with his soldiers, to the plaza, where they commenced chopping at the *rollo*[1] with axes, but as it was thick, and made of very hard guayacan wood, it was like cutting at flint, so that the steel flew from the hatchets, while the *rollo* received no particular harm, and some prognosticated that it would remain there, as representing justice, and the name of the king, by whom it had been erected; and not by traitors. The great hardness of the wood was attributed to that cause. However this might be, the *rollo* remained standing with honour.

Aguirre, hating the name of the king, then passed onwards with his soldiers to the royal treasury, and, without waiting for the keys, or for the officers to give him an account, he broke the doors to pieces, and robbed a large quantity of gold and pearls, being the king's fifths and the royal revenues; his men also destroyed the books, containing the accounts of the treasury.

The traitor, now that he saw himself master of the city, issued a proclamation, under pain of death, that all the inhabitants of the island should appear before him with all their arms, offensive and defensive, and that no one should leave the city under the same penalty. He then ordered a pipe of wine, of more than forty arrobas,[2] to be brought to the fort, from the store of a merchant, so that his soldiers might drink and be merry. They emptied the pipe of wine in two hours.

4. The traitor was informed that a merchant, named Gaspar de Plazuela, had ordered a vessel belonging to him, that was coming from the island of Santo Domingo, to be

[1] A column of wood or stone, often erected by the Spaniards as an emblem of jurisdiction.

[2] Arroba = 25 lbs.

concealed; so he caused the merchant to be arrested, and
ordered him to be killed, if the vessel did not make its
appearance.

He ordered some of his most trusty soldiers to prevent
the inhabitants from hiding their wares and other property,
by visiting all the houses, and making a list of all they
found, especially of goods, wine, and provisions, commanding, under the severest penalties, that nothing should be
taken from the sequestered property.

This was done by his satellites, and even more, for they
took all the silk and linen clothing, and much wine and eatables, filling the fort with some, and taking the rest to
rooms, stores, and shops, whose owners were commanded,
under pain of death, not to remove the smallest portion.

Aguirre possessed himself of a certain quantity of merchandize, which was the property of the king, dividing it
amongst his soldiers. He ordered that all the canoes and
piraguas in the island should be brought to his port, with
the intention of breaking them all up, so that no one should
leave the island, and give notice of his proceedings. Thus
ended the work of the first day, and then they retired to rest.

The traitor found this island in the most prosperous state,
full of provisions, merchandize, and money, and most abundant in pearls, for in the past years the pearl fishery here,
and in the neighbouring island of Cubagua, had been very
successful. In consequence of the depredations of these
tyrants, it sank from a state of great prosperity, and has
not raised its head from that time.

Great indeed was the grief of the inhabitants at seeing
their governor and alcalde prisoners, their wives captives,
their daughters abused, their homes burnt, their estates and
lands sacked, their cattle slain; and this grief was augmented,
seeing that all this misery was brought about by the hands
of Christians, who were not ignorant of the crimes they were
committing, before God, and by a traitor who was lost to

Christian feelings.   They throw all the blame of this
terrible state of things on the covetousness of the governor,
who, if he had not been tempted to leave the city, as he did,
might have defended it; but as he went, he was made
prisoner, and so he remained.

CHAP. XXIX.

1. *For the love of a roving life, like that which these traitors led, some
soldiers of the island join them, which causes no little detriment.—
2. Aguirre sends to take a ship that was in Maracapana, belonging
to the Provincial of Santo Domingo, but fails.—3. The Provincial
of Santo Domingo determines to go in his ship, to the port of Burburata, and other parts, to give notice of the proceedings of Aguirre.
Aguirre orders provisions to be collected.—4. Aguirre addresses the
people of the island with feigned words, and even with lies.*

1. The evil example, treasons and roving life of the
tyrants, was the cause that some of the soldiers belonging to
the city and island followed their example, having the same
inclinations, and not being punished for their violence,
robberies, and insolence, like unto the soldiers of the traitor,
for such had become their trade; they were rather favoured
by Aguirre, particularly those who exceeded the others in
mischief, and boasted that they were against the king.
Aguirre considered this a most important political element,
that the more culpable his soldiers were, the firmer hold had
he on them, and that they would not leave his protection,
fearing the justice of the king.   So some soldiers, on the
island, determined to put themselves under Aguirre's
banner, offering to follow him wherever he went, and to lay
down their lives as his vassals, and with no less loyalty than
those followers whom he had brought with him.   The tyrant
gladly admitted them into his band, advancing their pay out
of the government funds he had robbed.   Thus he bound

them to serve him, as they had promised, for any other conduct would have cost them their heads. He then gave them permission to become as great villains as the rest, and this was exactly what they desired. They joined the other soldiers, and led them to those spots, of which they knew, where the inhabitants had hidden some of their property, merchandize, clothes, jewels, and strings of pearls. They effected these robberies secretly, and divided the plunder; but these acts were the cause of much greater evils, destruction, and cruelties than if they had merely joined in the forays; for as these fellows knew every corner of the island, for it was not a large one, they gave information on all points, showing to the Marañones, the estates where some persons had fled to, or had their wives and children, as they thought, in safety.

Amongst other things these new soldiers informed Aguirre that, in the port and small village of Maracapana, there was at that time a provincial of the order of Santo Domingo, named fray Francisco Montesinos, with certain settlers and soldiers, occupied in the conversion of the Indians, whom his majesty had committed to his charge; who had a fine, large, and well armed ship, which could be easily taken and brought to the island, and would serve them well for their voyage to Nombre de Dios.

This was just such a piece of information as would please the tyrant, and no time was lost in getting one of the brigantines ready, with eighteen soldiers, under the command of a captain named Pedro de Monguia, with a negro as pilot, who knew the navigation of the coast well. They were ordered not to touch anywhere, but to sail direct to where the provincial was, to take possession of the ship, and bring it to Margarita.

Monguia started, and just outside the port he fell in with Plazuela's vessel (until the arrival of which, its owner was to be detained in prison), which he sent in, after having boarded it, and Diego Hernandez, a Portuguese, with three companions, devoted to Aguirre, entered the port of Margarita; so this saved the life of Plazuela.

Monguia continued his route, and when nearly within sight of the port of Maracapana, he and some of the soldiers weighed the matter they were upon (thinking they ought not to be so vile and wickedly intentioned), and decided that their lives would be in safer keeping if they remained with the provincial, than if they returned to Aguirre. They resolved to inform the provincial of all they knew; for Monguia, and those who thought with him, considered that when fortune ceased to befriend them in the path the traitors were taking, their end would be miserable, and that they would all have cruel deaths.

3. All Monguia's companions did not think with him, for they were now so accustomed to the life they led with Aguirre, that it would be almost death to them to leave it; however, at last, some had to feign acquiescence, others were forced to submit, and they stood right for the provincial's ship, who received them with pleasure, but with calmness, until he was informed of the cause of their coming, and of the extraordinary news they continued to give him of what was going on at Margarita. This so excited him that, not trusting the soldiers (although they had made known to him their good intentions), he had them disarmed, and was most cautious of them, which they could not object to, as such conduct would have shown that they were not innocent, and without blame as to what might have happened up to this time; for they protested that the deeds of Aguirre did not meet with their approval. Fray Francisco Montesinos determined to sail immediately in his ship, accompanied by the Marañones, and to inform the authorities in the port of Burburata, which is under the government of Venezuela, and in the island of Santo Domingo, and, in his route, to pass by Margarita and see if he could not attack and rout Aguirre.

Aguirre had made up his mind, the moment he had despatched Monguia, that he had the provincial in his power, and that he and his band would get away to Nombre de Dios, with all celerity and ease. In order that there might be no delay, on the score of provisions, when the ship arrived, he ordered the inhabitants to bring six hundred sheep and some bullocks to him, so as to salt them down, also a large quantity of cassava, ready for the arrival of the ship.

The tyrant was anxious that his men should be well cared for in the houses in which he had placed them: he did not send his men to some of the principal houses, in order that their owners might send food to himself and to the soldiers of his guard, who were generally in the fort. During the day the soldiers were in their quarters, eating and drinking, also in evil doings; at night they slept in the fort in an open space, and as it was a hot country, each laid himself down wherever sleep overtook him, for they were so vile and common a lot, that they perhaps had never had better resting places.

4. Aguirre caused some of the principal, and nearly all the other inhabitants, to assemble in the *plazuela* of the fort, with the object of explaining away the disgust they felt of the soldiers quartered on them; and to console them with his accustomed untruthful expressions, saying, " My very dear friends, be it well known to you, that my arrival in this island with my companions is not with the object of settling here, neither to offend any of you, but rather to render you good service; for, God is my judge, that I did not intend to remain here more than four days; but my ships came in such a bad state, that it was impossible to continue my voyage with them, and, not finding here any other vessels to meet my wants, I am obliged, now that Providence has proportioned me the ship of the Reverend Father Provincial, to await its arrival, rather than build others, which would detain us

here a much longer time than if we waited for that of the
Provincial. But be you sure that, as soon as the ship
arrives, we will leave your country and continue our voyage, for which I have begged of you to prepare, without loss
of time, the necessary provisions for us ; and this has likewise been the reason, as I will explain to you, why I have
imprisoned the governor and other caballeros, so that there
might be greater facility and security that we could supply
our wants with our money ; for, as I have already often said,
I do not wish that either my soldiers or myself should take
these things, without paying the highest prices for them ; and
this I again repeat, for I well understand that you wish to be
most favourable to us, or that fearing us, you let us have what
we require at a lower price than the real value ; in the sale
of a fowl for two rials, the seller must be a loser, and by the
same rule in all the other provisions ; thus I command, that
for less than three rials and upwards, no fowl shall be sold
to a soldier, and in same proportion all other articles, and I
give my solemn word and honour that when I leave I will
give very ample satisfaction and reward for the kindness
you have shown, and intend to show us."

The inhabitants saw plainly that these words of Aguirre
were false, for it was evident that his acts belied his words ;
it was of little use to raise the prices of the various articles,
to those who had no idea of paying the just value, or who
even took what they required, without payment or even by
force, and often such things as the captains and soldiers
had no use for, merely to do evil to the poor inhabitants.

CHAP. XXX.

1. *Aguirre kills one of his captains. Four of his soldiers desert.*—2. *Two of the deserters found ; Aguirre orders them to be hung. He intends to kill a monk of the order of Santo Domingo.*—3. *Aguirre informs his soldiers how he intends to proceed in his tyrannies.*—4. *He places his brigantines with their bows towards the shore, fearing that his soldiers might desert ; and he destroys the houses and estates of an inhabitant, who had fled.*

1. Aguirre became uneasy and fearful of one Enriquez de Orellana, whom he had made captain of the ammunition, and this without more cause than he had found on other occasions, when he wished to destroy any one: even if what had been reported to Aguirre was true, that Orellana had got drunk, on the day they came to Margarita. However, true or not, he ordered him to be hung, without allow-ing him to confess, although he begged for it. Aguirre gave the command of the ammunition to one Anton Llamoso, who had been sergeant of his guard, and so faithful was he to Aguirre, that he held the post until the death of the tyrant.

Some of the soldiers saw how insecure their lives were, for when they appeared to be in the greatest favour with Aguirre, he, on the most trivial suspicion, made away with them ; so they bethought them how to escape from him. They were delayed in their project, seeing that the island was so small, and so well known to the inhabitants, whom Aguirre had so subjected, that he would oblige them, under the severest penalties, to search out and capture the soldiers, when they were missed ; also that day and night, their chief was most vigilant with his guards and sentinels, placed everywhere in the town, and on the roads leading from it, so that it was next to impossible to escape with safety. However, with all these difficulties in sight, they determined to try ; so four soldiers, two and two, named Francisco Vasquez, Gonzalo de Zuñiga, Juan de Villatoro, and Luis Sanchez del Castillo, at a certain hour of the night, fled from the city.

When this was known to Aguirre, he was furious and raved like a madman, foaming at the mouth with rage and passion, for he believed that if he did not give himself up to such like demonstrations, and give peremptory orders to find them, all his men would desert and leave him.

He instantly commanded that the strictest search might be made by the inhabitants, against whom (so that it should be the more effective) and against the governor and the rest whom he had in confinement, he spoke most ferociously, and, with a thousand bitter oaths, told them that they had secreted his soldiers, and consequently knew where they were ; and that if they had not, the men were on the island, and could not escape from it ; and if they did not wish to see the entire destruction of the island, they would go and find the deserters ; and, independently of giving him the greatest pleasure, he promised to give two hundred dollars reward for bringing to him each of the four soldiers.

2. He, moreover, threatened to execute the governor, if he did not issue his mandate to find the soldiers. This the governor had to do, knowing that the tyrant was as good as his word, or even more so. Aguirre sent in search of the deserters, with certain of the inhabitants who knew the country, some soldiers who had recently joined him, and also some of his Marañones.

Some in fear of Aguirre's vengeance, others in the hope of reward, after much search, found Juan de Villatoro and Luis Sanchez, who, when they were brought into the presence of the tyrant (without allowing them confession), were immediately hung ; and Aguirre reproached them with ferocity, whilst they were being executed, for having intended to return to the service of the king. In confirmation of what he uttered, after they were dead, he commanded that an inscription should be put over each, with these words: "These men have been executed, because they were faithful vassals of the king of Castille." Then, with his serpent's tongue, he said over the dead bodies : " Let us now see if the king of Castille will give you life again."

In sight of such proceedings against the two soldiers, many who were thinking of deserting, were shaken in their resolve and began to vacillate, fearing similar punishment.

Whilst the execution was going on, a monk of the order of Santo Domingo passed the spot, and when Aguirre perceived him, he ordered him to be killed ; which would have been done, had not the inhabitants who were present, succeeded by their prayers and intreaties in saving his life. For a time the monk was spared, but shortly he fell a victim, as we shall see.

3. When Aguirre was not occupied in these cruelties, or in designing them, he made known to his soldiers the sort of justice (or rather injustice) he intended to deal out; promising himself that he would succeed in all he intended, by reason of the good principles he had inculcated in that island; and thus he told them repeatedly the manner he intended to command, and to dispose of affairs.

He said that one of the most necessary proceedings for the well-being and preservation of the Indies, was to cut the throats of all the monks they fell in with, of the orders of San Francisco and Santo Domingo, also those of the other orders, excepting the Mercedarios. He said that the monks disturbed the liberty that was necessary for the soldiers, for their conquests, and the subjection of the natives. Then he declared that he would execute, with cruel torments, all bishops, viceroys, presidents, oidores,[1] governors, lawyers, and procuradores, who came in his way, for that all these persons had entirely destroyed the Indies. After these, he thought

---

[1] Auditors or judges of the Royal Audiences.

S

of destroying all the caballeros of noble blood, because they were likewise opposed, as a matter of duty, to the vices of the common soldiers. After these he would destroy, without sparing one, all public women, and even those who were not chaste ; having come to this determination by the hatred he felt for Doña Inez de Atienza (for we have seen that she was of this last class), on account of the many troubles she had caused him. It was not likely that these were mere words, for, during his tyrannous lifetime, he executed all who came within his grasp ; for he was the cause of the death of his governor Pedro de Ursua; after that of Don Fernando; then a priest was his victim; then Doña Inez, and many others; he was also the murderer of monks; of the governor of Margarita, as we shall see; of an alcalde, and of a regidor; and if he did not cause more deaths, it was because he had not the opportunity.

Similar feelings were entertained by many of his soldiers, if only to follow his execrable example. Some time was passed in these councils, and also in boasting, in mustering his forces, and instructing them in the art and subtleties of war, which they were to employ in the attack, retreat, and defence, letting them know that he did not intend to give battle to any captain sent against him, excepting to the king in person, because, as to all the rest, he intended to rout them by his stratagems, and knowledge of the art of war.

4. Until he received the news of what had occurred in Maracapana, to those he had sent to take the provincial's ship, although some time had passed, he did not consider it a great delay, feeling confident that the ship would be brought to him. But he still distrusted the faithfulness of his soldiers, and feared that they might become disgusted with the life they led, and might take possession of the brigantines (or some of the inhabitants of Margarita might do the same), and, running away with them, give information against him. He, therefore, had the brigantines placed with

their bows in shore, intending, in case the ship of the provincial did not arrive, to hurry on the completion of another that was building in the port, and thus leave the island.

At this time an inhabitant of the city, named Alonzo Perez de Aguilar, not liking the neighbourhood of Aguirre, laid his plans for escaping from the town, and afterwards from the island ; and, although Aguirre used every means, in the hope of arresting him, Aguilar escaped. The traitor, not being able to have his person, vented his tiger's rage upon the houses belonging to Aguilar. He went, accompanied by some of his satellites, to destroy the houses, as if they had been the property of a traitor to his king ; he caused them to be pillaged, unroofed, and then levelled to the ground, so that there was not one stone upon another, and strewed the ground with salt: this vile spirit also caused the slaying of the cattle, the destruction of the estates, lands, and all he could find belonging to Aguilar.

CHAP. XXXI.

1. *Aguirre kills a captain, named Juan de Turriaga, and buries him with pomp.*—2. *Aguirre threatens the people of Margarita with his vengeance, in case the provincial of Santo Domingo takes his men in Maracapana.*—3. *The provincial's ship is seen making for the island, the traitor prepares for defence.*—4. *Aguirre, observing that the provincial's ship had anchored, puts the inhabitants into the fort as prisoners, and determines to kill the governor, and his companions.*

1. Aguirre had not recovered from the rage in which he had perpetrated his last horrors, when it was augmented on his being informed that one of his captains, named Juan de Turriaga, had shown himself friendly to the soldiers, by having some poor men at his table, who held him in great respect, for his goodness of disposition. As flowers are rendered poisonous by the pestilential spider, so Aguirre

said of this captain that he was his enemy, and acted in this friendly way to the poor men, in order to make a party, with the object of killing him. Aguirre, having made up his mind, doomed Turriaga, and, to strike terror into the hearts of soldiery and people, he arranged that Turriaga should die. He delegated this bloody act to his maestro del campo, Martin Perez, as a faithful satellite to his tyrant chief. Perez selected some of his friends among the soldiers, who, with arquebuses and other arms, went stealthily one night to Turriaga's quarters, whom they found at evening meal with some of his comrades. Turriaga, on seeing Martin Perez enter, rose from table, to receive him with the honour due to his rank, as maestro del campo. Turriaga had scarcely uncovered himself, bowing and approaching Perez, when the arquebuses were discharged at Turriaga by some, then others rushed at him with their lances and swords, when he fell to the ground, dead, bathed in his own blood. The murderers then sallied out of the house, communicating to Aguirre that his enemy was no more.

Early the next morning Aguirre (for Turriaga was a Biscayan, like himself, and he wished to show respect to one who had followed and served him) gave orders that he should be buried with all pomp, as it is the custom to bury captains, and other distinguished soldiers. Aguirre himself was present at the funereal honours, with his troops, showing all the signs of mourning, with arms trailing, and muffled drums. It was the opinion of the better portion of the soldiery that the tyrant Aguirre had killed this captain more because he was a good, affable, and generous man, than for any reason he had to suspect him in any way.

2. The tyrant began to be anxious about the delay of Monguia with the provincial's ship from the port of Maracapana, for already many more days had passed than he had given him. He imagined that the provincial had killed Monguia, or had imprisoned him and his party. These

thoughts changed his previous feelings of joy, that he should
take the provincial's ship, into sadness.   His suspicions
caused him to bellow out his ungovernable rage with
horrible threats, saying to his soldiers and the inhabitants,
that if that friar (the provincial) had imprisoned or killed
his people, he would resort to unheard of modes of vengeance,
slaying, with every species of cruelty that could be thought of,
all the men and women in that part of the country (yet, even
if this act had been committed, they were not culpable);
he would not even spare the child at the breast, but would
wash the public places and streets with their blood, also
that the water courses of the city of Margarita should run
with blood: after which, not one stone should be left standing on another, all the houses should be burnt, a thousand
monks should be sacrificed, with the most painful deaths;
and if the provincial, the Friar Francisco Montesinos, fell into
his hands, he would flay him alive, and make a drum of his
skin, as an example to all.   This wicked one also ordained
that after death he should be flayed, and that a drum should
be made of his skin, in the wars of heretics against catholics.
These and other threats, with the acts he consummated,
rendered the poor inhabitants of Margarita very sorrowful,
so that they looked upon their lives as not worth a maravedi,
and felt their condition to be hopeless when they saw the
tyrant's ferocious countenance, the violent movements of his
person, stamping on the ground, and foaming at the mouth,
when he spoke to them.   All that he said met with the approbation of his captains and soldiers.

3. Such was the terrible situation of the inhabitants of
Margarita, after the provincial had left Maracapana in his
ship, and had given information along all the coast of Cu-
maná, in the port of our Lady of Caravalleda, two leagues
to the east of the port of the country of Caraccas, called
La Guayra, and in the port of Burburata.   The provincial then returned to Maracapana, and to the island of

Margarita, with the intention of trying his fortune, and seeing if he and his followers could not defeat the tyrant.
When his ship was seen in the distance, from the city of
Margarita, as if coming from the port of Burburata, the
news was given to Aguirre, who thought the ship was being
brought to him as a prize. This calmed the fury he was in,
in some measure, and mitigated the terror of the inhabitants,
for they feared the tyrant would put his dreadful threats
into execution upon mere suspicion only.

At that time a piragua, with a negro from Maracapana,
entered the port of the city (which was then near the shore,
although afterwards the city was removed three leagues
inland, where it now is), bringing news to Aguirre of all
that had happened there to his soldiers, and that his men,
with others brought by the provincial, had come to attack
him. On hearing this news, his fury was redoubled, and he
added to former threats, others more terrible, against the provincial and his followers.   He began to put these threats into
execution before the ship anchored, by seizing the inhabitants,
their wives and children, imprisoning them in the fort,
putting the greater number in irons, and doubling those of
Juan de Villandrando, and others who were already in prison.
He repeated to these unfortunate persons how he intended
to serve them, and that the water-courses of the town
should run with blood.

The provincial's ship was now nearing the island, and,
judging from the course it was steering, Aguirre was told
it would go into a place five leagues distant from the city,
known as Puerto de Piedras.

4. With this information, and having the ship in sight,
the tyrant put himself on the defensive.   He also caused
horsemen to be placed at certain distances, from the city
to Puerto de Piedras, so that when the ship came to anchor,
they should make signs one to another, and he would thus
be informed without loss of time.   That he might not be in

want of officers to accompany him, when he went in person
to the defence of Puerto de Piedras, he gave the post of
alferez-general to Alonso de Villena, who held that appointment under Don Fernando.

The spies, like true traitors, shortly made it known to the
tyrant that the provincial's ship had anchored in Puerto de
Piedras. This was not pleasant information for Aguirre,
but he began to arm his men, to go against the friar; and
such was his rage, that pious Catholic ears were horrified at
his blasphemous and heretical words. When all was ready
to march to the front, a most barbarous thought came upon
him, so as to terrify his soldiers afresh, and force them to
follow him, and thus prevent their desertion to the king's
side. It was as follows (and not without the concurrence of
the more wickedly intentioned of his captains and soldiers),
that before they went, they should kill the governor, the
alcalde Manuel Rodriguez, the alguazil mayor Cosme de
Leon, one Caceres the regidor, and one Juan Rodriguez, a
servant of the governor's, who were in prison. This vile act
having been determined on, that very night, when all the
lights of the town were extinguished, he ordered these prisoners, who were confined high up in a room in the fortress,
to come down to a saloon. The prisoners suspected his vile
object, and death-like was their fear; which, being perceived
by Aguirre (who always liked to be present at these scenes), he
began to console them with feigned words, telling them to
have no fear; that if there were any among them who cared for
his life, and had faith in what he promised, he would give his
word, that although the friar had with him as many trees
and thistles as there were on the island (for the island was
full of such, and very prickly, as I can well vouch for), and
they fought against him, and if in the battle all his companions were slain, none of those he had as prisoners should
suffer, or be in any danger.

CHAP. XXXII.

1. *Aguirre arranges for the execution of the governor and his companions in captivity.—2. They kill the governor and his companions. Aguirre summons his soldiers to see the dead bodies, and makes his observations upon the matter.—3. He explains, and gives his reasons for their death.—4. Aguirre orders the bodies to be buried, and sends the inhabitants back to prison. He leaves his maestro del campo in charge of the city, and then sallies forth against the provincial.*

1. The prisoners were slightly consoled by Aguirre's words, although the very reverse succeeded as to anything in their favour ; for he was a false traitor, and never kept his word, and if he did anything, it was the very reverse of what he promised, as we shall see in what happened concerning the prisoners. He caused the rest of the inhabitants, and their families, to leave the fortress, so that they might have no idea of his designs. It is said that the principal mover in this affair was a soldier, one Gonzalo Hernandez, a Portuguese, a friend of Aguirre's, who informed the traitor that Don Juan and the other prisoners were conspiring against him, and that they had sent messengers and arquebusses to the provincial, begging of him to land his people, and give Aguirre battle.

The traitor (irritated by what the Portuguese said to him), and fearing the provincial, thought that it was not good policy to leave enemies in the rear, although they were prisoners, so he determined to kill them before he left the city, and thus to meet his ecclesiastical foe, a warlike churchman. It was nearly midnight, and the hour for such deeds, when he ordered one Francisco de Carrion, a mestizo, his alguazil, to go quickly with certain soldiers, and strangle the governor, and his imprisoned companions, who were in the lower apartment. This alguazil, and his men, lost no time in obeying the traitor's wishes ; they quickly got hold of some negroes, cords, and other articles necessary for perpetrating the deed, and, descending to the lower apartment, they told the prisoners to pray to God for his mercy, and to show such contrition for their sins as became Christians, for that they were about to die.

2. The governor's expectation that Aguirre would keep his word (in a matter of such gravity) gave him confidence that the traitor would not break it, nor cut short his days so soon: and he replied by asking what this meant, for that only a short time since the general had left them, and had given them his word, not only that they should not be killed, but that no harm should come to them. The alguazil, and his men said, notwithstanding what had been told them, that they must die, and advised them to pray to God, which was what they ought to do.

The unfortunate prisoners did so, seeing that the bloody business was about to take place, and with greater speed than was necessary; for these ministers of wickedness began by strangling the governor, after him the alcalde Manuel Rodriguez, then the alguazil Don Cosme, who was crippled in his hands and feet. The bodies were then laid together, and covered with some mats so as to hide them, when the murderers went up stairs to where Aguirre was, and, having given an account of what they had done, they showed demonstrations of pleasure, as if what they had done had been for the service of God.

As it was near the middle of the night, the traitor considered it would be as well to inform his soldiery of what had taken place; so he called his men into the lower room, where the dead bodies were, and, by the light of many candles, he ordered the mats to be raised. The bodies were exposed, and he, pointing to the corpses, spoke thus:

"Well do you see, O Marañones! in the bodies now before your eyes, that, independently of the crimes you committed in the river Marañon, by slaying your governor Pedro de Ursua, and his lieutenant Don Juan de Vargas, by

T

making a prince of Don Fernando, and giving your oath of allegiance to him as such, you have divested yourselves of all rights in the kingdom of Castille, you have forsworn allegiance to the king Don Philip, by swearing to make perpetual war upon him, and you have signed your names to the act. You afterwards added crime to crime; you executed your own prince and lord, many captains and soldiers, a priest, and a noble lady; and, having arrived at this island, you have forcibly taken possession of it, dividing the property found in it amongst yourselves, that which belonged to the king Don Philip, as well as that of individuals. You have destroyed the books of the treasury, and committed sundry and divers wickednesses. Now you have killed another governor, an alcalde, a regidor, an alguazil mayor, as well as other persons, whose bodies you now have before your eyes.

"So now you must open your eyes, and see each for himself. Be not deceived by any vain confidence; for having committed so many, and such grave and atrocious crimes, be ye sure that ye are not safe in any part of the world, excepting with me; for supposing the king were to pardon you, the relations and friends of the dead would follow you, and take vengeance. Thus I counsel you not to leave me, to sell your lives dearly when the occasion offers, and to let all be of one mind; for against such a union, all the force that may be sent against you will be of little avail. Let each man mark well what I have said, for it is a question of life and death."

4. As soon as his speech was finished, he ordered that two graves should be made, and the bodies were buried therein. In order that the inhabitants might not have one peaceful night in their houses, he commanded (for it was now about two in the morning) that their wives and children should be thrust into the fortress, to their great fear and affliction, and he had them secured as they had previously been. They

had their suspicions as to what had taken place, and that Don Juan de Villandrando and his companions had been killed, although Aguirre and his followers denied what they had done. The traitor left the prisoners in the fortress, in charge of his maestro del campo Martin Perez, and, at daybreak, he marched with eighty arquebusiers to Punta de Piedras, where the provincial had anchored.

Martin Perez, with the Marañones who had been left to guard the fortress and town, caused a feast to be made that day, when Aguirre departed, which was on a Sunday. They had his tables spread with great show and profusion, the transports blew joyous blasts, the generous wine ran freely, which made them talk merrily, and excuse themselves for what had been done. But this, as will be seen, cost the life of the maestro del campo.

CHAP. XXXIII.

1. *The people of the port of Burburata send tidings to the governor of Venezuela, and to the cities of his government, and that of Merida, concerning the acts of the traitor.*—2. *Pedro Bravo de la Molina sends information to the Royal Audience of Santa Fé, and to the other cities on the road.*—3. *Preparations are made by Pedro Bravo de la Molina, in the city of Merida, to resist the traitor, if necessary.*— 4. *The licenciate, Pablo Collado, is not unmindful of his duties, in the towns under his government.*

1. The padre Fray Francisco Montesinos, having advised the people of the port of Burburata as to Aguirre's doings, they likewise sent on the news to the towns in the government of Venezuela, particularly to the governor, the licenciate Pablo Collado, who was just then in the city of Tocuyo, and who sent orders to the men of Burburata to send their wives and children away, as well as their property, in case Aguirre should come there. This order was hardly

necessary for the men of Burburata, seeing that they were dwelling on the sea-shore, and were few in number, without means of defence, for they had, already, broken up their homes, and put their families in safety, as soon as they received the news from the provincial, the men returning to the port of Burburata. The governor sent advices to the city of Trujillo, recently settled by Captain Diego Garcia de Paredes, to that of Merida, also a recently settled jurisdiction, governed by Captain Pedro Bravo de la Molina, a man of noble blood, and who gave proofs of the same in all the acts of his life, but more especially in what concerned Aguirre.

The governor of Venezuela ordered both cities to be prepared for defence (as it was reported that the traitor might pass that way), begging of Pedro Bravo de la Molina, as he was out of his jurisdiction, to have all the soldiers ready that he could possibly get together, to go against Aguirre, which would be rendering a service to God as well as to the king, and to the governor it would be rendering a great service; and, as Diego Garcia de Paredes was in that city, retired with some soldiers who had separated from Collado's jurisdiction, on account of certain difficulties they had had with him in the city of Trujillo, shortly after Paredes had settled it, he begged of them to return at once to the city of Tocuyo; and he gave them his solemn word of honour that no more should be said relative to their former disagreements, but that he would be thankful to them for their assistance, seeing that he was menaced by the traitor.

2. The news having been received in the city of Merida by the governor, Pedro Bravo de la Molina, in the month of August, 1561, he immediately appointed certain of the citizens of that place, with a captain, to go to the town of San Cristoval (to which place it was not possible to go without a strong escort, on account of the warlike Indians who dwelt between one town and the other, in the valleys of the Bayla-

dores de la Guta, Saint Bartholomew, and other parts), to tell them the news, whence it could be sent to Tunja and Santa Fé (Bogotá) to the Royal Audience, to which Molina wrote, as well as to the Governor Pablo Collado, so that all the cities might be prepared to resist the traitor, should he enter these provinces. This being done, Pedro Bravo busied himself in making arrangements for the soldiers and inhabitants, whom he was to take with him to Venezuela, communicating to them his plans and stratagems of war, particularly if the traitor had a large force, that of the jurisdiction of Venezuela being small to resist him. The traitor might arrive at the city of Merida, where it was necessary there should be a guard of sturdy men (in case they should be obliged to go to Venezuela) to guard that town against any rising that might occur on the part of the natives, for the country had but lately been settled.

3. Molina sent some soldiers from the city, to be on the look-out at certain distances on the road, and the post from Trujillo would advise him, as to Aguirre's advance and intentions. He also ordered that some soldiers should go onwards to Tocuyo, where they would know (because there they would find the governor in person) when the traitor might land, advising the governor, Don Pablo Collado, not to diminish his force in sending him news, for that he wanted more men than he already had.

The inhabitants and soldiers of Merida were perfectly agreed (and I make this distinction because in these lands we call *vecinos*, those settlers or inhabitants of the towns who have *encomiendas* of Indians, all the rest being transient, and called soldiers), and were of one mind, that their persons and property, even to the last maravedi, should be placed at the service of their king and lord, whereby it was well known to the world what loyal vassals the sovereign had, and how desirous they were to shed their blood in defence of his royal crown, especially against those who had rebelled against him.

Don Pedro Bravo gave sincere thanks to all the in-habitants, on his own part, and on that of the king.

4. During this time the governor of Venezuela was not idle in the cities of Tocuyo and Barquisimeto, doing all in his power to protect his government; for it was apparent to every one that no means of defence should be omitted, see-ing that Aguirre had a large number of well-armed fol-lowers, and that the numbers of the royal forces were small to cope with him, so that although prepared, they were in a state of consternation.

CHAP. XXXIV.

1. *Preparations ordered by the Royal Audience of Santa Fé, and officers appointed.—2. Orders are issued that the people of the various cities of the kingdom shall be ready for all exigencies, and what the governor Pedro Bravo de la Molina has to do in Merida.—3. The governments of Popayan, Santa Martha, and Carthagena, are ordered to collect troops, and various opinions as to sallying forth against the traitor. —4. Investigations are made, to see if there are, in the kingdom, any soldiers connected with the Peruvian mutineers. The royal seal guarded in Santa Fé.*

1. It was the beginning of the month of September of the same year, 1561, when the news arrived at the city and audience of Santa Fé. The oidores and licenciados Alonso de Grageda, Melchor Perez de Arteaga, Diego de Villa-franca, and Angulo de Castejon were there. All the cities in the kingdom were in great commotion, on becoming ac-quainted with the cruelties committed by Aguirre, as well as by the great number of armed followers he had with him; so the oidores, without leaving anything undone to put a stop to these terrible excesses (for all this tierra firme was suffering on account of the rebellions that had happened in various parts

of Pirú), sent to all the cities and towns of the audiencia of the new kingdom,[1] commanding that men and arms should be in readiness, appointing as captain-general (in case it should be found necessary for him to go against the traitor) the Mariscal Don Gonzalo Ximenez de Quesada (who then only had this title and was regidor of the city, until the following year of 1568, when he received the title of adelantado of the new kingdom), a successful and valorous personage, and one whom the whole country respected for these qualities, and because he had discovered and conquered the country. Captain Hernan Vanegas was chosen as maestro del campo, a settler of the city of Santa Fé. He was from Cordova in Spain, a cavalier of high standing and bravery, of which he gave many proofs in the conquest of Santa Martha, and in his discoveries in the same kingdom, his conquests over the Panches, and in the founding of the city of Tocayma.

2. For captains of horse were nominated Juan de Cespedes, an inhabitant of Santa Fé, and Gonzalo Suarez Rondon, an inhabitant, and one of the founders, of Tunja ; as captain of infantry, Juan Ruiz de Orejuela of Santa Fé, but originally from Cordova in Castille, all conquistadores and founders in the new kingdom, as was also Gonzalo Rodriguez de Ledesma, native of Zamora in Spain, who, on this occasion, was named by the Royal Audience captain of the guard of the royal seal, which was in Santa Fé.

In each town a captain was named to be in charge of men, arms, and horses, so as to be in readiness if wanted. Letters of thanks were sent to the city of Merida, for the information afforded by Captain Pedro Bravo de la Molina, and abundance of provisions for the use of that part of the country, should the traitor go there. The people of Merida were ordered on no account to leave the city, although the gover-

---

[1] The kingdom of New Granada, then governed by the *Audiencia Real*, consisting of a president, and four *oidores* or judges.

nor of Venezuela should send for help, but to remain with all their people, advising the Royal Audience, by the post, of all the news that came to them respecting the landing of Aguirre; and if it happened (on account of the little opposition the traitor met with in the government of Venezuela) that Aguirre had the intention of passing into the kingdom of Santa Fé by the city of Merida, they were to take away all the provisions from the town and vicinity, and abandon it, for they were not in sufficient numbers to resist the army he had under his command.

3. The Royal Audience did not omit to advise the governments of Popayan, Santa Martha, and Carthagena, commanding their respective governors to be in readiness with their people, should help be required; and should the traitor come into their governments, to do their utmost against him, as became loyal vassals of the king.

All the cities of the new kingdom having collected their men, it was found (leaving a sufficient number to protect the towns of Santa Fé, Tunja, Velez, Pamplona, Ybague, Tocayma, Mariquita, and the town of San Cristoval) that there were one thousand five hundred soldiers, four hundred pikemen, more than two hundred arquebusiers, and the rest rodeleros (men armed with shields), and horsemen, ready and well found for the field. It was ordered that the people of each town should be practised in the art of war weekly, so that when required, they might be used to military affairs. All this being done, various opinions were expressed by the several officers and the old soldiers of Santa Fé and Tunja, as to the best plan of proceeding against the traitor, when the time came, some considering that the surest method was to await him in the *riñon* (kidney) of the kingdom, in the province of the city of Tunja towards Pamplona, where he would enter the settlements and vast valleys called the Zemiza, because it was an open plain country, where cavalry could act and provisions were abundant ; that neither one nor both of the oidores should be absent, so that the Audiencia should be there, representing the person of the king.

Others considered the best plan would be that the captain-general with his men (it not being necessary that any of the oidores should be of the party) should march to Pamplona, wait for Aguirre between that town and San Cristoval, in the valley of Cucuta, and give him battle in the open country ; for the traitor and his army would necessarily arrive fatigued and worn, having had to march over a very heavy country, and thus there were hopes of defeating him.

These discussions rose to such a pitch, and each party so loudly sustained its views, that it was feared some difficulties might arise, if the Royal Audience did not silence them at once, by informing them that for the present all that was required was that they should be merely in readiness. This stopped further discussion, but no expense was spared in arranging their arms, horses, and provisions, neither were splendid dresses and adornments, the fruits of vanity, forgotten, which are the usual accompaniments of a military life, in which the greater portion of their own money was expended, for the king did not give them a maravedi.[1]

[1] The poet Don Alonzo de Ercilla, the author of the *Araucana*, and one with whom " Spanish poetical genius and heroism were one feeling," heard of the atrocities of Aguirre at Lima, after he had left Chilé. He at once determined to go against the traitor, but arrived too late to share in the operations which led to Aguirre's overthrow.

In Canto xxxvi, part ii, of the *Araucana*, he says,—

" Costa a costa, y a veces engolfado
Llegue al Callao de Lima celebrado.
Estuve alli hasta tanto que la entrada
Por el gran Marañon hizo la gente,
Donde Lope de Aguirre en la jornada
Mas que Neron y Herodes inclemente
Paso tantos amigos por la espada,
Y a la querida hija juntamente,
No por otra razo y causa alguna—
Mas de para morir juntos a una.

4. It was considered of no little importance to make careful inquiries in all the provinces of the new kingdom, to see if there were any soldiers who had been concerned in the rebellions in Peru of Gonzalo Pizarro, Francisco Hernandez Giron, Alvaro de Oyon,[1] and other turbulent men, so as to keep a watch over them : for it was to be supposed that they had not forgotten their evil inclinations, and would rather join the traitor Aguirre, than the king's party.

During the time that these suspicions and fears of the traitor continued in the New Kingdom (which was from the period when they first received the information, to Christmas of that same year, when the news they desired came to them, that the traitor's army had been destroyed, and himself killed in the city of Barquisimeto), every night thirty armed men guarded the Seal of the Royal Audience, under command of Captain Ledesma.[2]

> Y aunque mas de dos mil millas havia
> De camino por partes despoblado,
> Luego de alli por mar tomè la via
> A mas larga carrera acostumbrado,
> Ya Panama llegue, dó el mismo dia
> La nueva por el ayre avia llegado
> Del desbarate y nucerte del tyrano,
> Saliendo mi trabajo y priesa envano."

Ercilla was then aged twenty-nine, and he had been eight years in America. After a long illness in Tierra Firme, he returned to Spain in 1562.

[1] A soldier who, a short time before, had excited a revolt in Popayan.

[2] The seal of the Royal Audience was received at Bogota, in the same way as if it had been the king of Spain himself. It is of silver, and very large, and is now deposited in the National Museum, at Bogota.

CHAP. XXXV.

1. *Aguirre marches with his soldiers to Punta de Piedras, whence he returns to the city. He is told unfavourable things of his maestro del campo.*—2. *Aguirre has his maestro del campo killed in the fortress. Some prisoners escape.*—3. *A horrible thing occurs to one Llamoso, relative to the body of the maestro del campo.*—4. *The Marañones and soldiers of the provincial see one another.*

1. Aguirre, with his eighty well-armed soldiers in good order for battle, left Margarita for Punta de Piedras, and, having arrived there, discovered that the provincial had set sail, and was steering towards the city. Aguirre marched back as quick as he could, so as to arrive before the ship, and be fully prepared for his enemy. The maestro del campo Martin Perez, hearing of Aguirre's return, went out to meet him, with the arquebusiers who had remained with him, and gave him a grand salute and joyous reception. They embraced each other, as if they had not met for a long time, entering arm in arm into the fortress, where Aguirre found the same order amongst the imprisoned inhabitants, as when he had departed.

One of his captains of infantry, named Christoval Garcia, who had been a caulker, either from the enmity he bore the maestro del campo, or because he desired to have his post, succeeded in discrediting him with Aguirre; for, knowing his chief's bitter and suspicious disposition, and that it would require but little to get him on bad terms with the maestro del campo, or even to have him killed; and giving a colour of truth to his malice, by an appearance of zeal for the honour of his general, he said to him that same day, that the maestro del campo harboured much evil in his heart, that he had asked many of his friends to kill Aguirre on the first opportunity, and to take the men and ships to France, for which purpose he had got his friends together, when they agreed to carry out his views ; they had had a great feast in the fortress, the moment Aguirre had left for Punta de Piedras, when the trumpets and arabales played, with other signs of rejoicing. He supplicated Aguirre that he would look to this matter, and not allow so open a treason to go further, for if he should lose his life, what would be the fate of his trusty followers?

2. Aguirre gave him his thanks, asking if he had any other witness to these doings. Garcia said, yes, that a little mestizo page of the maestro had been present at the conspiracy. The boy was brought into Aguirre's presence, most probably taught by Garcia, as to the answers he was to give, and said that he had been present at the whole of the proceedings.

Besides this, Aguirre was informed that, on the same day, when Martin Perez was in the plaza, the soldiers had spoken amongst themselves, saying, if anything should happen to Lope de Aguirre with the provincial's people, who was then to govern them? That this difficulty had been resolved by Martin Perez, who said : " Am not I here, and ready to serve you all ; I will do my duty right well, should the old man fail us." These two statements, whether false or true, were considered by Aguirre to be sufficient reasons for killing the maestro del campo, for which purpose he chose a little bearded monkey called Chaves, who, although still young, was learned in every species of villany, and some others of a similar stamp, belonging to his guard, and commanded them to kill Martin Perez (whom he sent for) the moment he came into the fortress. They were on the watch, and as soon as he came into the room where Aguirre was (unaware of the treason), to inquire what were his orders, the little Chaves came behind him, firing his arquebuss, and wounding him badly. The rest rushed on the victim with daggers and knives, wounding him in the head and body, so that his bowels and his brains were seen. The wretched maestro del campo, now in the agonies of death, wandered about the fortress with a portion of his brains and bowels out of his body, imploring confession with loud cries. The murderers followed him, when he fell, and Chaves rushed on him and cut his throat. These horrors, committed by these ministers of Satan, disturbed the inmates of the fortress, and the imprisoned inhabitants saw little else before them but the cruel fate of the maestro del campo; so they (both men and women, blinded by the fear of death) hid themselves in the upper rooms and other obscure parts of the fortress, and under their beds; and there were persons who broke open the windows of the turrets, so much strength did fear give them; and one Maria de Trujillo, the wife of Francisco de Ribera, the alcalde, threw herself into the street from a high window. God, in his mercy, was pleased to save her from death, by reason of the force of the fall. There were also one Domingo Lopez and one Pedro de Angulo, inhabitants of the town, who threw themselves from a high turret, fled, and hid themselves, thus saving their lives.

3. The rest of Aguirre's people were in the plaza, under some apprehension, and murmuring in consequence of what they had heard had taken place in the fortress. The traitor, hearing this, appeared at a window, and told them not to be uneasy, for that the noise they had heard in the fortress was caused by his having commanded Martin Perez to be killed, his son and maestro del campo, because he had wished to mutiny and kill him, and then go away with the people; so those who were in the plaza were quieted.

Aguirre had been told that Anton Llamoso, captain of the ammunition, and one of his great friends, was one of the conspirators with Martin Perez; and Aguirre, seeing him pass before him, and near to the body and the murderers, who had their arms in their hands, said to Llamoso, "They also tell me that you were one of the party with the maestro del campo; how was this? Was this friendship? And dost thou hold so lightly the love I feel for you?" Those who had slain Martin Perez, and were now steeped in his blood, desirous of other deaths, had scarcely heard Aguirre's words to Llamoso, when they came near to both, awaiting Aguirre's signal to murder Llamoso.

The great fear that fell upon Llamoso, however, did not prevent him from making explanations to Aguirre, backing them up by many oaths, mixed with a thousand blasphemies against those who had falsely accused him, and saying that treason had never entered his thoughts, and that Aguirre ought to believe him, for the affection he had always had for him and his doings; and, when it seemed to him that Aguirre was not satisfied with his words, he rushed upon the body of Martin Perez, which was almost cut to pieces, and, before those who were present, he threw himself upon it, shouting, "Curse this traitor, who wished to commit so great a crime! I will drink his blood!" and, putting his mouth over the wounds in the head, with more than demoniac rage, he began to suck the blood and brains that issued from the wounds, and swallowed what he sucked, as if he were a famished dog. This caused such horror to those who were present, that there was not one who was not turned sick at heart by the scene. Aguirre was satisfied of his fidelity, and so it turned out, for there was no one who sustained him, until his last hour, like unto this Llamoso.

4. The provincial's ship could not arrive at the port of the city before Monday morning, having left Punta de Piedras on the previous day (Sunday), in consequence of contrary winds. This day, early in the morning, they anchored half a league from the land, out of range of Aguirre's artillery, but the provincial was near enough to cause the traitor some inquietude.

Aguirre prepared for defence, hearing that the provincial

would land some of his men.   He collected some of his soldiers, and marched towards the beach, near to the ship, taking with him five brass falconets, which he brought with him from the Marañon.

All were charged, ready for the provincial's men, when they should land. The boats of the provincial's men, having approached those of Aguirre, within hearing distance, they upbraided the traitor's men, telling them that they were cruel traitors, disloyal and mutinous to their king, indeed, anything that came uppermost; they also received a reply from those of Aguirre, in no very measured terms, coupled with a thousand blasphemies, because those in the piraguas and galleon would not land, or leave the boats where the royal standard and flags were hoisted.

CHAP. XXXVI.

1. *Lope de Aguirre writes to the provincial.*—2. *The provincial replies from his ship, and then sets sail. Aguirre hangs two soldiers.*— 3. *Opinions as to whether it was politic of the provincial to communicate with the traitor.*—4. *The opinions and objections resolved.*

1. Aguirre, seeing that the provincial's people would not land, returned the same day to the fortress, whence he wrote the following letter to the friar :—

THE LETTER OF AGUIRRE TO THE PROVINCIAL.

" Magnificent and Reverend Sir,—It would give us much greater pleasure to celebrate your paternity's reception with boughs and flowers, than with arquebusses and discharges of artillery, because it has been told to us, by many persons, that such would be more generous ; and, if we are to judge by the proceedings we have this day observed, which are greater than we had been led to expect; it would seem that your paternity is a lover of arms and military exploits : and thus we see that you imitate the honour, virtue, and nobility, which our forefathers attained sword in hand.   This I do not deny; neither do these señores who are here, and who came from Pirú by the river Marañon, to discover and settle new countries, some of us maimed, some halt, and some of sound body.   Owing to the troubles in Pirú, we sought to find a land, miserable as it might be, to give rest to our poor bodies, which are covered with more seams than are pilgrims' weeds, and we would have remained and settled there, had we not, after many troubles, passed from the river, and into the sea, hungry and menaced even by death ; and let those who may come against us, take into account that they come to war with the ghosts of dead men.   The soldiers of your paternity call us traitors, but they should be chastised, they should not say so, because to attack Don Philip, king of Castille, is the work of grand and noble souls ; for, if we were engaged in mean occupations, we could pass an orderly life, but we know no other trade than to make cannon balls and sharpen lances, which are the sort of money current here.   If there was any necessity to go into details, we might make it known to your paternity, that Pirú owes much to us, and we might relate the cogent reasons we have for doing what we do, but of these things I will say nothing.

" To-morrow, please God, I will send to your paternity copies of the edicts that have been made amongst us, each man being at liberty to do as he thinks best. There are those, with you, who swore fealty to Don Fernando de Guzman as their king, and denaturalized themselves from the kingdoms of Spain ; and they mutinied, and usurped the powers of justice, and pillaged estates ; amongst these were Alonso Arias, Don Fernando's sergeant, and Roderigo Gutierrez, his chamberlain.   Of the other señores we need take no account, because such discourse would be trifling ; although, as to Arias, he would not be mentioned, had he not been a good rope maker. Rodrigo Gutierrez was rather well to do, but he had a downward look, a sign that he was a great traitor. Then there was Gonzalo de Zuñiga, a man of Seville. Know then, your paternity, that he was a great buffoon, and his tricks are these : he was in Popayan with Alvaro de Hoyon, in the rebellion against his majesty, and when his captain was about to fight, he deserted him and fled ; and, having escaped, he was in Pirú with Sylva in the mutiny and robbery of the royal treasure, when they killed the judge, and then he ran away again. He is such a coward that, as long as there is anything to eat, he is diligent, and in the hour of battle he flees, but his signatures will not desert. I am sorry that one man is not here, namely Salguero, because we want him much to watch over our sheep, because he understands that business well. As to my good friends Martin Bruno, Anton Perez, and Andres Dias, I kiss their hands. As to Monguia and Artiaga, may God pardon them, and if they are alive, I beseech your paternity to let me know ;[1] and we should all like to be together, and that your paternity were our patriarch : for, after believing that God is no more than any other, all the rest is moonshine.

" I beg of your paternity not to go to Santo Domingo, because we believe that you will be dispossessed of the office you hold there.

" In your reply, I beseech your paternity that you will write to me, and let us treat one another well in this war. God will bring trouble on all traitors, and the king will restore the loyal to life, although up to this time we have seen no one resuscitated by a king ; he cures no wounds, he restores no one to life. May the most magnificent and

---

[1] All these men, respecting whom Aguirre writes to the provincial, were the soldiers who were sent to capture his ship, and deserted to him.

reverend person of your paternity, be in great and increasing dignity.

" From this fortress of Margarita, I kiss the hands of your paternity. Your servant,

" LOPE DE AGUIRRE."

2. Aguirre sent this letter, by some Indians in a piragua, which was received by the provincial, and seen by his followers, who roared with laughter, for it appeared to them to be the nonsense of a buffoon, rather than the reasons of a captain-general. The provincial replied as a learned and religious man should, advising Aguirre to abandon his road of errors and to turn into the path of loyalty and service to his king, which was of great import to him for the security of his conscience ; but if, through his blind obstinacy he would not do so, the provincial charged him as a Christian, to have reverence for churches and all holy things, and the honour of women, and, for the love of that God to whom he would have to give account of his doings, that he would stop the shedding of blood, and the continuance of cruelties in that island ; that Monguia and Artiaga were alive, and were faithful servants to his majesty, and, that in what they had done by entering his service, they had complied with their obligation as Spaniards. This answer was sent by the Indians who brought Aguirre's letter. The provincial then got under weigh, and returned to Maracapana, sailing from thence to the island of Santo Domingo, where he made known all the news concerning the tyrant, and his cruelties.

Whilst the correspondence was going on with the provincial, and his ship was at anchor, two of Aguirre's soldiers, one named Juan de San Juan, and the other Paredes, were observed on the beach, reposing under the shade of some cactus trees. Amongst those who saw them, there were not wanting some who were not friendly to them, who told Aguirre that these two soldiers were hiding, and awaiting an opportunity to desert to the provincial's ship. This was sufficient for the tyrant, and he had them immediately hung at the *rollo*,[1] without even allowing them to confess.

3. There were some who considered the provincial's visit to Aguirre ill timed, for the traitor, seeing an opposing force so near, and suspicious of a larger one being sent against him, killed the governor and the others; and also, as the provincial made this demonstration, he might have done something more, by landing his people, for with them and some of the inhabitants, who had fled to the woods, but who would have joined them, he might have made a show of his forces, and might have got away those of Aguirre's party who had been obliged to follow him against their will, seeing that they would find protection with the king's forces; so that at least the tyrant would not have left the island with so large a force as he brought to it.

4. To these views there were two replies : one was that those who had fled to the woods, had received no notice of the provincial's approach, neither was it known that the tyrant had any men with him against their will; but rather, from their acts, it was to be believed that they followed him cheerfully. The next reason was that, had the provincial landed his party, greater misery would have resulted, for the cruelties of Aguirre and his fierce butcheries, were such, that had the inhabitants and the provincial's men not been able to join, more would have been imprisoned, and the threats he had fulminated against the defenceless people would have been put into execution to the utmost on man, woman and child. As the provincial and Aguirre did not meet, it would seem that the former did not err in not landing ; moreover, it is

---

[1] The *rollo*, or pillar, emblematic of jurisdiction, was used as a gallows, and also as a garrote. The culprit, being placed against it, the strangling cord was passed round his neck, and round the pillar, and then tightened from behind.

requisite to take into consideration the provincial's holy zeal, which never did wrong to any one, and if crimes followed, it was not his intention that such should happen.

CHAP. XXXVII.

1. *Aguirre prepares to leave the island, and kills a soldier.*—2. *He has flags made, and blessed in the church, on the feast of the day of our Lady of Assumption.*—3. *Aguirre makes an oration to his captains, and ensigns, on giving them the flags.*—4. *A soldier escapes from Aguirre, on account of which he kills two others, also a woman.*

1. Aguirre began to be desirous of leaving the island, but he found his steps rather retarded, for he had sunk his brigantines, and the provincial's ship had escaped him, and he had only three small barks, insufficient for his soldiers, arms, ammunition, and provisions, so he commanded the ship to be finished, which the governor had in the dockyard. He was informed that there were some carpenters, who had hidden themselves amongst the inhabitants, and he ordered them to bring the carpenters to him, saying that they should be well treated; and, as the people were suffering so much from the traitor, and wished to get rid of so wicked a guest, they sought out some carpenters for him, so that the ship might be finished, and thus shorten Aguirre's stay.

Doubtless there were occasions for the inhabitants to escape from the city, and to fly from the dangers that always menaced their lives. This was known to Aguirre, and, as his efforts to catch them were insufficient, he took vengeance on their houses and estates by robbing and destroying them, rooting up their crops, cutting down their trees and demolishing their orchards; and, as it appeared to him that these

punishments did not fill up the measure of his will, because
they were not mixed with human blood, he decided upon
killing one Martin Diaz de Armendariz, cousin of the governor, Pedro de Ursua, who came with the traitor very much
against his will.[1] He was considered a sort of prisoner, and
Aguirre thought of leaving him behind, and sent him out
of the city, to remain on an estate, with orders not to leave
it until the traitor should have left the island. There this
soldier lived, doing harm to no one, when the traitor changed
his mind, it appearing to him that it would not be politic
to leave enemies in the rear, so he sent certain of his soldiers
to where Armendariz was, with orders to strangle him, which
was done, without confession, for the murderers knew that
this would give greater pleasure to their general, Aguirre.

2. As he was now arranging his departure from the
island, amongst other things he caused three flags to be
made of the silk he had stolen. They were of the colour
that represented his cruelties, namely black taffety, spotted
with red crossed swords, which represented the blood he
shed, and the cause of lamentation and mourning. He
ordered these flags, when finished, to be blessed in the
church, as if such a ceremony could do him service.

The traitor ordered that, on the Day of Assumption of our
Lady, the 15th of August of the year 1561, a solemn mass
should be said in the mother church, to which he went,
with his followers in warlike array, he himself going in the
vanguard as the general. On the way to the church he saw
the king of spades, out of an old pack of cards, in the street,
on the ground; he stooped down and picked it up, but he
soon threw it from him, as it appeared to him that by doing
so he showed his disdain for the king of Castille; and, madman as he was, he began to stamp on the ground, swearing
a thousand oaths against his majesty, and, snatching the card

---

[1] Probably a son of Ursua's uncle, Miguel Diaz de Armendariz, the
juez de residencia in New Granada. (See page 1, and the Introduction.)

from the ground with great passion and rage, tore it to pieces. This madness of his was imitated by his more particular friends among the soldiery, who joined him in shouting a thousand blasphemies against God and his saints.

Having arrived at the church, and the flags having been blessed (by the priest who said the mass), the traitor handed them to the captains and ensigns, saying that he confided them to their valour and loyalty; that, as he was satisfied of their persons, he gave them the flags, so that they might march under the flags, to follow, defend, and guard his person, going out into the field on all occasions with the flags, against any sort of warriors who might oppose them; that they might make war upon all who opposed them; that the obstinate towns were to be sacked, but he charged them to respect the churches and female honour, but nothing else. They had full liberty to do as they pleased, for as they had made a new king, they could make new laws. This gave the soldiers great pleasure. When they left the church, accompanying their general back to the fortress, they were all most joyous that he had given them such broad licence to commit crimes; and, as to the exceptions mentioned by the traitor, respecting their veneration for churches and the honour of women, they well knew that in breaking them, they would receive the same punishment as for any other crimes, which were greater praises and rewards to those who committed the more heinous, so that the soldiery might be more satisfied. These exceptions were merely to flatter and deceive the inhabitants, who were present. The rovers were not moved by any zeal for the service of God; to whom we should give infinite thanks, that He put a bridle on them, so that they did not sow the seeds of any heresy, for the abominable way of their lives might have produced heresy.

4. Not the least culpable, in every species of horror, was Alonso de Villena, for which reason his life had been spared

up to this time. Aguirre was now set against him, for certain words of little importance it was said he had made use of against his chief, for which he received a severe reprimand, and he was not in favour as heretofore. This caused Villena to be fearful (for he knew Aguirre too well, and that it did not require him to be very angry with any man, to kill him, although he might be his best friend), and he began to search for means of flight, to return to his devotion to his king, without pain of death, for he considered himself as condemned, for having been concerned in the murder of the governor Ursua, and in nearly all the others that had been perpetrated. To these were added fresh fears, should he fall into Aguirre's hands, after he had deserted. This soldier wished it to be understood by the inhabitants, that he fled from Aguirre, fearing he would kill him.

It was bruited among some of the soldiers that Villena wanted to kill Aguirre, and this coming to the traitor's ears, he sent to some of his friends to lay hands on Villena, and kill him. But Villena was advised in time by his spies, that Aguirre's soldiers were after him, so he escaped by a false door, and hid himself in the woods; and, although the strictest search was made, he was not found. It was made public that Villena was sought, that he might be executed, because he wanted to kill Aguirre; so he gained favour with the inhabitants of the island. But this caused the death of some of his friends, as of one Dominguez, alferez of Aguirre's guard, and one Loaysa, (a great friend of Villena's). Aguirre declared it to be impossible that they were not in concert with Villena; so, without any further evidence, the traitor determined to kill them, and employed one Juan de Aguirre to do it, who stealthily came upon Dominguez, and killed him with numberless stabs of his dagger. Loaysa was strangled, without being allowed to confess. Aguirre then arrested the lady of the house where

these two men lodged, one Anna de Rojas, a married and
excellent woman, accusing her of being privy to Villena's treason, and of not having informed him. She was
hung on the *rollo* in the centre of the plaza. That this
execution might be the more solemn and celebrated amongst
these traitors, a squadron of arquebusiers entered the
plaza when she was about to be executed, and whilst
hanging and half dead, they fired one after the other at her,
in presence of their infamous commander, who applauded
the best aims they made at the heart and head of the poor
creature, and at whose wretched death they remained most
joyous.

<hr>

CHAP. XXXVIII.

1. *Aguirre orders an old man to be killed ; he likewise does the same to a*
   friar of Santo Domingo. He also commands another friar to be
   killed, to whom he had confessed.—2. Of another who was strangled,
   which caused much sorrow in the town.—3. The traitor hangs an
   old man and a woman ; he also does ridiculous things to some soldiers.
   —4. One Francisco Fajardo comes to the island of Margarita from
   Caraccas, with some people, with the intention of routing Aguirre.

1. This good woman's husband was named Diego Gomez.
He was old and crippled, and at that time was very ill at a
farm, with a friar of the order of Santo Domingo. It seemed
to Aguirre that the old man had participated with his wife
in the treason of Villena, so he sent his head-constable,
Paniagua, to strangle him, which he did, taking with him,
as an assistant, a Portuguese soldier, named Manuel Baeza,
with two others. When they had killed the old man, the friar,
it would appear, blamed them, or else, to give pleasure to their
general (who hated priests), they strangled the friar on their

own account. They buried both in one grave, returning to Aguirre with an account of what they had done, which gave him great satisfaction. Aguirre also had great pleasure in killing another religious man of the same order, of an exemplary life, and much beloved in the island. He had confessed to this friar, more out of form than for the health of his soul, and, in discharging his conscience, the friar severely reprehended him, and, with holy exhortation, urged him, as he was bound to do, to step aside from the evil road he was going, and to follow that of God and his king, and not to have the weight of so many murders on his conscience. This exhortation was a bitter draught, and the good inspirations that God offers to those who have turned their backs upon him, are not heeded by them, but rather held in hatred, and they will not see, or take counsel (as those that are blind) of those who put these lights before them. Not only did this traitor not take heed of what this blessed friar said, but he conceived a mortal hatred for him, so that he would not see him again, or even hear his name mentioned; and he was often on the point of killing him, but did not then carry his intention into effect, in consequence of the friar being held in great esteem; until the head constable, Paniagua, had killed the other friar at the estate. Then Aguirre charged him with the execution of his confessor, for it seemed to him that Paniagua would bring eager hands to this new work of death, as one who had already dispatched a son of the church on his own authority, and that he had better be the instrument of death for the confessor; and so Aguirre gave him the order to go and kill his confessor, which he did without loss of time.

2. He met with the confessor in the road, although some say he found him in the church, and dragging him out, he thrust him into a house, where he told him he had been sent by his general to kill him; to which the confessor re-

plied, that if such was the case, he hoped he might be allowed to pray to God. Permission having been given, he threw himself with his face on the ground, and said the Psalm of the Miserere, and other holy prayers, when those ministers of wickedness took him up from the ground to kill him. He then said that he offered himself up to God, in a pure and simple spirit, for his sins, and he prayed they would give him the most cruel death they possibly could: he then clasped his hands towards heaven. The executioners put the cord into his mouth, and from the back began to tighten the rope and strangle him with such violence, that his mouth was broken to pieces; but, seeing that he did not die outright under this species of cruelty, they lowered the strangling cord to his throat, and again twisting it, he died. Such was the end of his exemplary life.

The inhabitants of the city, nay, of the whole island, were sorrowful indeed at the death of the holy man, and he was looked upon as a martyr, having been sacrificed for having done his holy duty in regard to the sacrament of confession.

3. They were now rapidly finishing the ship and arranging for the embarkation of Aguirre, his cruelties also were increasing, and it appeared a philosophical maxim, that the natural movement is stronger in the end than at the beginning; as cruelty was, as it were, naturalized in this traitor.

One of the soldiers, named Simon de Sumorostro, now an old man, repenting of what he had done, and not wishing to continue with Aguirre, on account of his cruelties, begged to be left behind, saying that he was now too old and sickly to follow the wars. Aguirre replied that he might remain, and the old man left his presence with joy. Aguirre then called some of his ministers, and said to them, "Old Sumorostro has asked permission to remain behind, and I have granted his request, go and see that he is safe; that, during my absence, the inhabitants and authorities may do him no ill."

But the soldiers knew well the meaning of the traitor, and they went after the old man, and took him straight to the *rollo*, and there hanged him. This prevented others from asking the same favour of Aguirre, but some of them arranged for their flight.

Aguirre also hanged a certain Maria Chaves on the *rollo*, because a soldier who lodged in her house had fled, and she had not given information as to the projected desertion. The amusements of this tyrant consisted in oppressing his fellow creatures ; as happened to a young man, who unintentionally had not paid him a visit. He was ordered to appear at the fortress, and, after Aguirre had severely reprimanded him for his want of attention, he ordered the little beard he had to be rasped off, washing his face before and after the operation with fetid urine, while the traitor (with some of his friends) laughed immoderately at the scene. When it was over, the young man was ordered to present four fowls to the fellow who acted as the barber. The same was done to one of his solders, named Alonso Cayado, because he was a good man, and an enemy to the cruelties practised by his comrades ; so it appeared to the traitor that he was a useless person, but not having then decided as to his death, he had him brought into his presence, he being in the plaza, and, before the assembled crowd, had him shaved as the young man had been, saying that he thus punished him for not having on a certain occasion fallen in, in the ranks, in time. These barbarities were common, when he was in a happy mood, and did not wish to kill his soldiers ; but there were occasions when, for the most trivial occurrence, his victim was doomed to death.

4. They were now nearly ready to embark, and were only waiting for the people to go on board the ship, and set sail, when there appeared off the island one Francisco Taxardo, inhabitant of the town of our Lady of Caraballeda or Caraccas, which country was in course of conquest by him. He

had started to oppose the traitor, on receiving the news from the provincial. He came to the island with other inhabitants, in piraguas, accompanied by a good number of Indians with their bows and arrows, with the intention of seeing what could be done against Aguirre. He might have succeeded had he come sooner, and had not Aguirre been on the point of starting ; for had the inhabitants been assisted before, the traitor might have been overthrown, but they could not do this alone, for they were so few in number ; neither did Francisco Taxardo do anything, for the same reason ; for, although he landed with his men, and came near to the town, it was under cover of a wood, from whence he shouted to Aguirre, and called upon the traitor's soldiers to come over to him, and he also called to the inhabitants, offering protection to all those who joined him, as he was under the king's banners.

Aguirre was suspicious that Taxardo had more men with him than he chose to shew, and, for fear of his soldiers going over to the king, he would not march out, but carefully guarded his men in the fortress, closing the gates, and allowing no one to go out. Taxardo did not dare to leave the cover of the little wood, which Aguirre would have cut down, but for the fear that those he sent would desert from him.

Aguirre told his men, that Taxardo's reason for inviting them in so friendly a way was merely to have them in his power, and that when he had them, he would take vengeance on them for the deaths they had caused in that island, and elsewhere.

CHAP. XXXIX.

1. *Aguirre embarks with all his people, and, whilst doing so, he causes his admiral to be killed.*—2. *The traitor sails, but changes his route, by going to the port of Burburata.*—3. *He is becalmed, which retards his voyage.*—4. *They burn a ship they find in the port, and the inhabitants advise the governor of Venezuela of Aguirre's arrival.*

1. The traitor's fears were excited at the arrival of Taxardo, and it caused him to change his views as to embarking his people, so that Taxardo's party could do no harm with their arrows. Aguirre got his men out of the fortress (it being inconvenient for them to sally from the gate) through an opening he made high up in the wall, and they went down by a ladder one by one, and embarked, whilst he, and some of his friends, kept guard; until there only remained a few men, including his admiral Alonso Rodriguez, one of his old friends, who was not a little culpable in past crimes. He, seeing that the waves wetted Aguirre, begged of him to retire, so that he might not get wet. This observation so raised his anger that, drawing his sword, he cut the admiral's arm off. He then ordered him to be attended to, but, immediately changing his mind, the traitor ordered him to be killed, which was done, his attention and politeness to his chief having cost him his life ; although some said that the admiral, who was occupied about the vessel, complained that the people would be uncomfortable if three horses and a mule, sent by Aguirre, went, and that it was this that incited him to this sanguinary act.

When all the people were embarked, and Aguirre was about to do the same with his guard, he went with them to the house of the priest of the town, named Contreras, and taking him much against his will, made him embark also. All being on board the three vessels, after having been

on the island forty days, and having robbed and destroyed
many estates, they left the inhabitants in the greatest misery,
and it required many years for them to recover from such a
visitation.

2. Aguirre stole more than fifty cross bows, many swords,
lances, and other arms which were in the fort; three good
horses and one mule, and all the horse trappings they could
lay their hands on, with the idea of finding some horses
wherever they might land. The soldiery who embarked
numbered one hundred and fifty men, for, although when
they came to the island they numbered about two hundred,
some fifty had deserted, including those who joined the provincial, in Maracapana, with Monguia, and those who were
killed. Aguirre left the island on the last Sunday in the
month of August of 1561.

Aguirre was aware, or conjectured, that the provincial had
given information concerning him to the whole coast, even
as far as Nombre de Dios and Panamá, so that at the various
points there would be armed forces to oppose him, and to go
from Nombre de Dios to Panamá would be very difficult,
for he might be easily routed. He soon decided to stand
out to sea from the island of Margarita, and then changed
his course for the port of Burburata, with the intention of
traversing the government of Venezuela, to the new kingdom of Granada, from thence to Popayan and Pirú, without
considering the great difficulties that might intervene during
so long a journey, and so he ordered the pilots to steer for
the port of Burburata.

3. He did not think himself quite certain of the people in
two of the vessels. He sailed in the new ship, but he did
not allow the others to have a cross-staff, to observe the lati-
tude, or a compass, so they had his vessel in sight to follow
during the day, and at night he hoisted a light. His voyage
was not so prosperous as he had expected, (and as is generally the case thereabouts, in consequence of the wind being

aft, so that it is only a two days' voyage from the island of Margarita to the port of Burbarata), and owing to a succession of calms, he was eight days at sea. He attributed this delay to the bad management of the pilots, and he menaced them with death, believing that, as he was so long in seeing his port, the pilots were taking him elsewhere. This caused this most impatient being to give utterance to a thousand blasphemies and heresies against God and his saints; saying at times that if God had made the heavens for the wicked and cruel people such as he had with him, he would not go there; at other times, raising his eyes to heaven with an infernal look, he said, "Oh, God! if thou wilt do me a favour, do it now, and the glory of it guard for thy saints!" Observing that the calm continued, he would declare that he did not believe in God, that he was a great robber, that until now he had been on his side, but that now he had deserted him and gone over to his enemies; and thus he said a thousand other nonsensical things against the sea, winds, and tempests, in which he was joined by his soldiers, who echoed his words. When he blasphemed they did the same, when he abjured they did so, when he was murderous they followed his example, and when he was a robber they joined him; and as he was a traitor they all were; such is the power of the heart over the other portions of the body, such also is the divine goodness and forbearance until the fitting time has come. However, in spite of all these blasphemies, these traitors were at last permitted to arrive at the port of Burburata, on the seventh of September; when they anchored in great joy and, without remaining in the ships, they immediately landed.[1]

[1] "Agiri spoilt all the coast of Caraccas and the province of Venezuela, and, as I remember, it was the same year that Sir John Hawkins sailed to Saint Juan de Lua in the *Jesus of Lubeck*, for himself told me that he met with such a one upon the coast that rebelled, and had sailed downe the river of Amazons."—Raleigh's *Guiana*, p. 23.

Aguirre, however, could not have been the pirate met by old Sir

4. The first act of the traitor was to set a merchant vessel on fire, the owners of which, knowing of Aguirre's approach, had discharged her cargo and scuttled her, but there being no great depth of water, a portion remained exposed. The part out of the water was set on fire, which gave a light to the traitors all that night, during which they remained encamped on shore, and Aguirre would not allow any of his Marañones to move until the morning.[1] The inhabitants of the town, who were a short half league from the coast, had, on the first news about the traitor, taken their precautions as to the safety of their property, as did also other towns in the various *repartimientos* (large grants of land). When they saw Aguirre entering their port, they took all their goods away, and, as they could not defend the place, they abandoned it. As soon as the traitor had landed, with his followers, the people sent to inform the governor, Pablo Collado, who was waiting for Aguirre in the city of Tocuyo.

The governor, perceiving that he would be obliged to show a front to Aguirre, and seeing that those he had with him were few in number, ordered that the neighbouring forces should join him in Tocuyo, and, fearing that he would not be strong enough for the enemy, if he was the attacking party, he determined to harass them,

John Hawkins, as he was killed in 1561, and Hawkins did not sail from England, in the *Jesus of Lubeck*, until 1564, and did not reach the West Indies until the following year ; when he disposed of a cargo of slaves at this very port of Burburata. He probably heard of the doings of Aguirre at this place.

Burburata, in Humboldt's time, was nothing but a port of embarkation for mules. In the early days of the Spanish colonies, it was an important place.

[1] At this point of Aguirre's career, Piedrahita takes up the narrative, the details of which he collected from Pedro Simon, Pizarro's *Varones Illustres* (*Vida de Diego Garcia de Paredes*), and Castellanos' *Elegias de Varones Illustres.*

by taking all provisions out of their reach, and keeping them on the alert for ambushes at night, for none of them knew the country, nor the passes, which were very rough in places. A royalist force had been assembled, and Gutierrez de la Peña, an inhabitant of the city of Tucuyo, had been appointed general. Fresh information was sent to Pedro Bravo de la Molina in the city of Merida, informing him that the enemy was already on the threshold, begging of him to come with all the men and arms he could muster, and supplicating afresh captain Diego Garcia de Paredes, and the rest of the settlers in the government of Venezuela (who, as we have said, had retreated to the city of Merida), to send succour, and to come and serve the king on so pressing an occasion ; promising them oblivion for past occurrences.

CHAP. XL.

1. *Garcia de Paredes goes from Merida to Tocuyo, with some followers, sent by the governor.*—2. *The governor of Venezuela sends to the governor and inhabitants of Merida to come and assist him.*—3. *The governor of Merida goes with twenty-five soldiers to Tocuyo.*—4. *Aguirre's men find a pilot in the town of Burburata, who was one of those who had passed over to the provincial.*

1. Although, on the first news received from the governor, Pablo Collado, Diego Garcia de Paredes and his companions had not come from Merida, they were yet on the alert, like good and faithful vassals, to go and serve his majesty, and on receipt of the second notice, they, being

Z

ready, marched forth to Tocuyo, where they were received
with open arms, particularly by the governor, who thanked
them heartily for their assistance. The governor named
Garcia de Paredes as his maestro del campo, offering him
explanations of what had occurred, and giving him to
understand how much he appreciated him. He added that,
in consequence of Paredes having been absent when they
had to prepare against Aguirre, he found himself, as it were,
caught between the arch and the wall, and was in such a
strait, that he had named Gutierrez de la Peña general.
He, therefore, begged of Paredes that he would accept the
office of maestro del campo; assuring him that although
Peña had the title of general, he (Paredes) would have the
command in the field, and the charge of all. Paredes accepted the office, thanking the governor, and offering at the
same time to lay his life down for the king.

The governor and the maestro del campo went together
to the city of Barquicimeto, where they found Gutierrez de
la Peña, drilling the people he had got together; for
although it had at first been determined to muster the forces
in Tocuyo, it was afterwards found more convenient to do
so in Barquicimeto, because it was a more open country,
and nearer to the port where the traitor had landed.

Pedro Bravo remained in Merida, to follow Garcia de
Paredes, with all the people he could possibly collect. He
soon gathered together the principal people of the town,
when it was determined to send a second message to the city
of Santa Fé, and, although they had been ordered not to
abandon their city to go to the assistance of the governor,
even if they knew of the entry of the traitor into the province of Venezuela; yet it was considered of more importance to the king, to arrest the steps of Aguirre, which would
also ensure the safety of their city.

These two points being resolved on by Pedro Bravo and
the inhabitants, they determined to dispatch three soldiers,

with particulars of their views, to the city of Pamplona, and
from thence to Santa Fé. Of these, one was named Andres
de Pernia, but he, although a brave man, and one of the best
soldiers in the conquest of these lands, knowing the difficulty of traversing the country of so many warlike Indians
as there were between their city and the town of San
Cristoval, told the governor, that he dared not go with so
few men, for that they would surely be killed on the way.
But as Pedro Bravo and the inhabitants considered that
they could not spare more than three, it was agreed that it
would be more reasonable to go and assist Venezuela with
all their men. So advices were not forwarded to the Real
Audiencia, until more accurate news could be sent of the
intentions of the traitor, and of the route he intended to
take. All this turned out well, and they saved themselves
from great expense.

3. Following out the second plan they had determined on,
Captain Pedro Bravo was ordered to get twenty-five of his
best men ready without loss of time, and to go with them, to
the help of the licenciate Pablo Collado. As to talk about
the power of the law is not quite the same as to fight for it,
there were some who were backward in coming out to show
a front to the traitor, their view of the case being that their
forces, and those of Venezuela, were insufficient to resist so
considerable a body of the enemy as they were led to believe existed; that their own city would be victimized, and
that those who would be left to take care of the city, would
not be able to put down any rising of the Indians. But the
high spirit of Captain Pedro Bravo, and his zeal in the
service of his majesty, induced him to desire to act so that
the traitor's steps might at once be arrested, for it would be
much more difficult to do so, when he had penetrated further
into the country; for he would then have picked up some
soldiers like himself: so Bravo said that it was not well for
him or his reputation, nor for that of the city, to be back-

ward in the least, in such zeal as they had already shown
for the service of their king. He took the arrangement on
himself, and ordered those who had been named, to be ready
the next day early in the morning, and he resolved to take
by force, such as did not go willingly; so that the few who
had made these excuses, seeing the governor's resolution,
conformed to the wishes of the others, and they all left at
daylight on the following morning for Tocuyo, in the name
of his majesty, and with their banner flying. Journeying
rapidly, they arrived at their destination in a few days, where
they were much required.

4. The traitor Aguirre had hopes, during the night when
he was encamped on the sea-shore in the port of Burburata
(as had happened when he landed at the port of Margarita),
that the inhabitants would pay him a visit, and, like the
others, bring him some presents, to appease him, and induce
him not to commit crimes, as he had done up to the present time. But the night having passed without anything
having taken place, at daybreak on Monday, the 8th of
September, he sent a party of his picked friends to the town,
to examine it, and ascertain the views of the inhabitants,
also to bring back with them to camp, such fresh provisions
as they could lay their hands on.

Aguirre's men, on their arrival at the town, found it
abandoned, and only one soldier there, named Francisco
Martin, a pilot, who had left Margarita for Maracapana, with
Captain Monguia, and the other soldiers, who had passed
over to the provincial. He had remained on land, desirous
of returning to the traitor again. This pilot, although he
had fled with the inhabitants of the port of Burburata, on
Aguirre's arrival, had, as soon as he could slip away from
them, returned to the town to await his old companions, and
he showed great signs of joy on the arrival of the Marañones. He returned with them to the camp on the sea-
shore, and, in the presence of Aguirre, offered his services

afresh. Aguirre accepted them with pleasure, embracing him, thanking him for his constancy in following him, and declaring that he should be well cared for.

CHAP. XLI.

1. *Aguirre is informed that some soldiers, who are friendly to him, are in that part of the country. He sends in search of them.—2. The traitor kills a soldier. He burns his vessels, and takes up his quarters in the town.—3. The soldiers look about for horses, so as to sally forth with them. The traitor declares war against the king of Castille.—4. The whole country is in a state of ferment ; the robberies of the soldiers ; they find the alcalde, and a tradesman of the town. Aguirre sends to the town of Valencia for horses.*

1. The traitor, having pleased this Francisco Martin with words and acts, and having treated him as he did the other malefactors who were loyal to him, began to ask him how it was that he and the others abandoned him, and went over to the provincial, in Maracapana. Martin tried to satisfy Aguirre, and to prove himself innocent, and that it had never crossed his thoughts to be a traitor ; saying that Pedro de Monguia, Artiaga, and Rodrigo Gutierrez had deceived him as well as his companions, and, first carefully taking their arms from them one by one, had entered the port, and, when near enough for the provincial to hear them, had shouted "Long live the king," and given themselves up. Martin said he could not prevent this, neither could his companions, for they were disarmed. Nevertheless, they did not enter the service of the provincial, as could be seen ; and, when the provincial came to this port, they had escaped from him, their intention being to wait for Aguirre, should

he come there, and choose to receive them back. He added
that he alone had shown diligence in returning to the
town, that the others were in the woods, rather persecuted
by the inhabitants, and that they were in a most miserable
condition, almost without raiment, and starving : thus, without doubt they would return to Aguirre's service, when they
knew that he was there. This recital gave great joy to the
traitor, for he now knew that he had people of his party in
Tierra Firme. He gave Martin a good suit of clothes, and
handed him a letter, full of the most friendly offers to the
others, despatching him in search of those who were in the
woods, to read the letter to them, and to tell them how
desirous he was to serve and favour them.

2. Francisco Martin made strict search, and, being unable to find them, he returned to Aguirre's camp, where
he remained, aiding in the cruelties committed by the
rest, until he received his merited payment in a miserable
death.

In continuation of crimes, such as he had committed in
the island of Margarita, Aguirre caused one of those soldiers
to be killed, who had joined him in the island. The victim
was a Portuguese, named Antonio Farias, and he was murdered for having asked, when he stepped on shore, if it
was an island or the main land.

It was now past mid-day, and all hands had landed from
the vessels that had been brought by Aguirre, so he determined to take up his quarters in the town, he and some of
his particular friends remaining behind to burn the ships, which
was done, the object now being to afford no opportunity for
any of his followers to desert. He then went to the town
(leaving the ships on fire), where he took up his residence,
taking greater care than he had hitherto done of the safety
of his person, for he feared that some soldier or another, finding himself on the main land, might kill him and easily
escape, an end the tyrant merited for his crimes.

Still, he need not have had these suspicions, for his followers were desirous of committing all sorts of horrors, and of having such a chief to command and assist them, who would be the more satisfied the greater the crimes, and they knew it would be impossible to find such another sanguinary commander.

3. As this locality did not quite suit the traitor, he sent out parties of his soldiers to hunt up horses, so as to prosecute their march. Although they used their best efforts, they could only collect twenty-five or thirty saddle horses, the rest being unbroken mares.

The inhabitants had counselled the Indians to beset the route of Aguirre's followers with poisoned arrows, which brought them to death's door. They returned to Aguirre, who, to show his sorrow for the sufferings of his men, began to excite himself, and get into a towering rage, uttering a thousand blasphemies against God and his saints, also a thousand threats against the inhabitants of the town, and he commanded a proclamation to go forth, declaring a war of fire and blood against the king of Castille and his vassals, with pain of death to any of his soldiers who did not execute this bloody mandate, only excepting those who came to serve him voluntarily, and with pleasure. This war was solemnly proclaimed through all the streets of the town, to the sound of trumpets and kettle-drums.

4. The traitor, having given permission to the soldiers most in his confidence, to go out and pillage, amongst other places they came to the estate of one Benito Chaves, an alcalde, four leagues from the town, who was there with his wife, and a daughter, married to one Julian de Mendoza. They left the women, robbing what they could, and taking the alcalde to Aguirre; so that he might give an account of the country, and of the rest of the inhabitants.

Other soldiers laid hands on one Pedro Nuñez, a tradesman, who, on being brought before the traitor, was asked why all the people had fled from the town. The man replied that it was from the fear they had of him. Aguirre then asked him to say what they thought of him and his followers; but Nuñez, suspecting the object of this question, excused himself from answering, saying that he did not exactly know. Aguirre resumed his inquiry, telling him to answer without any fear, and that no harm should come to him, on account of any statement he might make.

The poor tradesman, being thus pressed, replied that the inhabitants believed that his worship and his followers were cruel Lutherans. This caused Aguirre to become inflamed with anger, and, taking off his helmet, he threatened to throw it at him, saying, " Stupid barbarian! and art thou such an ass as to believe this? I do not dash my helmet at thee, because at some other time I shall chastise thee for thy ignorance, even unto death."

It was necessary for Aguirre to remain in that town longer than he wished, so as to break the horses they had stolen, otherwise the animals would have been no use to them. Meanwhile his soldiers committed every species of excess, destroying all the cattle they could lay hands on, also all the property of the inhabitants they could find, some of which had been buried; they consumed provisions and other things with prodigality, and what they could not use they wasted; for, finding some pipes of wine, hidden under refuse, they brought them to the town, and cooked all their food with wine ; others stood the pipes up, knocked the heads in, and bathed themselves in the wine. These scenes gave Aguirre great pleasure, and he even amused himself in the same way. Seeing how long they were detained in the town, he wrote a letter to the inhabitants of Valencia, which is seven leagues to the east, in which (as absolute lord) he sent to tell them that he did not intend to pass through their town, so as not to delay his march to the new kingdom of Granada, and thence to Pirú, but that he ˙ was desirous that each inhabitant should send him a horse, for which he would faithfully pay the value, and this he trusted they would be all of one mind in doing, which would give him pleasure. If, on the contrary, they did not accede to his demands, he and his soldiers, should they pass that way, would take vengeance on them.

The inhabitants took no heed either of his letter, or of his threats.

CHAP. XLII.

1. *Aguirre kills a tradesman, also a soldier in this town of Burburata.—* 2. *Two of his soldiers desert from him. He begins his march on foot, for want of horses.—3. Aguirre leaves his camp on the road, and returns to Burburata, where he gets drunk with his companions; three desert.—4. Disturbances in the camp whilst Aguirre was at Burburata, two soldiers are killed.—5. Opinions amongst the Marañones relative to the death of one. The tyrant is informed of what had happened, and returns to camp.*

1. Amongst the soldiers who were turning things upside down in the country, to find occupation for their thievish hands, there was one who dug up a jar of olives belonging to the tradesman, named Pedro Nuñez, who was still a prisoner. He had put some pieces of gold into the jar, hoping thus to save them ; and, when it came to his knowledge that a soldier had found his hidden treasure, he went to Aguirre and besought him to see that the gold was given up to him, as the soldiers had eaten the olives.

The traitor commanded the soldier to be brought before him, and, having asked him about the jar of olives and the gold, the soldier replied that it was true as to the olives, but not as regarded the gold. Aguirre then asked the tradesman

A A

how the cover of the jar was fastened on, when he replied, before the soldier, that it was sealed with pitch. The soldier swore this was not the fact, and, to prove the other had spoken falsely, he brought to Aguirre a cover that had been closed with plaster, saying that this was the cover the jar had been closed with, and not one with pitch; so Aguirre, who had not forgotten what he had formerly said to Pedro Nuñez, when he wished to dash his helmet at him, said that any one who could tell such a lie of a soldier, would lie as to every thing else, so he had him strangled.

On the following day, a soldier of the Marañones, named Juan Perez, feeling unwell, left the town and sat himself by the side of a clear running stream. When Aguirre passed that way, and saw him, he said, " What dost thou do here, Perez?" The soldier replied that he was not well, and was merely reposing there. Aguirre observed that if Perez was unwell he could not continue the march, and that it would be as well for him to remain in the town. Aguirre returned to the house, when he commanded Perez to be brought before him, saying that he was not well, and that it would be as well to cure him; but instead of this, he hung Perez, although great efforts were made to save the soldier. Aguirre replied with great anger to those who interceded, telling them not to speak in favour of any man who was so lukewarm in war; and so he ordered a placard to be put on the dead man, notifying that he had been executed for being useless and backward. In these, and other cruelties, the traitor and his Marañones passed the time which was requisite to get the horses ready for the journey.

2. All being nearly ready to march towards Valencia, to which place he intended to go (probably because the inhabitants had refused to send the horses, and had not answered his letter), two soldiers, named Pedro Arias de Almesta, and Diego de Alarcon, disgusted with their position, and unsatisfied as to their security in regard to the maddened violence of

Aguirre, came to the conclusion that, as he was on the point of starting, he would not look after them if they fled; so they both deserted together. When this was known to the traitor, he sent forth a troop of trusty followers to search for them, to the estate of the alcalde Chaves (who was still a prisoner in the town), and he ordered his wife and daughter to be brought in. They having been brought, he ordered Chaves to go and find the two deserters, and told him that if he did not do this, he would take his wife and daughter with him to Pirú, but that if he succeeded, he would restore them.

Having destroyed the town, he loaded the horses with his artillery and munitions of war, and, as their number was only just sufficient for this work, the soldiers had each to carry his own arms and provisions; so they all sallied forth on foot, even Aguirre's own daughter, and the wife and daughter of the alcalde, besides other females, who had continued with them since they had left Pirú.

Aguirre left three sick soldiers in the town, namely, Juan de Paredes, Francisco Marquina, and Alonzo Ximenez, who, being unable to proceed, had to be left behind. This was considered a marked favour on the part of Aguirre, that, now being worn out and useless, he did not hang them; perhaps it was because they had been his accomplices in all his cruelties.

3. They were all marching on foot, at no great distance from the town, and going up a hilly track, when they descried a piragua in which some Spaniards came, bound for the port, and the traitor, putting his trust in no one (for his bad conscience gave him mortal fears), determined to return to the town, and get hold of those who came in the piragua. So he continued his march quickly up the hilly route, and on the descent on the other side he halted his men, so that they could not be seen from the port. Here he left his party in charge of his great friend, Juan de Aguirre,

his majordomo, with orders that no one was to move from that spot until he returned.

At nightfall, he took with him twenty-five or thirty arquebusiers (cross-bowmen), trusted friends, and returned to the town, when they began to ransack the houses, and search for the people who came in the piragua, and not finding them they took possession of one of the houses, and sat themselves down to supper, on what they had brought with them; but they drank so much wine from a pipe that had been left, that all the soldiers were half drunk, but Aguirre was dead drunk. Now would have been the moment to kill the traitor, for there were none to defend him, all being under the influence of drink.

Subsequently his more sober companions were glad that they did not kill him, as it was not God's will that Aguirre should die then.

This drinking bout turned out well, for three soldiers, named Rosales, Acosta, and Jorge de Rodas, during the dark hours of the night, left the party and deserted. These were sought after but not found, although they merely hid themselves in the town, in the hope that those of the piragua would come in that night, or the next morning, and take them.

4. There were not wanting dissensions in the camp during this absence of Aguirre in the town; for on that same day (there being no water in the camp, and it being very hot, their thirst caused them to search for water), the soldiers took vessels and went into the woods, which were very thick, in search of water, at a distance from the camp in some little ravines, in which (they being so secret and narrow, and being apparently safe from the traitor), some of the inhabitants of Burburata were secreted, who, having had information from some Indians, their spies, that the soldiers were coming thither in search of them, broke up their camp and went further into the forests. The

soldiers, having arrived at the watering place, and perceiving fresh marks of people, sent some of their Indian
servants to hunt through the woods, and see if they could
not find the people who had left these signs. The Indians
began their search, and far in the interior of the woods
they came upon some huts, where the Spaniards had been,
and, on examining these sylvan habitations, many things
were found belonging to the poor creatures who had fled
in such haste, and amongst them a cloak, which was well
known to belong to one Rodrigo Gutierrez, one of those
who had gone off with Monguia, and returned to his allegiance to the king, under the provincial.

They found, in the cloak, a deposition which Rodrigo
Gutierrez had made before the judge of Burburata, appended
to which there was a declaration against Aguirre by Francisco Martin, a pilot, corroborating the statement of Roderigo
Gutierrez.

This cloak was brought into camp with other articles, and
Juan de Aguirre, having taken due note of it, and seeing
how much all this proved in regard to Francisco Martin,
went to Francisco Martin, who was a prisoner for an affair
he had had with one Anton Garcia, and stabbed him to
death, and so he paid with his life, for having returned again
to his tyrant master, when God had once, in his mercy, set
him free from such companions.

5. It so happened that whilst they were killing the soldier,
and discharging an arquebuss so as to finish him off, one of
the Marañones, named Harana, wilfully or by accident, sent
a ball at the other soldier, Anton Garcia, who was imprisoned with the pilot, and killed him. This caused much
consternation amongst the rest of the soldiers, who accused
Harana of having killed him on purpose, whilst others defended him, and said that the death was accidental; but he
gloried in the deed, and said publicly that he had killed him
because he was going to run away that night, that he was

well killed, and that he would take the act upon himself, for he was sure that his general would be glad of it.   But with all this Harana perceived that the dissensions did not cease —indeed, they increased, and there was a prospect of a recourse to arms.   If this had happened Juan de Aguirre would have got the worst of it; so he went in haste to the port of Burburata, to give notice to the traitor of what had passed and was passing in the camp.

The traitor left the town for the camp, when the murdered remained dead, and the living in life, and what had happened gave pleasure to Aguirre, particularly as regarded the act of his friend and majordomo, Juan de Aguirre.

CHAP. XLIII.

1. *Aguirre marches, but with much trouble, towards Valencia. He becomes ill on the march.—2. They arrive at Valencia, and find it deserted by the inhabitants. Aguirre becomes worse, but recovers, and then kills a soldier.—3. The alcalde, Chaves, takes two soldiers in Burburata, and sends information to Aguirre; one of them runs away. —4. The traitor manages to lay hands on the inhabitants of Valencia, and on another soldier.*

1. On the following day Aguirre went from Burburata to his camp, and began his march to Valencia, by very rough roads indeed, at times being obliged to go on hands and feet in climbing the mountains.   The laden horses suffered particularly, they had to lighten their burdens, and, as the country was a very hot one, their difficulties were increased.   So Aguirre ordered the soldiers to take the baggage which the animals could not carry, independently of their provisions and knapsacks ; and he also obliged some of his captains, and the principal persons of his party, to take a portion of the baggage which the animals had been

unable to carry. Aguirre himself took more than his share, marching amongst the men, and crossing deep openings in the hilly ground, where the horses had to be unladen to pass ; and, in passing the artillery, they all had to assist, so great were the difficulties they had to suffer. They were eight days going from Burburata to Valencia, which brought a sickness upon Aguirre, in consequence of the weight of the things he carried, and the horrid state of the road.

On the day he got to Valencia he became much worse, so that he had to be carried in a hammock by some Indians, whilst some soldiers shaded him with a flag, and he was so out of temper, that when he stopped under the shade of a tree, he shouted to his soldiers, " Kill me, Marañones ! kill me !" which they might easily have done, and they were afterwards even sorry they did not do so, for thus they would have escaped the punishment from their king, which they richly merited for their terrible crimes.

2. When the inhabitants of Valencia received the news of the arrival of Aguirre in the port of Burburata, they gathered together what they had in their houses, and, with their families, went in canoes to some islands situated in a large lake called Tarigua, inhabited by friendly Indians, where they erected huts, so Aguirre could not lay hands on them, and only found their cattle, which he freely helped himself to.[1] When some soldiers, who had been sent in

---

[1] This lake, called *Tarigua* by Padre Simon, is the lake of Valencia, or of Tacarigua. It is larger than the lake of Neufchatel, the land which surrounds it is flat and even, and it has fifteen islands, which rise up like buttresses from the water. It is situated in the rich valley of Aragua, which forms a basin between granite and calcareous mountains of unequal height, separating it from the coast on one side, and from the *llanos* of the interior, on the other. The rivers direct their courses towards this inland lake, which is closed in on all sides, and are there taken up by evaporation.

The town of Valencia, on the banks of lake Tacarigua, was founded in 1555 by Alonzo Diaz Moreno, and is twelve years older than Caraccas. It was at first only a dependency of the port of Burburata.— *Humboldt.*

advance, entered the place, they found it deserted, and the houses empty. They billetted themselves as they liked, selecting the best habitation for Aguirre, in which he took up his quarters the night he arrived. He became very ill here, and in a few days he was reduced to a skeleton, and at the point of death. In this state he could easily have been killed by any one, for there were no guards to watch over him, and the people went in and out of his quarters to see him, as they pleased. However, after a time he got better, and the way he showed his thanks to God, who had spared him, was to utter blasphemies against his Creator and his saints, and against the people who had left the place, calling them barbarians and cowards, for such he said they must be, " for not one soldier or Indian had joined his party, which was so honourably employed in warlike doings, as true men who had loved war, and followed the profession of arms since the beginning of the world ; war was so honourable a career that the angels in heaven had had theirs." In this manner he jumbled up all sorts of absurdities and heresies, which were hateful even to the ears of those soldiers of the band who were like himself.

The soldiers, finding the houses empty, and that there was nothing in them to destroy, burnt them to ashes. They also laid hands upon the cattle for food, and on the horses to ride, and to carry their baggage and warlike stores. The traitor, having somewhat recovered, issued a proclamation that no soldier should go further from the town than within gun-shot, without his permission, under pain of death. This was a net, in which he knew he would catch some of them, and thus shed blood, for it appeared to him, in consequence of his sickness, that too many days had passed without an execution.

It so happened that a soldier named Gonzalo, who had the post of paymaster (this office was nominal, for the only payment in that camp was that which each man purloined), and to whose knowledge the proclamation had not come, left the town without his license, to catch some parrots; and for this offence Gonzalo was killed, the moment Aguirre was made aware of his having done so.

3. Chaves, the alcalde of Burburata, was very anxious to find the two soldiers who had deserted from Aguirre, for the traitor had taken his wife and daughter with him as hostages, until the soldiers were found. He was assisted in the search by his son-in-law, Don Julian de Mendoza, his friends and servants. After a time the soldiers were found, and, being chained, Mendoza was charged to take them to Aguirre, and so liberate his wife and mother-in-law. They started, but Pedro Arias became so cast down with fear, at the thoughts of the rigorous punishment to be expected from Aguirre, that, whilst on the journey, he threw himself on the ground, saying that he would go no farther. Don Julian observed that such a determination was of little consequence to him, for that the head of the deserter would be sufficient for Aguirre. The soldier replied that Don Julian might cut it off if he thought fit, but that he would not move from that spot. But Don Julian was serious in his view of the case, and, without more ado, he drew his sword with one hand, and with the other, lifting up the soldier's beard, began cutting his throat. The soldier Pedro Arias, feeling that Don Julian was in earnest, implored him to desist, promising to do his best in going onwards, although seriously wounded.

At last they arrived at Valencia, when the deserters were exchanged for the two women. Aguirre immediately ordered Diego de Alarcon to be hung and quartered. The culprit was dragged through the streets, the common crier shouting, " This is the sentence commanded to be put into execution by Lope de Aguirre, the great chief of the noble Marañones, on this man, because he is a faithful vassal of the king of Castille, that he be dragged to the place of exe-

cution, hung, and quartered; and such is the fate of those
who act like him." His head was cut off, and placed on the
rollo which was in the plaza. Aguirre, passing by this
spot, and seeing the head, shouted, with a devilish laugh,
" Ah! are you there, friend Alarcon? How is it the king
of Castille comes not to bring thee to life?" With regard to
the other soldier, Pedro Arias de Almete, as he was a good
penman, and as Aguirre required him as his secretary,
he was not executed, but attention was paid to the curing of
his wounds. This was looked upon as a miracle, because for
much less things than desertion, Aguirre hung his followers
in pairs.

4. The traitor now ordered Christoval Garcia, a ship
caulker, with a party of soldiers, to do their best in getting to
the island where the inhabitants of the town had taken refuge,
to lay hands on all the effects they could, and to bring them
to Aguirre. Garcia started, and arrived at the lake, which
was deep, but he found no means of getting to the island.
He did his best to make rafts of canes, but, on embarking,
they settled down on one side, and let their cargo into
the water; and, as Garcia saw no other mode of accomplish-
ing his object, he returned to the town. This unsuccessful
operation vexed Aguirre much, particularly as his men had
been unable to lay hands on any of the inhabitants. He
was, however, somewhat appeased by receiving a letter
from Chaves, the alcalde of Burburata, in which he stated
that, desiring to serve him, he had imprisoned Rodrigo
Gutierrez, who was the owner of the cloak in which the
deposition had been found, and one of the three soldiers
who, with Captain Monguia, had been the cause of the desertion of the party to the king's side at Maracapana, and who
also had remained in Burburata when the father provincial
arrived; and that, if Aguirre sent immediately for him, he
should be given up. This information delighted the traitor,
and he sent off Francisco Carrion, his principal alguazil,

with twelve soldiers to fetch the deserter. Gutierrez, having been informed of what Chaves had done, fled to the church; and Carrion tried to get him out, but the priest defended the man; so the alcalde was imprisoned, and guards were set over him. This, however, gave time for Gutierrez to get rid of his chains, and fly for safety to the woods. The alcalde feared for his own life, for having disappointed Aguirre of another victim; however, the alguazil and his men returned to the traitor, who, on hearing of this unsuccessful result, was very angry with the alguazil, particularly for not killing Chaves, in revenge for the escape of the soldier.

CHAP. XLIV.

1. *The traitor allows the priest of Margarita to return to his dwelling, on condition that he forwards a letter Aguirre had written to the king. —2. The alcalde of Burburata informs the traitor as to the preparations the governor is making to oppose him: Aguirre kills three soldiers.—3. A sentinel informs the town of Barquicimeto, that Aguirre is marching on it, the inhabitants fly.—4. Ten of Aguirre's soldiers desert on the march, at which he becomes very wroth, and utters ten thousand blasphemies, as was his custom.*

1. Aguirre had brought Father Pedro Contreras, the priest of Margarita, with him to Valencia, who had often begged to be allowed to return to his flock. In the end this was conceded, but he was made to take his oath that he would cause a letter written by the traitor to be sent to the king of Castille, and, if the letter could not be forwarded at once from Margarita, to send it to the Royal Audience of Santo Domingo, or by any other channel, provided it reached the hands of the king. The priest at first objected to take the oath, but seeing how important it was for him to escape from the traitor, and thus save his life, he did

so. He returned to the port, and thence to the island of
Margarita, and did his best to forward the letter to the
king, although it was a most audacious piece of com-
position, and as full of absurdities as the individual who had
written it, for in it he showed his little talent and sense, but
the cruelty of his disposition was most apparent. The letter
began thus : " King Philip, a Spaniard, son of Charles the
invincible, etc."; but we will not extract more, as its extra-
vagancies are not worth printing : however, many copies of
the said letter are to be found in these countries of the Indies
and other parts, some of which I have seen.[1]

[*Francisco Vasquez*, *MS. Relacion*, pp. 79-86. " At
this time the tyrant wrote a letter to the king Don Philip,
our lord, which was as evil and shameful as himself."

LETTER FROM THE TYRANT LOPE DE AGUIRRE TO
KING PHILIP II.

" King Philip, a Spaniard, son of Charles the Invincible!
I, Lope de Aguirre, thy vassal, am an old Christian, of poor
but noble parents, and native of the town of Oñate, in
Biscay. In my youth I crossed the ocean to the land of
Peru, lance in hand, to perform what is due from an honest
man, and, during fifty-four years, I have done thee great
service in Peru, in the conquest of the Indians, in forming
settlements, and especially in battles and encounters which
I have fought in thy name, always to the best of my power

---

[1] Old Father Simon's loyalty was horrified at the idea of printing
Aguirre's treasonable letter to the king of Spain. A copy is now, however, inserted in this translated edition of his text, taken from the
manuscript narrative of Francisco Vasquez, one of Aguirre's followers ;
and no scruple is felt in doing so, because Simon's account of Aguirre's
cruize is copied almost word for word from Vasquez, without any
acknowledgment.

There is another copy of this very curious letter, somewhat abridged,
in *La Historia de Venezuela por Don José de Oviedo y Baños* (1723),
lib. iv, cap. vii, p. 206 ; which appears to have been taken from some
other manuscript, and not from that of Vasquez. Humboldt (in his

and ability, without asking thy officers for payment, as will appear by thy royal books.

"I firmly believe that thou, O Christian king and lord, hast been very cruel and ungrateful to me and my companions for such good service, and that all those who write to thee from this land deceive thee much, because thou seest things from too far off. I, and my companions (whose names I will mention presently), no longer able to suffer the cruelties which thy judges and governors exercise in thy name, are resolved to obey thee no longer. We regard ourselves no longer as Spaniards. We make a cruel war on thee, because we will not endure the oppression of thy ministers, who, to give places to their nephews and their children, dispose of our lives, our reputations, and our fortunes. I am lame in the left foot, from two shots of an arquebus, which I received in the battle of Chucuinga,[1] fighting under the orders of the marshal Alonzo de Alvarado, against Francisco Hernandez Giron, a rebel, as I and my companions are now, and will be until death: for we now know, in this country, how cruel thou art, that thou art a breaker of thy faith and word; therefore, even if we received thy pardon, we should give less credence to it, than to the books of Martin Luther.

"Thy viceroy, the marquis of Cañete, a bad, effeminate,

Narrative, iv, p. 257, note A,) has made some extracts from the version of Oviedo; and Southey (who had never seen either the work of Oviedo, or the manuscript of Vasquez), in his account of Aguirre's voyage, copied these extracts from Humboldt's *Narrative*. Piedrahita had never seen a copy of the letter.

Oviedo y Baños thus introduces this strange epistle. "Though the letter delivered by Lope de Aguirre to Padre Contreras, to be transmitted to the king, really does not deserve notice, yet, as a specimen of the madness of that man, we refer to it, that the reader may be amused for a moment by this fine letter, as being dictated by an owner of mules."

[1] Oviedo y Baños, in copying this letter, has put *Valley of Coquimbo*, instead of *Battle of Chucuinga*. Humboldt, in the extracts he made, has followed him, and Southey copied from Humboldt. Chucuinga or Chuquinga is in the Andes, between Nasca and Lucanas.

and ambitious tyrant, hung Martin de Robles, a man who had been distinguished in thy service, and the ill fated Alonzo Diaz, who had laboured harder in the discovery of Peru, than the tribes which followed Moses ; and Piedrahita, a good captain, who fought many battles in thy service ; and it was these men who procured a victory for thee in Pucara; for, had it been otherwise, Francisco Hernandez Giron would now be sovereign of Peru. Do not put any faith in the accounts of services which thy judges declare they have performed, because they are great fables, unless they call having spent 800,000 dollars out of the Royal Treasury, a service. Chastise them for their vices and evil deeds, for evil doers they certainly are.

"Hear me! O hear me! thou king of Spain. Be not cruel to thy vassals, for it was while thy father, the emperor Charles, remained quietly in Spain, that they procured for thee so many kingdoms and vast countries. Remember, king Philip, that thou hast no right to draw revenues from these provinces, since their conquest has been without danger to thee. I take it for certain that few kings go to hell, only because they are few in number ; but that if there were many, none of them would go to heaven. For I believe that you are all worse than Lucifer, and that you hunger and thirst after human blood ; and further, I think little of you, and despise you all, nor do I look upon your government as more than an air bubble. Know that I, and my two hundred arquebus-bearing Marañones, have taken a solemn oath to God, that we will not leave one of thy ministers alive. We consider ourselves, at this moment, the happiest men on earth, because, in this land of the Indians, we preserve the faith and the commandments of God in their purity, and we maintain all that is preached by the Church of Rome. We expect, though sinners in this life, to endure martyrdom for the laws of God.

" On leaving the river of Amazons, which is called Mara-

ñon, we came to an island inhabited by Christians, called
Margarita, where we received news from Spain of the great
conspiracy of the Lutherans, which caused us much terror
and alarm. In our company there was one of these Lutherans, named Monteverde,[1] and I ordered him to be cut
to pieces. Believe me, O most excellent king, that I will
force all men to live perfectly in the faith of Christ.

" The corruption of the morals of the monks is so great in
this land, that it is necessary to chastise it severely. There
is not an ecclesiastic here, who does not think himself higher
than the governor of a province. I beg of thee, O great
king, not to believe what the monks tell thee in Spain.
They are always talking of the sacrifices they make, as well
as of the hard and bitter life they lead in America. Be
assured that when they shed tears there, in thy royal presence, it is that here they may be the more powerful.
Wouldst thou know the life which they lead here? they are
engaged in trade, striving for benefices, selling the sacra-
ments of the church for a price, enemies of the poor, avari-
cious, gluttonous, and proud to that degree that, at the least,
every friar pretends to rule and govern all these lands.
They never desire to preach to any poor Indian, yet they
are possessed of the best estates. The life they lead is
surely a hard one, for does not each of them, as a penance,
have a dozen girls, and as many boys, who catch fish, kill
partridges, and gather fruit for them. Remedy this, O king
and lord, or else, I swear to thee, on the faith of a Christian, that heaven will punish thee, and great scandals will
follow. I say this to let thee know the truth, though neither
I, nor my companions, either desire or hope for thy mercy.

" Thy judges, too, each have 4,000 dollars a-year, besides

---

[1] Monteverde, who appears to have been a Fleming, was murdered
long before Aguirre reached Margarita. See p. 101. The blood-thirsty
maniac had committed so many murders, that he had forgotten the
order in which they came.

8,000 for expenses, and, at the end of three years, each of them has 60,000 dollars, besides land and other property. Notwithstanding all this we should be content to submit to them, if, for our sins, they did not force us to bow down and worship them, like Nebuchadnezzar. This is insufferable.

" Alas! alas! what a misfortune it is that the emperor, thy father, has conquered Germany at such a price, and has spent, in that conquest, the money that we procured for him in these very Indies! Most excellent king and lord, Germany was conquered by arms, and Germany has conquered Spain by her vices, of which we are here well rid, and are content with a little maize and water.

" Let wars spread where they may, and where men carry them, yet at no time will we cease to be obedient to the holy church of Rome. We cannot believe, O excellent king and lord! that thou canst be so cruel to such good vassals as thou hast in these parts; and I therefore desire that thou mayst know what thy ministers do without thy consent. Near the city of the kings,[1] and close to the sea, some lakes were discovered where fish were preserved; and thy wicked judges, for their own profit, rented them in thy name, giving out that this was done with thy consent. If this be so, for the love of God allow us to have some of the fish, for it was us who discovered the lakes.[2] Surely the king of Castille is not in need of four hundred dollars, which is the sum for which these lakes are rented : and, O most illustrious king! it is not in Cordova nor in Valladolid that we ask for this property. Deign to dole out charity, my lord, to the poor men who have laboured in this land;

[1] Lima.

[2] These are, no doubt, the lakes of Villa, near Chorillos, and about fifteen miles from Lima; where there is still capital wild duck shooting. Probably Aguirre had been punished for poaching on these lakes; but how strange that this petty grievance, of former years, should have occupied his mind under the circumstances in which he was then placed !

and remember that God is the same to all; that there is the same justice, the same reward, the same heaven, the same hell, for all mankind.

" In the year 1559, the marquis of Cañete entrusted the expedition of the river of Amazons to Pedro de Ursua, a Navarrese, or rather a Frenchman, who delayed the building of his vessels until 1560. These vessels were built in the province of the Motilones, which is a wet country, and, as they were built in the rainy season, they came to pieces, and we therefore made canoes, and descended the river. We navigated the most powerful river in Peru, and it seemed to us that we were in a sea of fresh water. We descended the river for three hundred leagues. This bad governor was capricious, vain, and inefficient, so that we could not suffer it, and we gave him a quick and certain death. We then raised a young gentleman of Seville, named Don Fernando de Guzman to be our king, and we took the same oaths to him as are taken to thy royal person, as may be seen by the signatures of all those who are with me. They named me maestro del campo; and, because I did not consent to their evil deeds, they desired to murder me. I therefore killed this new king, the captain of his guard, his lieutenant-general, four captains, his majordomo, his chaplain, who said mass, a woman, a knight of the Order of Rhodes, an admiral, two ensigns, and five or six of his servants. It was my intention to carry on the war, on account of the many cruelties which thy ministers had committed. I named captains and sergeants; but these men also wanted to kill me, and I hung them. We continued our course while all this evil fortune was befalling us; and it was eleven months and a half before we reached the mouths of the river, having travelled for more than a hundred days, over more than fifteen hundred leagues. This river has a course of two thousand leagues of fresh water, the greater part of the shores being uninhabited; and God only knows

how we ever escaped out of that fearful lake. I advise thee
not to send any Spanish fleet up this ill-omened river; for,
on the faith of a Christian, I swear to thee, O king and
lord, that if a hundred thousand men should go up, not one
would escape, and there is nothing else to expect, especially
for the adventurers from Spain.

" The captains and officers who are now under my command in this enterprise, and who promise to die in it, are
Juan Jeronimo de Espindola, a Genoese, captain of infantry,
admiral Juan Gomez, a Spaniard [then follows a long list],
and many other gentlemen. They pray to God that thy
strength may ever be increased against the Turk and the
Frenchman, and all others who desire to make war against
thee; and we shall give God thanks if, by our arms, we
attain the rewards which are due to us, but which thou hast
denied us; and, because of thine ingratitude, I am a rebel
against thee until death.

        (Signed)

                    " LOPE DE AGUIRRE, the Wanderer."

2. The alcalde, Chaves, showed by his conduct that he was
little better than the Marañones and their leader, and his
acts showed that he was rather for Aguirre than for his king,
for, knowing what the Governor Pablo Collado was doing in
Tocuyo, to resist the traitor, Chaves wrote another letter to
Aguirre on this subject, also informing him that the lieutenant-general, maestro del campo, and other officers, had
been appointed by the governor, and that they had procured assistance from the new kingdom of Granada, with the
intention of defeating him at Barquicimeto, or at Tocuyo.

This was not pleasant news for Aguirre, but he was
obliged to Chaves nevertheless, and made arrangements to
leave his present position at once, for the above mentioned
two places, for he considered that any delay on his part would
be dangerous, as it would give time for the governor to col-

lect more forces, and obstruct his march; so he ordered that, early on the following day, they should raise their camp and leave Valencia. On the night previous, for fear any of his people should desert him, he commanded that all his soldiers should sleep together in an enclosure belonging to his habitation, whence they could have escaped with the same facility as if they had been in the streets, for the walls of the enclosure were only of frail palings. But their desire to continue this loose sort of life prevented them from leaving the company of the traitor.

Aguirre determined, that night, to rid himself of those whom he considered would be troublesome to him on his march, namely three soldiers who had offended him, named Benito Diaz, Francisco de Sosa, and another called Cegarra. The cause of his anger with Diaz was that he had said that he had a relation in the new kingdom of Granada; and, as to the others, it appeared to him that they lent an unwilling hand in warlike affairs; so he strangled them secretly in a hut which was in the enclosure, and, in the morning, when he started, he ordered the hut to be set on fire, so that the three bodies might be burnt. He also left the town and gardens in ruins, and destroyed all the cattle. He then departed with his followers and ninety horses, proceeding to Barquicimeto by the direct road, which traverses the mountains of the province of Nirua, after having been in Valencia fifteen days.

3. The people of the two cities (by order of the governor Collado) had placed spies in proper places, to give notice when the traitor was advancing. One of these, the moment he saw the Marañones enter the mountains, started with great haste, and, as he came running into the city of Barquicimeto, he shouted to the people to arm themselves, for that the tyrant was fast approaching, and that he would be there during the day; but, as the inhabitants were unprepared (all the people of the district were not collected

together in the town with the general, Gutierrez de la Peña,
but some were in Tocuyo, making necessary arrangements for
defeating Aguirre), they fled to the woods, with their wives
and children, taking such of their property with them as
they could, in the confusion of their retreat, and leaving the
town empty.   The traitor arrived eight days after the flight
of the people.

4. Aguirre was now in the mountains, the track was bad
and rocky, and surrounded by thick forests ; so some of the
soldiers thought this was a good opportunity to desert, from
such vile companions.   Ten of them, one by one, hid themselves, without knowing where any of his companions were ;
so that, when this came to Aguirre's knowledge, it was too
late to catch them ; but he gave rein to his pestilent tongue,
shouting a thousand blasphemies against God and his saints,
as was his custom when angered, casting his eyes to heaven
with threatening looks, stamping wildly on the ground,
foaming at the mouth, and making vows of revenge, and
horrid oaths, saying, " Ah, Marañones ! how true it is what
I have said, that you would leave me in the hour of greatest
need, and that I should have to fight alone with the mountain cats, and monkeys of the forests ; better would it have
been had I died ere this, than that I should yield my life to
these vile ones of Venezuela !   Oh, thou prophet Antonico !
how well didst thou foresee the truth.   Had I but believed
thee, these Marañones would not have deserted." This he said,
alluding to a little page that he had, of whom he was very
fond, who often told him not to trust the Marañones, as they
would all leave him when it suited them to do so : so, when
any of them ran away, he remembered the warnings of
Antonico.

At this juncture Juan Gomez, Aguirre's admiral, came to
him and said, " Body of God ! Señor general, why does your
worship thus vex yourself ? The other day three men deserted
us ; but if thirty had done so, I would rather have had the

room than the company of such fellows, for there would
have been so many enemies less; but for the love of God!
there are many and strong trees hereabouts!" giving him to
understand by this observation, that, as he had executed
three of his men before he left Valencia, he could hang
such as he had unfavourable suspicions of, and in this way
rid himself of his present fears. Aguirre listened atten-
tively to this advice of his admiral, but did not consider it
politic to act upon it, as it might produce greater difficulties,
though subsequently he attempted such wholesale murder.

CHAP. XLV.

1. *Aguirre, marching from Valencia to Barquicimeto, comes to a mining
settlement, where he falls into some trouble.—2. The traitor advances
to the river of the valley of the Damas, where he rests a day.—3. Here
he determines to kill some of his men, but does not do so. One of his
captains comes from Margarita to Barquicimeto, and gives information as to Aguirre's forces.—4. The maestro del campo, Diego Garcia
de Paredes, reconnoitres the forces of the traitor.*

1. Three days had Aguirre been on his march, when he fell
in with a mining settlement, where gold was extracted; but
the inhabitants and their negro workmen had fled. In the
hurry of flight a large quantity of maize was left behind in a
hut, of which Aguirre was glad, for his party wanted provisions; still, he would have been better pleased had he been
able to lay hands on the negro miners, and add them to a
party of twenty others he had with him under their captain,
for he trusted that the negros would be of much use to him
in his projected warlike encounters, for he had already well
schooled these negros, and had told them they were free.
He allowed them the same licence as the Spaniards, to commit every species of enormity, and they exceeded the doings
of the white men in robberies, cruelties, and murders.

After a day's rest, Aguirre continued his route, when very heavy rains fell, soaking his people to the skin, and causing the track up the mountains to be so slippery that the unshod laden animals were continually slipping and falling, and even rolling backwards, to the great inconvenience of the soldiers.

At this the furious Aguirre suggested impossible remedies, accompanied by a thousand blasphemies and heresies against God and his saints, concluding with the following: "Does God think that because it rains in torrents I am not to go to Pirú, and destroy the world? He is mistaken in me." At last the miscreant became convinced that his blasphemous conduct did not aid the progress of the laden animals, so he ordered his soldiers, by the aid of hoes, and other instruments, to cut steps in the steep parts of the track, so that the animals might get some sort of hold, and thus get to the top.

2. Whilst the rear of this piratical crew were occupied in overcoming the difficulties of the road, the van, having no baggage, and the track being narrow and tortuous, so that they could not see each other, and being unmindful of the delay there might be in the ascent of the baggage and animals, went onwards without stopping. On Aguirre's arrival at the summit, his vanguard was not to be seen. This threw him into a violent rage, and he rode a-head as fast as possible, coming up after a time with his mayordomo and friend, Juan de Aguirre, and his captain of the guard, Roberto de Susaya, when he said, "I predict to you, señores, that if there does not arrive amongst us, from this district, forty or fifty soldiers, I begin to perceive that in the present state of mind of my Marañones, we shall never get to the new kingdom." Onward went the traitor after the vanguard, and coming up with it, he abused both officers and men roundly, ordering them back to the mountain pass they had descended, where Aguirre took up

his quarters for the night.   On the following morning he
gave orders that, during the march, the van of his followers
should be more attentive than heretofore to the progress of
the rear.   The march commenced, when they came to the
valley of the Damas, so called by the first Spaniards who
discovered this part of the country.   They descended into
the valley, and came upon a large ravine with a considerable
stream of good water, called Aracin (which I can personally
vouch for).   Near the stream a hut was met with, full of
maize, which was most opportune, and was the cause of their
resting a day at this spot, during which period they were informed of the arrival of some of the king's troops at Barquicimeto through their spies, who were posted at the entrance of the valley.

3. The traitor, seeing that he was near the town in which
Chaves, the alcalde of Burburata, had informed him that
the king's forces were collecting, began to have fresh
fears of some of his soldiers, and, communicating these
suspicions to certain of his well-tried captains, he told them
of his determination to kill all the suspected soldiers, as well
as the sick, some forty in number, for, with such an example,
the remainder would be true to him.   Some of the junta did
not agree with their commander, probably inspired from
above.   They said that if he did so his course would be less
secure with the others, for they considered if this occurred,
that in time their turn would come to share the same fate.
So Aguirre changed his mind as to this sanguinary proceeding, and his view of having only one hundred of his well-
tried friends, as his companions.

Some days before this, one of Aguirre's captains had
arrived at Barquicimeto, and had entered the king's camp.
This was an officer whom we have already mentioned, named
Pedro Galeas, who (a few days before the traitor had left Margarita), had been asked by the traitor if he had a flag.   Galeas
replied in the negative, when he gave him twenty yards of silk

to make one. On another day (the day before he embarked), Aguirre said, " Pedro Alonzo, hast thou a drum?" when he replied that he only had the case, but without parchment. The traitor then said to him, " Then, by the life of God! be not surprised if I make of thy skin, parchment for the drum." Pedro Alonzo Galeas gave the best answer he could, and retired from the presence of the monster, not without fear that he might be sentenced to death, for shortly afterwards a friend, as he passed him, told him that he had been doomed to die. Galeas kept well on the watch, and at night he escaped to the sea-shore, where he found Captain Faxardo, who had just landed, who as we have said came from Caraccas, with help for the island; and giving him an account of his danger, Faxardo provided him with a canoe in which he went to Burburata, when he gave information respecting the traitor, the number of his followers, and arms, and the reason of his desertion to save his life.[1]

About the time Aguirre was leaving Valencia, Galeas was coming to Barquicimeto, where he arrived simultaneously with General Gutierrez de la Peña, who had come from Tocuyo with his soldiers. Peña and his followers had some suspicion that Galeas might be a spy of Aguirre's, so they guarded him for some days, until they were satisfied with his good conduct, and expressions of sorrow that he had ever been in such vile company as that of Aguirre, of whose forces and arms he gave a full account (which was what the king's party most desired to know), assuring them

[1] Pedro Alonzo Galeas had been employed by Ursua, on detached service, on two occasions, see p. 26, p. 32, p. 35, p. 96.

On deserting Aguirre, he received his pardon, and continued to serve for many years, under the governors of Venezuela. In 1572 he was employed by the governor, Don Diego de Mazariego, to subdue the Mariches Indians, who, since their cacique had been impaled by Pedro Ponce de Leon, the former governor, had retired into the woods, and harrassed the Spaniards. He completely defeated them, and brought them under subjection again.—*Oviedo y Baños.*

also that, of the hundred and forty men he had with him, only fifty followed him out of choice, and that the rest only waited for the opportunity of being protected by the king's troops, to abandon the traitor. Galeas also informed the royalists of the best way to manage Aguirre; not to attack him in a pitched battle, but to retire before him, and in this manner the king's troops would be in no danger.

4. All this gave courage to Gutierrez and his soldiers, for they were somewhat doubtful of success, seeing how few their numbers were, and the scarcity of arms and ammunition, as was seen when the maestro del campo, Diego Garcia de Paredes,[1] went out with fourteen or fifteen men to reconnoitre the camp of the traitor.

All the troops were on horseback, but they had the most wretched saddles and bridles; their only arms were some badly made lances, and some Burgundian helmets, which

[1] Diego Garcia de Paredes was the son of a very distinguished officer of the same name, a native of Estremadura. When Pizarro returned to Spain, after his first discovery of Peru, young Paredes joined him, and was present at the landing of the Spaniards at Tumbez, and at the arrest of Atahualpa at Caxamarca. Paredes returned to Spain with Hernando Pizarro, and afterwards fought under the banner of Charles V, in Italy, Germany, and at Tunis. He again embarked for the Indies, and, having been some time at Nombre de Dios, he finally went to Venezuela, where he founded the city of Truxillo ; which he named after the place of his birth in Spain. This was in the year 1556. In 1559 Pablo Collado was appointed governor of the neighbouring district of Tocuyo ; while Paredes continued to govern Truxillo, until, in 1561, the Royal Audience of Bogota received tidings of the unheard of cruelties of Lope de Aguirre. Paredes lost no time in mustering his forces and marched to Merida, to assist the governor Collado, who appointed him maestro del campo, and where, as Simon relates, he took a leading part in destroying the traitor. He then sailed for Spain, with some of the banners of Aguirre, which he placed over the tomb of his father. These banners had the blood-red swords worked crossways upon them. As a reward for these services Paredes received the government of Popayan, and once more sailed for the Indies in 1563. He landed on the coast of Venezuela, with a small party, where he was killed by the Indians, who fired arrows upon his followers, from an ambuscade.—*Pizarro's Varones Illustres del Nuevo Mundo*, p. 399.

were merely dirty old hoods, made out of pieces of cloth of various colours, with two or three linings of cotton cloth; and the sight of such helmets provoked a smile, rather than confidence as to their utility for defence.

The general remained in Barquicimeto (whilst Paredes went out to look after the enemy) with the rest of the king's troops, some seventy in number, armed in about the same unsatisfactory manner as the party of Paredes. The general had only two arquebuses, one of them having no lock, and very little powder; neither could it be said that they were good horsemen, indeed only the captains had any pretensions to the art; as to the men, when mounted, they looked more like baggage than caballeros. Having made these warlike preparations the general, Peña, remained behind, not over comfortable, anxiously hoping for the success of the maestro del campo.

CHAP. XLVI.

1. *The maestro del campo, in a narrow part of the road, unexpectedly finds himself in Aguirre's camp. Both parties retire.—2. The general Peña takes letters of pardon from the governor, for Aguirre and his soldiers.—3. The king's party determine to await Aguirre's attack upon the town. Aguirre writes a letter of promises and threats.—4. The traitor's party show themselves to those in the town, but no action ensues.*

1. Paredes was on the march with his people towards the enemy, and Aguirre with his against the royalists, on the day he left the Aracin valley, the former entering the lower part of the valley of the Damas, the latter descending from the upper. Their track lay through thick forests, most difficult to march through, and by such a narrow path that one tra- veller had to follow behind another, and horsemen scarcely

had room to turn their horses. On such a road both parties were coming in opposite directions, without having an idea of each other's position, when suddenly they came in sight. They were so astounded at thus seeing each other, that the only determination they came to was mutually to retreat. Those who came with the maestro del campo (as they were mounted, the road very narrow, and their confusion considerable), whilst turning their horses, had some of their Morisco lances, and some of their Burgundian helmets, knocked off by the branches of the trees; and, as it appeared to them that there was no time to collect their fallen lances and helmets, they were left by the retreating soldiers. No less were the difficulties of the Marañones; they did not march armed, neither were the matches of their arquebuses lighted; they, however, lighted them at once, and commenced their march in the best way they could, suffering much from the obstacles of the road, until nightfall, when they encamped near a rivulet. They examined the arms and helmets that had been dropped by the soldiers of the maestro del campo, and jeering at one and the other, the traitor said to his people: " Do ye not perceive, Marañones, where fortune has brought ye, and where ye wish to fly to and remain ? Look at these helmets, brought by the galleons of Meliona! see how rich these vassals of the king of Castille are !" In this and a thousand similar ridiculous observations, in regard to the helmets, they amused themselves until two or three in the morning, when the moon rose, and they continued their march, Aguirre taking care secretly to place guards near to those he suspected, so that they might not desert.

2. The maestro del campo did not draw rein until he arrived at some savannas or open land outside the forest, where he proposed to form ambuscades, and rout the tyrant; but this plan did not take effect, for the Marañones, who were marching by the light of the moon, came upon the royalists, who decamped in haste from before Aguirre.

The maestro del campo, having twice been too near his enemy, returned with all speed to the city of Barquicimeto, from whence he advised the governor, who was still at Tocuyo, as to the state of affairs.

The military portion of the community held council how best to defend the place, and oppose the tyrant. They considered that they were not very safe within the city, inasmuch as they were on horseback, and had no arquebuses; while the traitors were on foot and had firearms, and if they took possession of any of the houses (as it was most probable), they could defend themselves and annoy the royalists and their horses at pleasure. The general Peña had many letters of pardon with him (for as the licenciate Gasca had done in Pirú, when he went against Gonzalo Pizarro and his followers, so had the governor Pablo Collado written these documents, and signed them in the king's name), which promised to all those of Aguirre's men, who would leave him and come over to the king's side, before they encountered each other in battle, full pardon for all the crimes which they had committed in this rebellion, promising them their lives in his royal name. With these there was a still stronger pardon for Aguirre, with a letter in which he was exhorted to abandon this rebellion, and join the king's forces, promising him that the governor would take no notice of what had occurred, but rather that he would place these matters at the pious feet of his majesty, with his strong recommendation that all should be confirmed that he promised in his royal name to him and his soldiers; but if he still persisted in continuing his present state of life, to save the lives of so many who must fall in battle, Collado proposed that Aguirre should meet him, and settle the question in single combat.

3. The king's party, having arranged to leave the city to Aguirre, distributed the letters of pardon in the houses, so that when the Marañones came in, they might easily find

them. Having done this, they took with them all the provisions, so that the traitor might find none there; and then they all separated, retiring to the heights of the open country, and having marched half a league, they encamped that night by the side of a stream, whilst Aguirre was journeying that same night towards Barquicimeto, arriving at noon within a league and a half, and also halting by a stream. Here he loaded his guns and pointed them in the direction of the road that came down from the town, placing his band so as to be in readiness for any emergency. The traitor now determined to send a letter to the town, by an Indian Yanacona, one of those he had brought with him from Pirú. In this letter he told the people of the town not to leave the place, for that it was not his intention to do them any harm; that he required some provisions and horses, which he would pay well for, and if any soldiers or others wished to accompany him to Pirú, he would allow them to do so, promising such persons most honourable treatment, and that when they got to Pirú they should have a pleasant life of it; but, on the contrary, if they fled from the town, he gave them his oath that he would burn it to ashes, destroy their cattle and plantations, and tear to pieces all the inhabitants that fell into his hands, and do his utmost to prevent any from escaping.

The royalists received this letter, and, taking due note of its extravagances, did not give themselves much trouble in replying to it, for they were well aware of the sort of friendship they had to expect from the traitor.

Aguirre rested that half day, and the following night; and the next day, Wednesday, the 22nd of October, in the year 1561, he put his forces in order of march, including his artillery, at the same time issuing an order, that if any soldiers went three paces out of the line of march, those who might be nearest to such an offender, were to kill him with their arquebuses, or in any other convenient manner.

Gutierrez de la Peña had not been unmindful on his side during the night, and the same Wednesday, at daylight, he, with all his soldiers on horseback (a little more than eighty in number), placed themselves on the heights just within firing distance of the arquebuses of the town, and west of it, from whence Peña could see Aguirre's camp, and that he was advancing rapidly, with the royalist force in sight. Aguirre now halted at the bottom of the ravine, and near to the first houses of the town, marshalling his people afresh. He placed his best friends well armed, in front, refreshing their memories as to what orders he had given them; in the rear were placed the baggage and servants, with the rest of his soldiers, and the march to the town was resumed. In the meanwhile the king's troops commenced descending to the houses, when Aguirre saluted, by firing his heavily loaded arquebuses with powder only, so as to make more noise, in the hope of striking terror into his enemy. He then ordered the firearms to be double shotted, and unfurling four flags and two standards, he continued his march, entering the town on one side, whilst the royalists did the same at the other; but as the town was small, they soon came near to each other.

The king's party had their doubts as to the prudence of attacking the traitor, and resolved, as they were so badly supplied with arms, in comparison with what Aguirre had, to retreat again to the heights, so there was no fighting; moreover, this would give time for those of the tyrant's followers who wished to leave him, to join the king's troops, for if they had come to a fight in the town, there was not a soldier under the traitor's banner who would not have sold his life dearly, as yet not knowing of the promised pardon.

CHAP. XLVII.

1. *Garcia de Paredes lays hands on some clothes and ammunition belonging to the traitor. His soldiers find the letters of pardon.—* 2. *Aguirre talks to them on this subject, they decide on following him.* —3. *Aguirre sets fire to the town. The maestro del campo fires into the enemy's camp. This vexes Aguirre.*—4. *Pedro Bravo de Molina arrives with men from Merida, where the governor had made him his lieutenant-general.*

1. Whilst the king's troops were retiring to the heights, the maestro del campo, Diego Garcia de Paredes, with eight companions on horseback, separated from the main body, and, unobserved by Aguirre's men, fell upon the traitor's rear, which had not as yet reached the town, taking four horses laden with clothes, powder, and other things, which were much needed by the royalists, as they were unprovided with them, and had not even powder for their few arquebuses.

Aguirre took up his quarters, with all his people, in a large square place, in the highest part of the town, surrounded by high mud walls with turrets, where the houses of a captain named Damian del Barrio stood. Here the traitor was somewhat protected from his adversaries, and felt more secure of many of his followers, of whom he had suspicion that they would desert.

The king's party could see their opponents from the heights, where they were encamped, anxiously waiting to see if any of Aguirre's men, who had found the letters of pardon, would desert him; but as he had shut them up in a guarded position, none of them could leave their quarters.

As night approached, the general left a troop of twelve of his best horsemen on the heights, and returned to his camp. Aguirre perceived that his enemy had moved, and, as his men were very anxious indeed to rob the houses, thinking they would find good pillage, he gave them leave to go to the houses, and strip them of all they could find.

However, as we have said, the inhabitants had removed all their property. They only found the letters of pardon for them, as well as one for Aguirre, accompanied by a letter, the reading of which rather disturbed him. He said to his soldiers : " I know, Señores, that you have found other letters of pardon written by the governor, in which inducements are held out for you to join him, promising pardon for all the wickedness you have committed up to the present time, and, as I am an experienced man in such things, and I wish you and myself well, I shall undeceive you : so put no trust in governors, nor in their papers or signatures ; think on the cruelties, robberies, deaths, and destruction of towns you have committed, you may be well assured that, as to the atrocities you have committed ; neither in Spain, the Indies, nor any other part of the world, have there been such men as you are, who have done such horrors; and I tell you, although the king in person wished to pardon you, I do not believe he would be allowed to do so, much less a licenciate such as Pablo Collado, for the relations and friends of those you have slain would hunt you to the death and kill you, for you will be always exposed to be murdered, you will be insulted and hunted like wild beasts, and called traitors. Just see what was the fate of Piedrahita, of Tomas Vasquez, and of other captains, in regard to the king's pardon, when, having served the crown of Castille the whole of their lives, there came a talkative little lawyer of no account, who cut their heads off ;[1] then what would happen to us, who have committed more murders and desperate actions in one day, than all those who have rebelled in the Indies against the king ? Let each of you think well on this ; be not too easy of belief ; do nothing in a hurry so as to repent afterwards ; and, as I have often said, nowhere are you so safe as in my company. As to having anything to do with these papers of the governor, they are bitter fruit and gilded pills, so that under a delu-

[1] Alluding to the executions of the marquis of Cañete, in Peru.

sive colour you would swallow poison. Let us reflect : if we at present have hunger and troubles, the future has rest in store for us ; if we have some difficulties before we get to Pirú, there we shall find abundance and happiness." Concluding, as he generally did when speaking on important occasions, " then let us sell our lives dearly, and do our duty."

3. Nevertheless each man apparently had his own particular view of the position of affairs. Aguirre, thinking that the houses of the town might give cover to the enemy, ordered them to be set on fire, only leaving a few, for the use of his arquebusiers. As the houses were of straw, some of the sparks set fire to the church, which was built of the same materials as the houses ; it is, however, said that the church was set on fire by a soldier named Francisco de Guerra ; but when Aguirre saw the church in flames (to give an idea that he had some Christian feelings), he immediately ordered that some ornaments and images of saints, which were on the altar, should be saved.

The king's troops, being aware of the reason why certain houses had been preserved, set fire to them when it was night, so that the only one remaining was that in which the traitor had his quarters.

During the night both camps were watchful of each other, but at daybreak Diego Garcia de Paredes, with some friends on horseback, and five arquebuses, which was the whole of the artillery even now in the king's camp (they had had only two at first, but were reinforced by three more), approached Aguirre's entrenchment, fired the arms, and made other disturbances, so as to disquiet the traitor and cause confusion. Aguirre ordered his men under arms, but it being still dark, it was some time before they could distinguish one another. He then ordered forty of his arquebusiers to sally out silently, and attack the maestro del campo. When they were within firing distance, they dis-

E E

charged their pieces, but without effect; neither did this operation cause any disturbance to those in the king's camp, who, without discomposing themselves, were well on their guard.

Each party retired to his camp; and it would appear as if God was so arranging these matters, that the traitor should be conquered, without more blood being spilt on either side, for enough had been already shed.

4. The governor, Pablo Collado (in consequence of indisposition caused by his apprehension as to the success of the king's arms), retired to Tocuyo, until captain Pedro Bravo de Molina, with his people, came from Merida, which was on the same day that Aguirre entered Barquicimeto. The governor had no intention of being present at any encounters with the traitor, notwithstanding the letter he had written to him (as some understood and published), advising him to come and cure himself of his malady in this New Kingdom, for that it was especially adapted for the improvement of his health; under the supposition that he might overthrow the traitor. Captain Pedro Bravo, perceiving the coldness of the governor, essayed to persuade him how important it was that he should be present in the king's camp, as representing his royal person, which would animate the soldiers to comply with their obligations, and in the hope that he would repay their exertions, and report to the king their conduct in his service, having seen with his own eyes what they had done; moreover, it would tarnish his honour if he did not go.

At first the governor made some excuses, referring to his peculiar attacks of illness, which had prevented him heretofore from joining the royal standard; but, as it was the desire of captain Bravo, he said he would make the effort to be found in the king's camp; the more particularly with the succours Bravo had brought with him, for which he was very grateful to the captain, and, seeing that he was a good and proper man, he named Bravo as his lieutenant-general, not only for this expedition, but for the district he was governor of, and he also gave him his commission as captain of the cavalry.

CHAP. XLVIII.

1. *Bravo accepts the posts conferred on him by the governor; they all leave Tocuyo for the king's camp.*—2. *Aguirre's letter to the governor, Pablo Collado.*—3. *Those from Tocuyo join the king's forces, when victory over the traitor is anticipated.*—4. *Two of Aguirre's soldiers desert to the king's side. The maestro del campo and captain Bravo catch some Indians belonging to the Marañones.*

1. At first the soldiers of Merida did not think that their captain ought to have accepted the offices he did, and that he ought not to march under the governor's banner, but rather go independently, as he came from another district, under his own flag, and with his own followers, to do what lay in his power, or even to show prodigies of valour.

But Pedro Bravo, by accepting the several important offices, considered he was acting in accordance with the rules of honour, as well as for the benefit of himself and his men, and, in truth, he served his king right well in all he did.

The governor, still considering that he had not conferred sufficient honours on Bravo, offered likewise to assist his soldiers and followers in anything they required. Some of the soldiers, in order to find out to what point the governor's liberality extended, rather than that they required it, said, although they had come most willingly to serve the king at their own expense, and what they required they were willing to pay for, they would, however, accept from his generous hands what they were much in want of, namely, shoes for their horses. The governor sent orders to a merchant to give each soldier, on his account, a dozen horseshoes, with corresponding nails ; he, however, gave instructions that they were only to have the horseshoes and nothing else ; and with this present he considered they were abundantly provided, and at little cost. Bravo's soldiers thanked the governor for his offer, but, as it really was not their wish to accept anything, the governor's offer of the horseshoes amused them.

The governor, Pedro Bravo and his men of Merida, and those who had joined him on the road, in the city of New Trujillo, (in all some seventy men), marched out of Tocuyo late in the day to join the king's forces ; and, having journeyed all the night (it being very hot during the day), at daybreak they met a messenger, the bearer of a letter to the governor, from Lope de Aguirre. The governor made a halt to read the letter, which he did to all his party.

2. "Most magnificent Señor.—Amongst other papers from you, found in this town, was a letter of yours directed to me, with more promises and preambles than there are stars in heaven, and, as regards myself and my companions, it was unnecessary for you to have taken such trouble, for I well know to what point your power extends, and how far you are able to oblige me, in your recommendations to the king. Most superfluous are your offers, as I know well that your position and power are but of poor account ; and, if the king of Spain had to pass through the conflict there is to be between us both, I would not accept them ; moreover, I will give you every advantage in arms ; but to me all you say is a mere artifice, and such as has often been resorted to against those brave men who conquered and settled this country. And you have come to rob them of the fruit of their hard-earned labour, saying that you come to do them justice, and the justice you offer them is to inquire how and in what manner they conquered the country, and for this you come to make war on them. The favour I ask of you is, that you do not

force us to come to blows; if we do, your gains will be few, for my companions make but light of your promise of pardon, and are prepared to sell their lives dearly. I have nothing to do with affairs in this part of the country; I wish to pay well with my own money, for the cost of some horses and other things; by this course you will preserve your district from the horrors of war. From what we have already seen of the things of this land, we will put wings on, and use our spurs well, not to be detained here; we have seen some of your hoods of helmets, or rather hats, and playthings of lances, thrown away by your soldiers in their hurry to escape from us. These things tell us what your forces are composed of. I return to the letter; it is of little use your saying that we were not acting as if we were in the king's service, I and my companions are only doing what our predecessors did, which is not against the king; for we hold him who commands us as our lord, and no other. It is a long time since we divested ourselves of our rights as Spaniards, and we refuse fealty to the king. We have made a new king whom we obey, and, as vassals of another lord, we may well make war against those we have sworn to fight, which is our business and not yours. And in conclusion I say, that according to the sort of behaviour you and yours adopt in our vicinity, so will we treat you. If you search us out you will find us ready for you, and the sooner you supply us with what we require, the sooner will we leave this land. I do not offer you my services, because you would hold them valueless. Our Lord preserve the most magnificent person of your worship, etc. Your servant,

"Lope de Aguirre."

3. The governor, having read this letter to his followers, said, "Would to God that the result of this war might be settled personally between me and Aguirre; for although he makes himself out so powerful, it might happen that I

should punish him as he intimates he could do with me; but, as God has so ordained it, let us give him thanks for all his mercies; our sins are the cause of so many evils, that even to this great distance have reached the sparks of the rebellions in Pirú, that make us so unhappy, and put us into such straits." This was said amidst such showers of tears and demonstrations of fear, as to cause the people to murmur, which continued so many days that it must have come to the ears of the governor.

The governor and his party continued their march, and arrived at the general's camp at midday, where they were received with every expression of joy by the soldiers of the camp, who were restored to new life by this timely addition to their numbers, and any doubts they may have had previously as to victory over the traitor were now converted into certainty; particularly in regard to the stratagem played off by Bravo, to give courage to the king's people, as well as to intimidate their enemies, for he reported that in Merida there was an oidor from the Audencia of Santa Fé, with five hundred armed men. Bravo himself had brought only two hundred men, which number appeared to him sufficient to counteract the intentions of the traitor.

This favourable news soon spread through the camp, and at nightfall a negro slave deserted to Aguirre, informing him of the arrival of Bravo, with a force of two hundred men, well mounted and armed.

The traitor heard this without shewing any particular signs of astonishment; but his soldiers became uneasy, and concluded, if this was true, that they must be now routed by the royalists; so several proposed to themselves to watch for an opportunity, desert to the king's camp, and so take advantage of the governor's pardon.

4. Although Aguirre had kept strict watch upon his men up to this period, he now increased his vigilance, and would not let them out of his entrenchment; this pre-

vented those who wished to escape, from doing so. But God prepared an opening for them to go over to the king's people; two of Aguirre's men, named Rengel and Francisco Guerrero, on the third day of their arrival, which was on a Wednesday, managed to get secretly out of the entrenchment to the king's camp, where they were well received, as it was of great importance to the royalists to know that there were very many in the enemy's camp only awaiting an opportunity to desert, which they could easily do. They said, that all the king's people had to do, to conquer the tyrant, was to, as it were, besiege Aguirre, and see that he did not obtain supplies of provisions, of which he was much in want, repeating that his men were most anxious to leave him, particularly captain Juan Geronymo de Espindola, Hernando Centemo, and ten or twelve of their comrades.

With this fresh information, and with what they had received through Pedro Alonzo Galeas, the king's party felt they could well assail the tyrant, and that, being in sight of him, they could prevent him from sallying forth in search of provisions, unless the whole of the traitors came out together.

On the same day the maestro del campo, the captain Bravo, and forty soldiers, including Rengel and Guerrero, went to within talking distance of Aguirre, when they commenced calling to the traitor's men to come out and join them, telling them not to dream of being victorious, as captain Bravo, with two hundred men, well mounted and armed, was there from Merida; that if they resisted he would cut all their throats; that they should come out at once, take advantage of the pardon, and thus save their lives. Whilst the king's people were thus talking to those of the traitor, they observed some male and female Indians, who were in the service of the Marañones, washing clothes in a ravine not far from Aguirre's position, so, leaving a number where they were, the maestro del campo and captain Bravo descended to the ravine with the rest, laid hands upon the Indians, and took them up behind them on their horses, all with the clothes they were washing.

CHAP. XLIX.

1. *Aguirre sends sixty arquebusiers to fire into the king's camp at night, but without any result.—2. The traitor comes out to the aid of his men, and prepares to resist the royalists.—3. Aguirre's fire makes no impression on the royalists. Captain Diego Tirado deserts from the traitor.—4. Another soldier tries to desert to the royalists. A mounted soldier of the king's party makes the circuit of Aguirre's entrenchment.*

1. The traitor was beginning to have some fears of his ultimate success, seeing that his men were deserting him, that the king's men showed so bold a front, and even came up to the walls of his quarters, and that his Indian servants were taken from him. With the concurrence of those he considered as his best friends, he resolved that sixty of them should sally forth in search of provisions that night, and fire into the king's camp, in the hope of doing them harm, and that about daybreak they should be retiring, for at that hour he would come out with the rest of his people to their help.

He gave the command of this expedition to Roberto de Susaya, the captain of his guard, and to Christobal Garcia, captain of infantry. They commenced their foray in the direction of the king's camp, when, after a time, they passed near to the captain Romero (who had settled Villa Rica, which he afterwards removed to another spot), who, with some companions, were coming from his town to help the king's party. Romero, in the stillness of the night, heard the trooping sounds of the sixty Marañones, and, putting spurs to his horse, he and his followers lost no time in galloping to the king's camp, and giving the alarm ; however it is said by some, that what Romero heard was not a noise caused by the Marañones, as they were far from the road he travelled on, but that it was caused by some wild mares and foals, which, scenting the horses of Romero's party, began to run about. As the whole country was up in arms, Romero might easily believe he had heard the footsteps of the enemy. The report had the effect of causing a goodly party, from the king's camp, to saddle at once and go forth, but they found no enemy, and returned to camp.

The sixty Marañones (who afterwards said they had heard no one during the night, neither had they come up with the king's camp) laid themselves down to sleep, and, at day-break, they were perceived by the royalist sentinels, who gave immediate alarm to their camp, when they all armed and went out in pursuit of the enemy.

2. The Marañones, perceiving this movement of the king's party, began to retire to their camp, and sent a soldier to Aguirre to advise him of their position, but, coming upon a portion of thick wood sufficient to protect their rear, whilst in front there were some ravines, they formed, and faced the royalists, who could not get near them with their horses, and so they stood looking at each other, until Lope de Aguirre with a troop came to the assistance of his men. The traitor was mounted on a jet black steed; the flag of his guard floated in the breeze (which was made of black silk, ornamented with two blood-red swords). Having joined company with the sixty arquebusiers, he made a movement as if he was coming from his cover to attack the royalists, who were about one hundred and fifty in number, all on horseback, for they had received people from Valencia, Coro, and the Burburata; still there were only five or six arquebuses amongst them all.

The royalists saw that, as long as the enemy remained in their present position, they could not get at them with their

F F

cavalry, nor do them any harm; so they made a movement as if retreating, when Aguirre left his cover and went after the royalists. Now it was that some of the king's people managed to get possession of the traitor's late position, preventing him from returning to it.

The king's party thought this a good moment to attack Aguirre at once; however they considered it more advantageous to commence skirmishing. Aguirre now implored a portion of his soldiers to lose no time in keeping up their fire; besides these, he had another troop with their loaded arquebuses, ready to fire, if the royalists attempted a general attack.

3. But it so happened (and it looked like a miracle) that being so near to each other, and many of Aguirre's party fighting with courage and the desire to do all the mischief they could, they did no harm to either man or horse of the royalists; some balls were seen, which, striking about half the distance they ought to have gone, amongst some horses, became as flat as cakes, sticking on the hair and skin of the animals, without wounding them. However, the king's party (although they had only five or six arquebuses) killed Aguirre's horse from under him, and wounded two of his soldiers.

During the skirmish a captain of horse (one of Aguirre's confidants, named Diego Tirado) mounted on a mare, and skirmishing in front of his party, thought this a good opportunity to desert to the royalists, and thus save his life (for he had taken many lives away whilst he had been with Aguirre); so, making rather a nearer gallop than usual towards the enemy, he made a dash towards the royalists, and got in amongst them, shouting " Long live the king, long live the king."

The governor and others received Tirado with much pleasure; when he told the royalists on no account to make an attack, as Aguirre had fifty armed arquebusiers in reserve, but to scatter themselves, so that he could not get a number of them together, and send in a heavy fire.

The royalists took this course, and to give more courage to those of Aguirre's people who wished to desert his flag, the governor gave Tirado his own horse, with instructions to go and skirmish in sight of the traitor, who was much affected on seeing that one whom he considered one of his best friends, had turned against him ; he, however, said to those about him, that he had sent Tirado on business to the governor.

4. At the same time that Tirado deserted from the traitor, his example caused another horseman, named Francisco Caballero, to try and effect his escape ; but he did not succeed.

Both parties were engaged in these skirmishes, without coming to a fight ; when one of the royalist soldiers, named Ledesma, being very well mounted, gave his horse the spur, going in the direction of Aguirre, who, seeing him advance, thought the soldier was deserting to him, and he shouted out to his men not to fire at the horseman, for that he was coming over to them. Ledesma, having arrived within thirty or forty paces of the traitor, was surrounded by the Marañones, when he, shouting "Long live the king," turned his horse and galloped back to his camp ; and, although the Marañones gave him a volley from their arquebuses, not a shot touched him.

CHAP. L.

1. *Aguirre, having fears of the desertion of his men, retires to his entrench-*
   ment. The royalists go to their quarters, but with hopes of victory
   over the traitor.—2. The traitor meditates on killing the sick and
   those soldiers he has fears of, but is dissuaded from this.—3. He takes
   their arms away from some of his soldiers, and drives away others,
   telling them to go and join the king's camp.—4. One of Aguirre's
   soldiers kills Pedro Bravo's horse. The traitor determines to return
   to the coast.

1. Aguirre became very angry, on seeing that his soldiers
were so near the enemy, and with such good firearms, and
that they did the king's people no harm ; that two of his men
had deserted ; and that his horse had been killed ; so, with
his accustomed fury, he said, "Marañones, is it possible that
a few herdsmen, with sheepskin jackets and hide bucklers,
thus shew themselves amongst us, and you do not bring
them to the earth ?" Aguirre made these observations in
consequence of his opponents wearing a sort of cloak made
of the skins of pumas or deer, much used in these countries of
the Indies ; their swords were rusty, their lances in a similar state. He also had his suspicions that his men, instead
of firing at the enemy, fired only into the air ; so he began
to retire to his entrenchment, having almost to drive many
of them, with a halberd he carried. Having got into his
quarters, a Portuguese, one of his great allies, named Gaspar
Diaz, secreted himself behind a door, armed with an *aguja*
or sharp instrument, watching for the coming of Francisco
Caballero (he who tried to desert to the king's party, but
failed), and, thinking he would please Aguirre by what he
was going to do, as Caballero approached, Diaz shouted
out, "Death to the traitor," and threw the *aguja*, which
caught the soldier in his *partes privadas*, causing him ex-
cruciating pain ; some others who came up would have
finished Caballero, had not the traitor (knowing that he had

not been very culpable) ordered that he should not be deprived of life, but that they should do their best to cure him.

The royalists, observing that Aguirre was retiring to his quarters, did the same, feeling, after what they had seen and done, that the victory would be for the king. They, however, placed a strong guard around their camp.

2. The traitor, seeing that his own people were doing mischief amongst themselves, began to rate them soundly, calling them cowards and women-hearted; that they had showed no prowess over their enemy, even with the great advantages they had over them in arms and in the affairs of war, and that it appeared to him that they made war with heaven, as they pointed their guns rather at the stars than at the men they had before them; this behaviour showed him their intentions, and if this was the way they continued the war, they would soon get the worst of it. The soldiers replied, that the reason why the balls did not reach the enemy was that the powder was bad.

Aguirre now placed some of his best friends at the gate of his quarters, as was his custom, to guard it, and prevent any one from going out. It was manifest to the traitor that many of his soldiers followed him unwillingly, and that the sick were an encumbrance to him, and, fearing that they would desert to the enemy, he considered it advisable to strangle all the unwilling and the sick; and, making a list of such as were to suffer, they amounted to more than fifty in number.

But, before putting this design into execution, he thought he would communicate with some of his friends; who could not help looking most seriously at the atrocity of the meditated act, and reflecting that if they sanctioned it, they would be blamed and severely punished by the king's party, in case they should be the victors, or perhaps God put it into their hearts to prevent the perdition of so many souls, in such a manner. They replied that the affair did not meet their approbation, for it might happen that, in the belief he was killing only the culpable ones, he might be destroying some who were only awaiting an opportunity to serve him well.

3. After much discussion, it was resolved not to carry the strangling into effect; but to disarm the suspected, and Aguirre urged his friends to keep a careful watch on them, giving his confidants directions, in case the suspected ones made any attempt to escape, to kill them all.

Aguirre now began to reflect on his projected return to Pirú, and that he had met with great impediments and resistance, and the idea flitted before him that he was not to be victorious, and that his men would abandon him. He considered, under these circumstances, that his best course would be to make for the sea coast with all his fol lowers, to embark wherever he could find vessels, change his route, and also his mode of life.

These views and fears of Aguirre were not unknown in the king's camp, and, with the idea of increasing his difficulties, thirty or forty of the royalist horsemen were always on the watch over his entrenchment, to prevent any of his party from sallying out in search of provisions, and also to encourage those who wished to desert. This being suspected by the traitor, he allowed no one to go out of his entrenchment, not even his confidants (for he began to have his doubts of them), to look for provisions, of which they were so much in want, that they were obliged to kill some dogs and horses to eat. The continuance of this state of things forced his confidential guards to leave their posts, and go over to the king's side by ones and twos. At sight of this, Aguirre's fears increased; but he still dissembled, and made it known that he had not lost confidence in his best followers, of whom he sent out a considerable number, armed with arquebuses, to watch the movements of the maestro del campo, and captain Bravo; who hovered about, near his camp, calling upon the traitor's followers to desert him.

Aguirre's armed troop of horse went forth, and soon a war of words commenced between the contending parties, the king's people calling the others traitors, which irritated them very much ; and they replied by a volley from their arquebuses. Bravo now tried to put an end to this mode of proceeding, telling his men that it was not politic to use such language to their opponents, particularly as they were of the same nation, but rather to speak to them in fair terms, and so try to induce them to come over to the king's side.

4. Whilst Bravo was thus speaking to his men, and not paying much attention to the enemy, one of them, named Juan de Lescano, a mestizo, considering that Bravo was one of the most active against his party, thought it a good opportunity to be revenged on him, by taking good aim at him with his arquebuse, the fire from which only killed Bravo's horse, which fell to the ground with his rider ; but God spared Bravo. Aguirre's men believed that Bravo had been killed also, so they raised a loud shout of triumph, for until this time they had not done any damage to the royalists.

The king's party, on coming up and finding that their commander was not hurt, returned the shout with a triumphant cheer, when the Marañones retired to their quarters. The royalists had been informed by recent deserters that Aguirre had formed the intention of proceeding to the coast, and that he had disarmed many of his men, observing at the same time that, as they appeared to have an idea of deserting to his enemy, it was not well they should go with their arms.

We now arrive at Monday morning, which was the vesper of St. Simon and St. Jude, the 27th of October, 1561, when Aguirre disarmed the greater number of his soldiers, and, being on the point of leaving his quarters, his soldiers said to him that, marching without arms, was as good as taking them to be slaughtered, for how could they defend themselves against the king's party ? This they said to the traitor in a courageous sort of manner, which appeared to Aguirre to look like a mutiny against him ; but he now considered it prudent on his part to return them their arms, making a virtue of necessity, telling them blandly, that he begged they would pardon him, for that this was the only error he had committed during the whole expedition, and that it was but just that they should look over it, also that his intentions were very different from what his acts might lead them to suppose ; however, some of the soldiers refused to receive their arms (for they were sorely offended at being disarmed), and Aguirre in person had to beg of them not to refuse.

CHAP. LI.

1. *The maestro del campo and captain Bravo come up towards Aguirre's entrenchment. Some soldiers go out to oppose them.—2. Captain Espindola, with a troop, deserts to the royalists, and all the rest of Aguirre's soldiers follow their example by various routes.—3. The maestro del campo sends news of the victory to the governor. Aguirre kills his daughter.—4. Aguirre is killed by two arquebuses fired at him. His head is cut off, and his hands are given to those from Merida and Valencia.*

1. Aguirre was now occupied in this move to the coast by daylight (although there were some who advised him to get out at night, so that he might not be observed by the enemy). He also desired to kill one of his captains, named Juan Geronymo de Espindola, for some bold words he had uttered, but there were none who would help him to execute Espindola. At this juncture, captain Bravo and Diego Garcia de Paredes came, accompanied by a considerable mounted force, towards Aguirre's quarters, having heard that he was about to march to the coast. They began shouting to the traitor's followers that he was deceiving them in all he was doing ; that they should trust him no longer, but come over to the king's

side at once. Whilst they were instigating the Marañones to desert, they perceived, as they had done some days before, other Indian servants at the stream which was near the entrenchment; so captain Bravo and the maestro del campo went out with fourteen or fifteen men, determined to catch them, telling those who remained on the heights that if they saw any of the traitor's men go forth to encounter them, to make a sign with a drawn sword: they then descended secretly to where the Indians were, but they were perceived by some of the Marañones, who were outside the entrenchment, trying to prevent, with their arquebuses, the advance of those whom Bravo had left on the heights. Aguirre, being informed of what was going on, sent Juan Geronymo de Espindola with fifteen arquebusiers to defend and bring the Indians in; this movement was observed by the king's party who were on the heights, who made the concerted sign by brandishing a drawn sword.

2. Although Bravo saw the signal, he pushed onwards, but when he descried Espindola and his companions on the plain, he thought it prudent to retire, and join his party on the heights, fearing the fire of their arquebuses, for the royalists had scarcely any firearms with them. Espindola and his party, seeing this, quickened their pace towards the retiring royalists, and, on nearing them, shouted "Long live the king, caballeros! long live the king!" this being heard by the maestro del campo and Bravo, they halted at once, awaiting the arrival of Espindola and his friends, when they mutually saluted each other in a most friendly manner. The Marañones declared themselves for the king, and were taken to the heights, each behind a royalist horseman.

Bravo now requested Espindola to remain in sight of Aguirre's quarters, in company with the maestro del campo, whilst he posted off to the governor with the deserters.

Aguirre was now seen to be outside his quarters, observing the movements of the royalists, and it appeared to them that his destruction was fast approaching, for as Espindola had deserted him, in like manner did the others, who, under plea of attacking the royalists, marched out in sight of Aguirre and joined the king's men, shouting "Long live the king, to whose service we come." The maestro del campo received them most courteously, and they begged of him to descend to the entrenchment, saying that those who were within would not defend the place, but would come over to him, for they were of the number that Aguirre put but little confidence in.

Whilst this was going on, the captain Juan de Aguirre Navarro, with some of his comrades, meditated on killing Aguirre, but did not find the opportunity. When they observed the maestro del campo coming down to their entrenchment, they sallied forth to receive him, offering their services to him, and crying out, as the rest had done, "Long live the king!" This was the last lot of the Marañones who remained under the traitor's bloody banner, for the rest of his followers, whilst Aguirre was watching operations outside his entrenchment, had escaped by an old gate, which Anton Llamoso was repairing (he it was who knocked out the brains of the maestro del campo at Margarita), who would not leave his tyrant master, saying that Aguirre had been his friend in life, and that he would live or die by his side. Meanwhile Garcia de Paredes, with his forces, was approaching Aguirre's quarters, to take the life of the traitor.

3. The maestro del campo, seeing that he had the victory in his own hands, despatched a mounted messenger to inform the governor and others as to the satisfactory state of affairs, and then marched straight on Aguirre's quarters.

The traitor, on seeing that he had been abandoned by all except Llamoso, asked him why he had not gone with the rest, and taken advantage of the king's pardon? Llamoso replied that he and Aguirre had been friends in life, and

that he would live or die with him. Aguirre made no reply;
he was crestfallen and lost; he went into an apartment
where his daughter was (who was now a woman) in company
with another female, named Torralva, of Molina de Arragon
in Castile, who had come from Pirú in company with the
traitors. She cannot have been of great age, for, in the year
one thousand six hundred and twelve, I saw her (she was
then very young) in the city of Barquicimeto. The devil instigated Aguirre to kill his daughter, so as to crown all his
cruel acts with this most bloody and unnatural one, that of
the destruction of his own flesh and blood. He said to
her, "Commend thyself to God, my daughter, for I am
about to kill thee; that thou mayest not be pointed at
with scorn, nor be in the power of any one who may call
thee the daughter of a traitor." Torralva tried to save the
girl, and even managed to take the loaded arquebuse from
the hands of the father, with which he was about to fire at
his victim; but Aguirre had a poniard, and with it he took
her life.[1] Having done this, he rushed to the door of the
apartment; but when he perceived that the king's forces
were upon him, his very hands lost the power of firing off
his arquebuse at them, so as to sell his life dearly; and,
in the most dejected manner, he threw all his arms on the
ground, and went and leant upon a miserable barbacoa or
bed place that was in the room (opposite that in which he
had killed his daughter). One of the first to enter (before
the maestro del campo), was one Ledesma, a sword-cutler
and inhabitant of Tocuyo; who, when he saw Garcia de
Paredes enter, thinking to make himself of importance,
said, "Here have I Aguirre as my prisoner." The traitor
replied, "I do not give myself up to such a villain as you;"
and perceiving Paredes, said, "Señor maestro del campo,
I beg that you, who are a caballero, will respect my rank,

---

[1] Castellanos makes Aguirre say to his daughter, "Die! because I
must die."

and listen, for I have many important things to say, for the good of the king's service."

4. Garcia de Paredes replied that he should be respected; but some of Aguirre's former soldiers, fearing if he were allowed to live it might go hard with them—for he might reveal what they had done during the expedition—persuaded the maestro del campo that the best, safest, and most honourable course was to cut off his head at once, and before the governor's arrival. This view of the case did not displease the maestro del campo, so he told Aguirre to prepare himself for death, and commanded two of his own Marañones to shoot him down with their arquebuses. This they did at once, and the traitor fell dead at their feet. It is, however, said that having received the fire of the first arquebuse in a slanting direction, he said it was not well aimed; but the second was fired at his breast, and he said, "That has done the business," and then fell dead. A soldier named Custodio Hernandez now fell upon the dead body, and, by order of the maestro del campo, cut the head off, and, taking hold of the hair, which was very long, he brought it out to show it to the governor, who was just arriving, thinking to do him honour.[1]

The maestro del campo (for it was his prize) sought for the flags and standards, and, going up with them to the chapel that was above the entrenchment, let them blow

---

[1] "At Cumana, before the earthquake of December 14th, 1797, a strong smell of sulphur was perceived near the hill of the convent o St. Francis; at the same time flames appeared on the banks of the Manzanares, and in the gulf of Cariaco, near Mariquitar. This las phenomenon is pretty frequent in the Alpine calcareous mountains nea Cumanacou, and in the island of Margarita, also amidst the llanos o New Andalusia, where flakes of fire rise to a considerable height.

"This fire, which is like the Will o' the Wisp of our marshes, does no burn the grass. The people call these reddish flames ' the soul of th traitor Aguirre,' and the natives of Barquecimeto believe that the sou of the traitor wanders in the savannahs, like a flame that flies the ap proach of men."—*Humboldt, Narr.*

out; but seeing that the governor was approaching, he went off to meet him, dragging the flags after him as a signal of victory. The governor was not well pleased that they had shot the traitor without his permission; but, concealing his feelings because the thing was now done, he ordered Aguirre's daughter to be buried in the Church, and the father to be quartered, and thrown out in the road.

The traitor's head was taken to the city of Tocuyo and placed in an iron cage, where it remained many days as a warning to evil-doers: his skull is still at the same place, with his flags; also the bodice and mantle of yellow silk worn by his daughter when her father killed her, with the poniard marks in them.

Captain Bravo, and his soldiers of Merida, as well as those of Valencia, to preserve a memorial of their doings in the king's service, wished to have some of the traitor's flags; to this the governor and his followers would not assent, but offered the hands of Aguirre to the towns of Merida and Valencia, so that they might place a hand on the *rollo*, in the respective towns. This was agreed to, Valencia having the left, Merida the right hand, which were carried to the said towns on the point of a lance.

The soldiers from Valencia took their leave, but on the road, it struck them that their portion of the booty (the hand of Aguirre) was of so little importance that they threw it to the dogs, who ate it; but it is true that those of Merida, on their way home, and passing the famous river Mototan, threw the hand that had fallen to them into that river, and in this way got rid of the bad smell which the putrefying hand was giving out.

The captain Pedro Bravo de Molina, with his people of Merida, had behaved so courageously on all occasions, particularly in this affair against the traitor, in which they had taken a principal share, that in due time the king largely rewarded them for such important services.

The general maestro del campo Diego Garcia de Paredes went to Castile to seek his reward shortly afterwards, and the king made him governor of Popoyan, which post he did not long enjoy.[1] General Gutierrez de la Peña was made a mariscal. He who profited least by the overthrow of Aguirre was the governor Collado, for the people of his district, having taken umbrage at some of his proceedings, took care to tarnish the good actions that he had done.

CHAP. LII.

1. *Gives an account of the country Aguirre came from, his character and customs.—2. His occupations during the year he was in Pirú.— 3. An account of the depredations he committed.—4. Although the governor kept his promise of protection, with some of the Marañones, yet some were punished.*

1. Lope de Aguirre was a Guipuzcoan of the town of Oñate, his parents were hidalgos, persons of fair standing, but whose names we have not been able to find. When the traitor was killed, he was a little more than fifty years of age, of short stature, and sparely made, ill-featured, the face small and lean, beard black, the eyes like a hawk's, and when he looked, he fixed them sternly, particularly when angry; he was a great and noisy talker; when well supported he was most determined, but without support he was a coward; he was very hardy, and could bear much fatigue, on foot as well as on horseback; he always went armed, and well protected, and never was without one or two coats of mail, a breast-plate of steel, sword, dagger,

---

[1] Diego Garcia never reached Popayan, having been killed by some Indians, when he landed on the coast of Venezuela.

arquebuse, and lance; he slept but little, especially at night, but he reposed during the day; he was the enemy of good men and good actions, particularly of praying, and he would allow no one to pray in his presence; so when he saw any of his soldiers with rosaries in their hands, he took them away, breaking them up, and saying that he did not want Christian soldiers, nor praying ones, that such occupations were only fit for monks and nuns, who understood such things; but that if necessary his men should play with the devil at dice for their souls. He sometimes told his men that God had heaven for those who chose to serve him, but that the earth was for the strongest arm; that he knew for certain there was no salvation, and that being in life was to be in hell; and that as he could not be blacker than the crow, he would commit every species of wickedness and cruelty, so that his name might ring throughout the earth, and even to the ninth heaven; that he would not spare his prisoners for the fear of hell, but that he would commit all the cruelties he had the appetite for; that belief in God alone would take any one to heaven; that he would show Adam's will to the king of Castile, to see if he had left him as his heir to the Indies.

2. Aguirre lived in Pirú more than twenty years, in a very different manner from the life he led in his last days, as he told the king in the letter he wrote to his majesty. His occupation in early days was that of a horse breaker, for himself, as well as for others, his own stock daily increasing. He was always of a turbulent disposition, and a lover of revolts and mutinies, and during the time he was in Pirú, he was engaged in nearly all them. It is not known that he had ever served under any noble banner, or even quite lawfully under the king's standard. He, however, went with Diego de Rojas amongst the Chunchos Indians; then with captain Pedro Alvarez Holguin, to the assistance of Vaca de Castro, but, just before the battle of Chupas, he hid himself

in Guamanga, so as not to be in that engagement. In the
rising of Gonzalo Pizarro, although he was nominated as
alguazil de verdugo (probably assistant to the public executioner), he remained in Nicaragua, and did not return to
Pirú, until after the battle of Xaquixaguana. Afterwards
he was concerned in several mutinies which did not succeed; and with Don Sebastian de Castilla in the affair of
the death of general Pedro Alfonso de Inojosa, the corregidor of Las Charcas; and, as one of the principal actors in
this mutiny, he was condemned to death, and would have
been executed, had he not escaped and hid himself. The
mariscal Alonso Alvarado caused a strict search to be made
for him, but without success. He then rebelled against the
king, with Francisco Hernandez Giron, but the oidores of
Pirú, having offered a general pardon to all those who had
been in mutinies and rebellions, if they would come in and
serve the king in the war against Francisco Hernandez, he
took advantage of the offer, and rallied under the royal
standard, when he was present in an encounter where he
was wounded in the leg; but he was not very much displeased, for his wound prevented him from being exposed
in the succeeding battle.[1]

[1] After the defeat of Gonzalo Pizarro, and the pacification of Peru,
as related by Robertson and Prescott, there were several commotions
before the land of the Incas quietly settled down to the dead level of the
Spanish colonial system, and the last hot blood was sent away down the
Amazons, under the weak guidance of Pedro de Ursua. Very soon after
the departure of the president La Gasca, a party of soldiers under Don
Sebastian de Castilla rose in Charcas, and murdered the corregidor,
Pedro de Hinojosa, and his lieutenant, Alonzo de Castro. The royal
auditors sent the marshal, Don Alonzo de Alvarado, to quell this revolt,
who crushed the insurgents with great severity by deaths, floggings,
and imprisonments, between July and November, 1553; when he received news of the rebellion of Francisco Hernandez Giron, in Cuzco.
The extreme severity of the marshal in Charcas, and the discontent of
the soldiers at not being permitted to use the Indians as beasts of
burden, enabled Giron to assemble a number of discontented spirits;
and, on the occasion of a wedding feast at Cuzco, on November 13th,

He mixed himself up in so many seditions in various parts, that he could not be tolerated in the country. He was driven from one province to another, and was known as Aguirre the madman.[1] In Cuzco they nearly hung him for

1553, he seized the corregidor, let the prisoners loose, and formed a rebel army. Giron then marched to Guamanga, to encounter the royal forces, and continued his advance to Nasca, on the coast of Peru, south of Lima, where he formed a regiment of negro slaves. Meanwhile Alvarado marched from Charcas, through Cuzco, in pursuit of Giron, and the two forces approached each other at Chuquinga, in the bleak region of the Cordilleras. A battle followed, in which the royal army under Alvarado was entirely defeated and dispersed. Giron then crossed the bridge over the river Apurinac, and passing Cuzco, encamped in the valley of Urcos. The royal army followed him from Guamanga, marched through Cuzco, and Giron retired before it, until at length he determined to make a stand at Pucara ; where he fortified himself in a strong position. On the approach of the royalists, however, he sallied out at night, a panic seized his troops, and they were thrown into confusion. Giron fled alone, but was captured, brought to Lima, and publicly executed. His head was hung up in an iron cage, beside those of Gonzalo Pizarro and Carbajal; but all three were soon afterwards stolen away at night, and secretly buried by some friends of the wife of Giron. In 1557 the viceroy marquis of Cañete arrived at Lima, and completed the pacification of Peru.

Aguirre was mixed up in the rebellions of Castilla, and of Giron, and was wounded at the battle of Chuquinga.

[1] A curious anecdote of a soldier named Aguirre, is given by Garcilasso Inca de la Vega (lib. vi, cap. xvii, del 2º parte), and it is very probable that this soldier was the identical Lope de Aguirre of the narrative. It is as follows :—" In 1548 a party of two hundred soldiers were leaving Potosi, on their way to Tucuman, with laden Indians carrying their baggage, though the judges of the Royal Audience had forbidden that services of this nature should be exacted from the natives. The licentiate Esquivel, who was the alcalde mayor, came out to witness the departure of the soldiers, and allowed them all to pass with their laden Indians, except the last, one Aguirre, whom he seized, and a few days afterwards he sentenced him to receive two hundred lashes ; because he had not sufficient gold and silver to pay the fine which was ordered to be levied on those who pressed Indians. The soldier Aguirre, having received a notification of the sentence, besought the alcalde that, instead of flogging him, he would put him to death, for that he was a gentleman by birth, and the brother of a man who was the lord of vassals in Spain. All this had no effect on the alcalde, who ordered the executioner to

a mutiny against the king, in which he was concerned with
Lorenzo de Salduendo (whom, as we have already seen,

bring a beast, and execute the sentence. The executioner came to the
prison, and put Aguirre on the beast : but all the principal people of the
town went to the alcalde, entreating him not to execute so rigorous
a sentence, and he at length consented to delay it for eight days. When
they came to the prison, they found that Aguirre was already stripped,
and mounted on the beast ; and, on hearing that the punishment was
only delayed for eight days, he said : ' I prayed that I might not be put
on this beast, and stripped naked, as I now am, but now that I have
come to this, I prefer to suffer at once, rather than bear the suspense of
eight more days.' On saying this, the beast was driven on, and he received the lashes, amidst the grief of both Spaniards and Indians, at
seeing so cruel and causeless a disgrace inflicted on a gentleman by
birth.

"Aguirre refused to proceed to Tucuman, but remained in Peru, and,
when the period of Esquivel's office expired, he followed him about,
with the intention of killing him, to avenge the indignity which he had
suffered at his hands. Esquivel went to Lima, a distance of three hundred and twenty leagues, but within fifteen days Aguirre was with him.
Thence the judge fled to Quito, a journey of four hundred leagues, but
in little more than twenty days Aguirre was there also. When Esquivel
heard of his presence, he made another journey of five hundred leagues,
to Cuzco ; but in a few days Aguirre also arrived, having travelled on
foot, and without shoes ; saying that a whipped man has no business to
ride a horse, or to go where he would be seen by others. In this way
Aguirre followed his judge for three years, and four months. Esquivel,
being tired of so many weary journeys, which were of no use, determined to settle at Cuzco, because there was a judge there, who was so
strict, that he thought Aguirre would not dare to attack him. He,
therefore, took a house, near the cathedral, and always wore a sword
and dagger, though arms were not worn by men of his profession ; saying
that he now had no reason to fear a little man like Aguirre. However,
on a certain Monday, at noon, Aguirre entered his house, and having
walked all over it, and having traversed a corridor, a saloon, a chamber,
and an inner chamber where the judge kept his books, he at last found
him asleep over one of his books, and stabbed him to death. The murderer then went out, but, when he came to the door of the house, he
found that he had forgotten his hat, and had the temerity to return
and fetch it, and then walked down the street. He passed the church
of San Francisco, and came to the open space on which they were building the nunnery of Santa Clara, where he met two young gentlemen,
brothers-in-law of one Rodrigo de Piñeda ; and said to them, ' Hide me!
Hide me !' without another word. The lads, who knew his story,

Aguirre killed). He was cast into prison, and although he escaped into the woods, he was much sought after by the asked him if he had killed the licentiate Esquivel; and he replied, 'Yes, sirs! hide me, hide me!' They then took him into the house of their brother-in-law, and concealed him in an enclosure where the bullocks were kept, at the back of the house, telling him not to come out on any account, nor even to raise his head, for fear some Indian should see him, and promising to bring him food, without any one knowing it. These boys, when they were eating their suppers at their brother-in-law's house, slipped bread and meat into their pockets, and, after supper, took the food to poor Aguirre. This continued for forty days. Meanwhile, when the corregidor heard of the death of Esquivel, he ordered the bells to be rung, and placed guards at the gates of the churches and convents, and on the roads leading from the city, so that no man could depart without permission; but no tidings could be obtained of Aguirre. At the end of thirty days the strictness of the watch was relaxed, and the sentries were taken off the churches, but not off the high roads, which were still carefully guarded. At the end of forty days it appeared to certain gentlemen, named Santillan and Cataño, that it would be well to rescue Aguirre from the severity of the judge, by taking him out of the city publicly, instead of attempting to effect his escape in secret. He was, therefore, dressed as a negro, for which purpose his hair and beard were cut, and his face, neck, hands, and arms up to the elbows, were washed with water which had been mixed with a wild fruit called by the Indians *vitoc*, that has the effect of making the skin black, but is of no other use. They then dressed him as a vile negro, and one day, at noon, they went out with him through the streets, to the hill called Carmenca. He walked on foot, before his masters, with an arquebuse on his shoulder. Thus they reached the outskirts of the town, where the guards were posted, who asked them if they had permission from the corregidor, to leave the city. One of them then said to the other, " Walk on slowly, while I go back to get the permit, and I will soon catch you up." The other then went on with his negro, until they had passed the jurisdiction of Cuzco; and, having bought a pony, and given Aguirre some money, he said to him, 'Brother! you are now free, and I can do no more for you.' He then returned to Cuzco, and Aguirre went on to Guamanga, where he had a near relation, a rich man, and one of the principal people of that city. This relation received him as if he had been his own son, and sent him away, after some days, well provided with necessaries. Thus Aguirre escaped, and this was one of the most wonderful things that happened in Peru in those times. The insolent soldiers said that if there were more Aguirres in the world, judges would not be so free and tyrannical."

If this murderer of Esquivel was the identical Lope de Aguirre, the

authorities, and it was for this reason that he joined the expedition of Pedro de Ursua, with the intention of attempting and committing all sorts of crimes and enormities. It was also reported that Pedro de Ursua's object in going on this expedition, was to return in arms against Pirú, as we have already mentioned.

3. Having arrived at the town of the Motilones, and, understanding that Ursua's intentions were different from what Aguirre had supposed, and that Ursua was faithful to his king, he proposed to kill him, and to raise Don Martin to be the general, he whom Ursua obliged to return to Pirú, but as this was not effected, Aguirre killed Pedro de Ursua and many others; and in the short space of five months and five days, the duration of the reign of his tyranny, he took the lives of sixty Spaniards; amongst them one priest, two monks of the order of Santo Domingo, four women, and his own daughter; destroyed four Spanish towns, pillaging all the estates he came near, of all of which he spoke very differently in the letter he wrote to the king; in which he said that the reason why he had rebelled, and thrown off his allegiance, was because his services had not been rewarded. We have seen the class of services he rendered, which we will not repeat here.

4. The licenciate Pablo Collado, governor of Venezuela, kept the promises of pardon he had made in the name of the king, with all those who had passed over to the royalist side, treating them well whilst he remained in his district; he also gave them permission to go where they thought

indignity he suffered at Potosi, and his long thirst after vengeance, may have been active instruments in forming his inexorably cruel character.

Lope de Aguirre was certainly in Peru at the time, leading a wild unsettled life. Padre Simon mentions that he fled from Cuzco to escape from the consequences of a crime he had committed there, and it is incidentally mentioned that the murderer of Esquivel was a short man, which agrees with the description of Aguirre, given by Simon.

proper; so they scattered themselves about Tierra Firma, sowing the seeds of mutinies and rebellions.

To arrest such a state of things the king, when he was informed thereof, sent decrees in the following year, 1562, from Madrid to all the provinces of these Indies, to arrest all the Marañones, wherever they were found, and to send them to Spain. However, none arrived there, for they fled, or otherwise evaded the royal mandate. But not all of them; for in the city of Merida, Pedro Sanchez Paniagua was taken prisoner and quartered, as one of the worst of the Marañones. The same was done to Anton Llamoso, the only one who did not desert Aguirre, by captain Ortun Velasco, in the city of Pamplona, the said Velasco being the chief justice.[1]

The Royal Audience of Santa Fé was not behind in issuing orders to arrest these Marañones, as I was well informed in the city of Santa Fé, by Francisco de Santiago, knight of the habit of Christ; and they succeeded in laying hands on Francisco de Carrion, the alguazil mayor of the traitor; Roberto de Susaya, his captain of the guard; captain Diego Tirado, Garcia de Chaves, Diego Sanchez de Balboa, and one Portuguese. All these were on their way to Pirú. They were punished in such a manner, that neither they, nor the rest of the Marañones, escaped the hands of justice; thus no one dared to commence new rebellions, for we have not seen any others (through the goodness of God), in these Indies, of any consequence, since the time of the " Tyrant" Aguirre.

[1] Castellanos remarks that Llamoso was the murderer of the lady Inez de Atienza, and that he was put to death in Pampluna, a city founded by Pedro de Ursua, the knight whom she had loved so faithfully. Ortun de Velasco had been the comrade of Ursua when he founded Pampluna, and, when Ursua departed in 1550, Velasco continued to govern that town for twenty years.

FINIS.

Printed in Great Britain by
Amazon.co.uk, Ltd.,
Marston Gate.